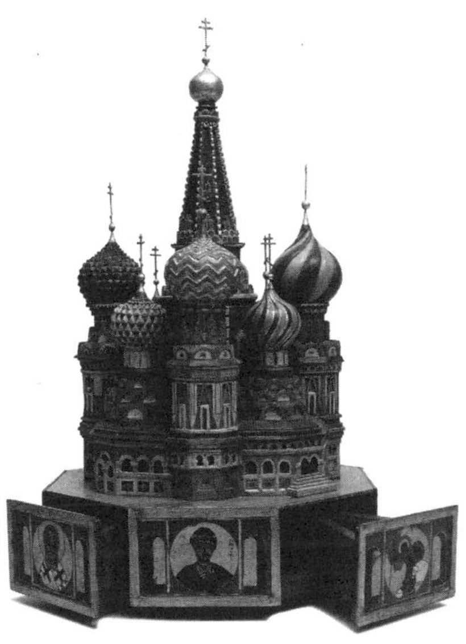

The Icon in Canada

*Recent findings from the
Canadian Museum of Civilization*

Compiled and edited by
Robert B. Klymasz

Canadian Centre for Folk Culture Studies
Mercury Series Paper 69

Canadian Museum of Civilization

CANADIAN CATALOGUING IN PUBLICATION DATA

Klymasz, Robert B. (Robert Bogdan), 1936–

The icon in Canada : recent findings from the Canadian Museum of Civilization

Mercury series, ISSN 0316-1854)

(Paper / Canadian Centre for Folk Culture Studies, ISSN 0316-1987; no. 69

Includes an abstract in French.
Includes bibliographical references.

ISBN 0-660-15964-3

1. Icons — Canada.
2. Icons, Byzantine — Canada.
I. Canadian Museum of Civilization.
II. Canadian Centre for Folk Culture Studies.
III. Title.
IV. Series.
V. Series: Paper (Canadian Centre for Folk Culture Studies); no. 69.

N8187.H84 1996 704.9'482 C96-980383-4

PRINTED IN CANADA

Published by
Canadian Museum of Civilization
100 Laurier Street
P.O. Box 3100, Station B
Hull, Quebec
J8X 4H2

Senior production officer: Deborah Brownrigg

Cover design: Purich Design Studio

Inside layout: Roger Langlois Design

Front cover: Harald Wodtke (b. 1939), Byzantine jewellery and music box, ca. 1974, carved and painted woods with gold leaf. Each of the eight triangular drawers displays an iconographic image on the front. The work is modelled after the Cathedral of the Intercession (St. Basil's) in Moscow. Photograph: Winnipeg Art Gallery.

Back cover: William Kurelek (1927-1977), field drawing, c.1973, interior of Ukrainian church in Chipman, Alberta. Photograph: Harry Foster.

Canadä

OBJECT OF THE MERCURY SERIES

The Mercury Series is designed to permit the rapid dissemination of information pertaining to the disciplines in which the Canadian Museum of Civilization is active. Considered an important reference by the scientific community, the Mercury Series comprises over three hundred specialized publications on Canada's history and prehistory.

Because of its specialized audience, the series consists largely of monographs published in the language of the author.

In the interest of making information available quickly, normal production procedures have been abbreviated. As a result, grammatical and typographical errors may occur. Your indulgence is requested.

Titles in the Mercury Series can be obtained by by calling in your order to 1-800-555-5621, or by writing to:

Mail Order Services
Canadian Museum of Civilization
100 Laurier Street
P.O. Box 3100, Station B
Hull, Quebec
J8X 4H2

BUT DE LA COLLECTION

La collection Mercure vise à diffuser rapidement le résultat de travaux dans les disciplines qui relèvent des sphères d'activités du Musée canadien des civilisations. Considérée comme un apport important dans la communauté scientifique, la collection Mercure présente plus de trois cents publications spécialisées portant sur l'héritage canadien préhistorique et historique.

Comme la collection s'adresse à un public spécialisé, celle-ci est constituée essentiellement de monographies publiées dans la langue des auteurs.

Pour assurer la prompte distribution des exemplaires imprimés, les étapes de l'édition ont été abrégées. En conséquence, certaines coquilles ou fautes de grammaire peuvent subsister : c'est pourquoi nous réclamons votre indulgence.

Vous pouvez vous procurer la liste des titres parus dans la collection Mercure en appelant au 1-800-555-5621, ou en écrivant au :

Service des commandes postales
Musée canadien des civilisations
100, rue Laurier
C.P. 3100, succursale B
Hull (Québec)

J8X 4H2

A b s t r a c t

The iconography of the Eastern Christian Church, rooted in the legacy of Byzantium, has profoundly influenced the nature of sacred art among large segments of Canada's population.

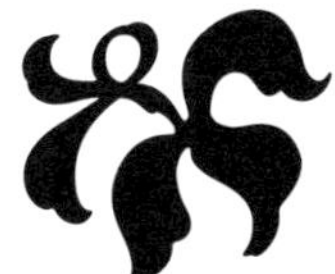 To enrich our appreciation of this living tradition, many of its aspects are explored, documented and analyzed. Although the volume gives prominence to ethnocultural, visual and religious dimensions, museological and technical concerns figure as well. An annotated bibliography supplements these findings and suggests a variety of areas that await further research.

Résumé

L'iconographie de l'Église orthodoxe, dont les racines remontent jusqu'à Byzance, a profondément influencé l'art sacré de certains groupes, au Canada.

Pour mieux saisir le phénomène, plusieurs aspects de cette tradition vivante sont ici explorés, documentés et analysés. Bien que les dimensions ethnoculturelle, visuelle et religieuse y soient traitées en priorité, on y fait également état d'aspects muséologiques et techniques. Une bibliographie annotée enrichit ces découvertes et suggère des domaines où pourraient s'effectuer de nouvelles recherches.

...the faith that caused my great-grandmother to bow before the icons and kiss the floor in front of the priest's hem every Sunday. That kind of faith I do not want; cannot imagine.

- Janice Kulyk Keefer, 1994

But the great icon in the Sophia Cathedral had reminded me of a beauty that no hatred, on earth or in hell, can defeat, alloy, dilute. There, by the Dnieper, I vowed to fight the black dogs, by whatever means I could find and to the death if need be.

- John Bentley Mays, 1995

I'm still not sure why I got the idea of making an icon, but I'm glad I did. The experience has marked my life.

- Jerry Bartram, 1996

CONTENTS

FOREWORD

At a recent meeting of the Museum's committee to review upcoming exhibition possibilities, one curator commented that the Museum seemed to be turning into an art gallery. He meant that by programming a series of exhibitions featuring recent works of art we were challenging the comfortable definitional boundaries of history and ethnology.

The comment served to remind us how much we have come to rely on artists, often the most creative and expressive individuals in society or community, to describe, summarize or challenge cultural meaning. In modern Canada, with its ubiquitous forms of material culture and social organization, museum curators seek out the artist's expression of regional, occupational or ethnic experience and use artistic traditions as a focus for examining cultural retention, adaptation and change. Works of art have become a primary focus for interpreting and understanding the diverse peoples of North America.

This collection of "findings" on the icon in Canada makes a valuable contribution, not only to the study of traditional art and ethnicity but also to museology. By including the voices of students, artists and devotees as well as scholars, the volume underlines not only the diversity of the data available but also the growing diversity of the museum audience.

Stephen Inglis

INTRODUCTION

by
Robert B. Klymasz

This foray into religious iconography began with research linked to two anniversaries: the millennium of Christianity among the Eastern Slavs celebrated in 1988, and the centenary of Ukrainian settlement in Canada marked in 1991. Prior to this, the Canadian Museum of Civilization had acquired several icons as incidental additions to the collections. With the gradual and unexpected discovery of many iconographers practising their art in various parts of the country, plans were laid for the development of a national icon collection at the C.M.C. Although fiscal restraints curtailed this programme of acquisitions, the research itself continued as part of curatorial preparations for an exhibition marking the bimillennium of Christianity.

To capture the full dimensions of this phenomenon in Canada, we adopted a broad approach that defined "icon" as an image linked to the east Christian, Byzantine tradition of religious iconography. Within the parameters of this working definition, certain formal features were seen as inextricable constants: the seeming flatness and disregard for perspective along with a general predilection for graphic rather than pictorial qualities — the traditional hallmarks of Byzantine-style iconography that in Canada continue to distinguish the icon from other expressions of religious art. Also, in spite of pressures to decontextualize the icon by looking upon it as a mere objet d'art, we found it important to recognize the icon's paramount, spiritual dimension as underlined by Claire Labrecque in her contribution to this volume, — even today, the realization of an icon represents a profession of faith on the part of the artist. It is certainly the primacy of religion that distinguishes these objects from the so-called "icons" that appear on computer monitor-screens and elsewhere today!

Six "Parts" constitute the body of this book. Part One features two analytic papers offering significant insights into the icon's continuing viability in two different parts of Canada , — Québec and the West: Michael Owen Jones focuses on the work of four iconographers to distinguish between folk and academic iconographers; Anne-Marie Poulin's paper traces in considerable detail the history and impact of the miraculous icon of Montreal, the *Portaïtissa,* and related phenomena. Part Two focuses on two exhibitions — one permanent, the other temporary — with contrasting presentations of the icon. The role of ethnicity as a determinant factor in iconographic production is broached in Part Three with its Ukrainian and Romanian surveys by Lesya Granger and Paula Vachon, respectively. Though seemingly peripheral to this volume's main concerns, the inclusion of Pauline Greenhill's notes on Portuguese *azulejos* in Toronto is an important reminder of how historic-geographical barriers that isolated variants of Byzantine iconography in the Old World have been eclipsed by contiguity and interchange in the New. In Part Four, three accounts written by iconographers themselves stand as rarities in a literature bereft of autobiographical narrative. Two are first-person statements by Vladimir Blagonadejdin and Tatiana Vartanova, iconographers trained in Russia and now based in Canada. Both reflect heroic strengths and inordinate commitments as fundamental drives that overcome extraordinary obstacles. The third member of this trio, Christina Senkiw, provides a telling glimpse into the nature and mechanics of transmission as pragmatic aspects of icon production today. Two "documents" focusing on technicalities in Part Five and an annotated bibliography in Part Six help delineate the vitality and complexity of the icon in Canada. Finally, in his "After-word", Andriy Chirovsky discusses some of the crucial theological underpinnings that are fundamental but often sidestepped in this field of investigation.

The legacy of Byzantium represents one of the great commonalities linking the peoples of Eastern Europe to one another. For over a million Canadian devo-tees, it is the icon that manifests a continuing, tangible connection to this legacy in way that is vibrant and extraordinary. The following materials suggest the diversity of this heritage but represent only initial probings into a field that is remarkably rich in history, mystery and tradition. Future research must continue the synchronic orientation initiated here in order to grapple with several large questions. — What happens when Byzantine-style iconography is transplanted from its native soil in the Old World to a different environment like Canada? How much is retained? What intrusions appear? What accommodations, graphic and functional, are made between conservative formulations developed over a period of centuries and the demands of our quickly paced, ever-changing society?

Many moments in this book reflect the support and interest of family, friends, iconographers and colleagues; their encouragement helped to dispel our hesitancy at entering into such deep waters. Indispensible , of course, was the active collaboration of those whose "findings" are published here. However, all would have gone for naught without the considerable production talents of Museum co-workers. My thanks to all!

ACKNOWLEDGMENTS

The Canadian Museum of Civilization gratefully acknowledges the following for permission to reprint excerpts from their works: on p. v, Janice Kulyk Keefer (from her "Kiev, November 1993" published in *PEN Canada Travel Anthology*, 1994, p.140); Penguin Books Canada Limited (from John Bentley Mays' *In the Jaws of the Black Dogs* [copyright © John Bentley Mays], 1995,p.163); and Jerry Bartram (from his "For the Love of God", *The Globe and Mail*, May 25, 1996,p.D5.

ICON PAINTERS IN WESTERN CANADA AND THE CONUNDRUMS OF CLASSIFICATION: WHO CREATES FOLK ART, WHEN, AND WHY?

by
Michael Owen Jones

"The great fear of the parish: they didn't want anything identified with Greek, and they were terrified it would be Russian. This ain't Russian," said Heiko Schlieper as we looked at his paintings covering the walls of St. George's Ukrainian Catholic Church in Edmonton. Andrew Baziuk, a local architect, modeled the building after a classical Byzantine church in thirteenth-century Ukraine. "What I did, basically, in my sort of mind's eye," said Schlieper, "I traveled back into the eleventh, twelfth centuries and pretended that I was a Euro-Slav who had studied in Byzantium, or a Byzantine who had gone to Kiev. While I used the Byzantine form, I Slavicized both line and color. Which means the line is simpler, and the colors are more blatant, fresher, purer colors, less sophisticated colors than you would have found in Byzantine work at that time." The result is a "synthetic" style, he said.

Contemporary icon painting in Western Canada is itself synthetic (or eclectic). It comprises diverse elements that, when combined, befuddle attempts at classification. St. George's is a modern Ukrainian Catholic church based on ancient Byzantine models; its iconostasis was made in Greece and its icons were painted by a German Canadian convert to Eastern Orthodoxy. St. Josephat's Cathedral, also in Edmonton, bears the sobriquet "Our Lady of the Comic Book" because its architecture and iconography mix Orthodoxy, Catholicism, and Modernism (Goa, 1989).

Keleher's survey (1989) of Canadian Ukrainian churches and their iconography illustrates some of the difficulties of classification caused by culture change and eclecticism (see also Stepovyk, 1991). The first category, a "pioneer model" of the late nineteenth-century "classic" iconography of Western Ukraine, "is not without its problems, since it comes from a degenerate period of iconography and theology. . . . There is often a good deal of folk religion in such parishes. Curious customs and religious practices, such as the particular form of liturgical chants, are preserved there, though forgotten in the Ukraine itself" (p. 49). Keleher's second and fourth groups — "Latinized" and "neo-latinized" — are comprised of Orthodox churches whose interiors look distinctly Catholic (e.g., lacking an iconostasis, having an image of the Sacred Heart of Jesus, or substituting the Trinity for the Pantocrator in the dome of the church). The third model includes churches that attempt to revive "authentic" Orthodox iconography; despite claims of strong Ukrainian national identity, however, Orthodox theological literature tends to be in English. The final category consists of "an attempt to combine all four of the models just described to create a 'modernist Orthodoxy.'" These parishes "take parts from various religious traditions, combining them into an inconsistent and incoherent mix" (p. 52). An eclectic model, it "is nothing more than a freakish fad. . ." (p. 54).

Differences in the ethnicity and religion of artists further confuse the classification of icon painting and other art in Western Canada (Isajiw, 1991; Jones, 1991; Klymasz, 1989, 1991). André Provost of Edmonton, Alberta, and Roger Desilets of Oakburn, Manitoba, claim French Canadian heritage. Taras Yuri Snihurowycz of Winnipeg hails from Ukraine. Vavara Rashid of Vancouver immigrated from Roumania, and Slavko Protic came from Yugoslavia. Heiko Schlieper (whose home is in Ottawa, not in the West) is of German descent. Edward Hartley, now in the Vancouver area, grew up an Anglican in English Nova Scotia and later converted to Greek Orthodoxy. Gary Robertson of Elma, Manitoba, had a Scottish father, Polish grandmother, and Ukrainian grandfather. Having rejected her parents' heritage, Gary's mother foisted Catholicism on him but in adulthood he reverted to the Ukrainian Orthodoxy of his grandparents, albeit with Anglicized liturgy because of limited knowledge of Slavic languages.

Media differ as well, adding another complication. Varvara Rashid and Heiko Schlieper paint with egg tempera while André Provost and Slavko Protic use acrylics. Others have chosen oils, for example Peter Lipinski, who was born in the Husiatyn district of Galicia and who became one of Alberta's earliest and most prolific painters (Bilash, 1994), and Anna von Kuegelgen, a Russian-German immigrant to Vancouver (both are deceased). Roger Desilets, who owns an apiary and learned candlemaking from a Polish immigrant, makes wax icons (Madonna and Child, and St. Dmitri) following a Bavarian tradition. Edward Hartley uses oil and sometimes egg tempera on cardboard. On a restricted income, Gary Robertson paints with anything he can find on whatever he can afford. Taras Yuri Snihurowycz, a professor of rehabilitative dental medicine, applies dental tools, techniques, and chemicals to create frames, pictures, and pendants. He has produced images on plywood, cork, canvas, soapstone, and chemically antiqued copper; used model airplane paint, oil, acrylic, and tempera; and made frames of wire, metal, wood, and ceramic (some of which he treated to appear like weathered bronze or ancient gold).

Generally speaking, icons as "windows on heaven" are pictorial representations of church dogma and abstractions following established canons rather than realistic portrayals given an individual interpretation (Barasch, 1992; Barida, 1977; Davies, 1994; Hordynsky, 1988; Quenot, 1991). But many of Taras Yuri Snihurowycz's icons depict elongated faces and tortured bodies. Peter Lipinski painted the face of God in the dome of St. Nicholas Ukrainian Greek Catholic Church (now preserved with two other churches at the Ukrainian Cultural Heritage Center), "a real no-no" iconographically, said Heiko Schlieper. Are these works, then, truly "icons"? Or are they more appropriately called "religious" paintings (Smart, 1989)?

Heiko Schlieper and André Provost claim to be largely self-taught as iconographers, a trait often cited as the hallmark of a folk artist (Hemphill and Weissman, 1974; Yelen, 1993). But Provost is a graduate of the Banff School of Fine Arts who freelances in stage management for opera companies. Schlieper is an academic expert who taught at McGill University for a decade and publishes on the history, religion, culture, economics, and politics of Byzantium and Eastern Europe (e.g., Schlieper, 1986). Moreover, Schlieper adamantly differentiates himself from folk artists "out of touch with the main centers of iconography" who paint "rather primitive figures" in a personalized, decorative way.

As a folklorist, I am concerned with questions of what folk art is, who creates it, and what it means to people. Many researchers, myself included, insist on traditionality as a distinguishing feature of folk art, labelling as folk artists those who model their activities on others' behavior and make objects based on precedents (Becker and Franco, 1988; Ben-Amos, 1984; Bronner, 1979; Bulger, 1980; Congdon, 1986; Teske, 1983; Vlach, 1986, 1988). Iconographers subscribe to convention, following rules regarding whom to depict and how to do so. Thus, all icons exhibit degrees of traditionality. Which exemplify folk art, and which fall into some other category?

Given all the complications, why try to classify? Grouping phenomena highlights their similarities while differentiating them from other things; it serves as an initial step toward understanding. Moreover, the proper identification of data orients the researcher to the discipline with methods and hypotheses most useful in analysis. In regard to folk art, classification assists in formulating theoretical models for teaching about art in educational settings (Congdon, 1986). Definitions provide conceptual tools for those working in the public sector as arts coordinators where decisions regarding what does or does not constitute folk art must be made and defended on a daily basis (Chinn, 1983). Developing library, museum, and archive catalogs and indexes of art and artists requires defining and categorizing information (Benedetti, 1987). Sometimes the intent of characterizing and classifying phenomena goes beyond academic or practical purposes to political ones; the history of folk art study reveals attempts in some quarters to define and control systems of knowledge (Metcalf, 1983, 1986). Clearly, then, definition and classification are important matters.

In order to develop one category, that of folk art, I describe four iconographers and their works. The artists include Gary Robertson who lives on a farm near Elma, Manitoba; Slavko Protic and Varvara Rashid of Vancouver; and Edward Hartley who lives in Surrey across the Fraser River from Vancouver. I then compare and contrast these individuals, noting similarities and differences regarding the context of learning and making art, the content of the art, and the concerns of the artists. Finally, I discuss concepts of art, folklore, and folk art. My purpose is not only to identify which iconographers create folk art, thereby addressing one of the many conundrums in classifying iconographers in Western Canada, but also to suggest more fully the role of aesthetic expression in people's everyday lives.

FOUR ARTISTS AND THEIR WORKS

The data in this section derive from more extensive field documentation of a dozen iconographers (see Jones, 1994b, 1995a). I include information about the artists here for comparative purposes in order to discuss concepts, not to present "biographies," "life histories," or "life stories" (Faulds and Skillman, 1984; Kirshenblatt-Gimblett, 1989; Oring, 1987; Titon, 1980). I have selected these four individuals because they and their work best illuminate the issue of who does or does not create folk art as well as when and why.

Gary Robertson

Of Polish and Ukrainian descent on the side of his mother, who married a Scottish immigrant, Gary Robertson was born in November, 1939. He lives with his dog on a 100-acre farm in a house of his own construction overlooking the Whitemouth River near Elma, Manitoba. While working as a shipping clerk for the Hudson Bay department store in Winnipeg he moved out of town at the age of 21. Eventually he quit his job at the store to become a postman in East Selkirk. "But they kept building up, building up. . . . This isn't for me. . . . From there I decided to quit work and do exactly what I wanted to do. That was 20 years ago" when he moved to his present farm.

It took him two decades to complete his home, constructing it out of logs from two pioneer houses in the area. He built a wooden dome on one (the nave of a chapel inside), an observation tower on the other, and a bell tower between the two. The section of his home to

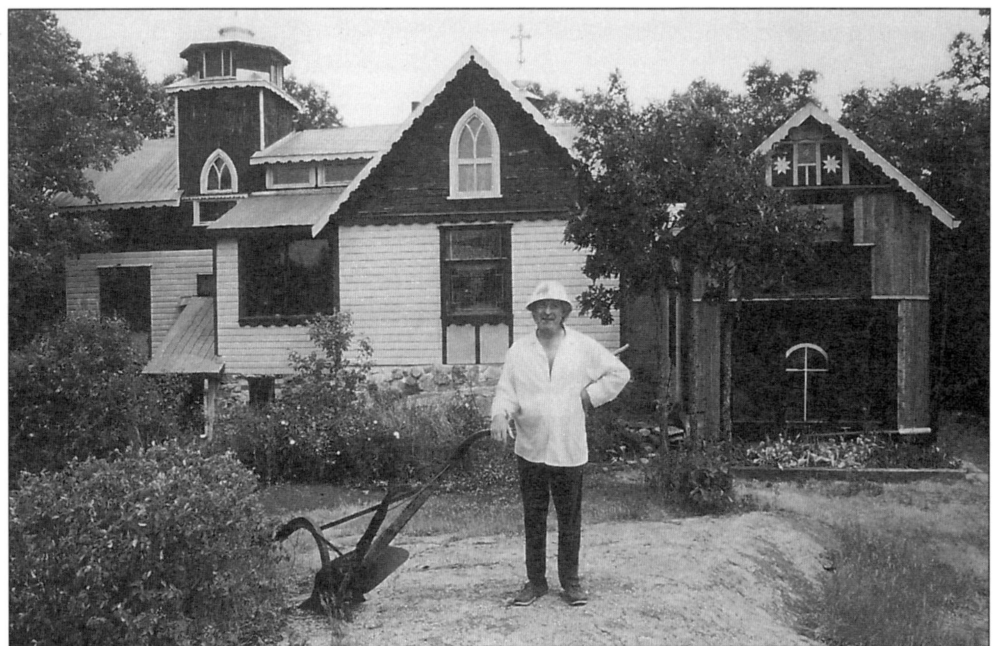

Gary Robertson and the "back" his house. Photo (1996): Michael Owen Jones.

the left of the entry contains a sixteen square foot chapel (half sanctuary, half nave) filled with perhaps four dozen icons that he has painted over the years. He obtained windows, siding, and stained glass from old churches, halls, and other abandoned buildings. He covered the roof in sheet metal, much of it salvaged.

The house features antique furniture and equipment as well as meticulously arranged, eye-catching displays of medicine bottles, tobacco cans, beverage bottles, dishes, and tea boxes among other items. He has adorned walls with his own paintings and textile pieces. Robertson has also chiseled Polish and Ukrainian designs on wooden beams as well as stenciled walls using a roller that he bought on a trip to Poland 25 years ago. Potted plants sit on tables, and vines climb the walls of the living room. The last room he completed is a green house, added to the east side of his log house.

Robertson has plans to enlarge the sun porch on the front of his house, to convert a third log building to a woodshed and storage room, and to build a bell tower to the west of the house. Although it has electricity and telephone, his home does not have indoor plumbing. He collects rain water in the summer through a drainage system from the roof to the basement, and snow in winter for cooking, drinking, and bathing. During warm weather he bathes in the river behind the house.

A triptych fills one corner of the dining room. Called "Madonna, Mother of God of Czestochowa," it replaces an earlier one purchased by the Canadian Museum of Civilization in 1993. Capped by rays from a cross salvaged from a church, the present triptych consists of six images. To the left at the top stands the Prophet Elijah below whom is St. Nicolas. On the right are St. John Padrom above St. George (Gary's favorites). In the center at the top are the Virgin and Christ child; below them Elijah rides to heaven in a fiery chariot. A white cloth covers the altar, the lower edge embroidered in red, green, and gold geometric designs. At the back are a printed prayer, a card depicting an icon, and a photograph of Father Semen Izyk, a local priest who died recently. "Old Father Izyk was thrilled with this chapel. Too bad he gave me a presentation [at a blessing in 1992] only in Ukrainian," which Gary does not understand well. On the wall to the left of the triptych hangs an embroidered piece by Gary above which is an icon of St. Mamas, the hermit saint. "Twenty years ago when I came here that's what the farmers nicknamed me: 'Oh, that's that old hermit lives down by the river.'"

Gary Robertson's mother and her brother rejected the ethnic language, customs, and Orthodox religion of their parents; she gave Gary to her parents to raise, demanding that he be an English speaking Roman Catholic. He lived with his grandparents most of his childhood and youth (they died a year and a half apart in the late 1960s), learning a bit of their household dialect (Polish, and a mixture of Polish and Ukrainian) as well as several Ukrainian customs and traditions from his grandfather, such as Easter egg dyeing, religious rituals, and embroidery and the making of traditional garments (the vest or *huppl* and the riding coat or *zupan*, which Gary wears on church holidays). In recent years he has tried to learn to read Ukrainian on his own. He has a small collection of works on Ukrainian churches and Byzantine icons (books, newspaper clippings, calendars), some of which serve as models and sources of inspiration for his paintings.

He painted his first icon when he was 15. It was a "small one of Our Lady of Poland with mantel," painted for his grandmother and based on a printed household icon of the "Black Madonna," "Our Lady of Czestochowa" (Kurelek, 1981:4), or the "Queen of Poland, with the scarred face" (Kostash, 1993:157). "I wanted to make something special for my grandmother, to bring home," said Robertson. "I was visiting my dad, my stepmother. . . . After that I was hooked." He began painting Ukrainian style Easter eggs about this time and also started an embroidered piece, finished only recently, that he worked on when emotionally troubled.

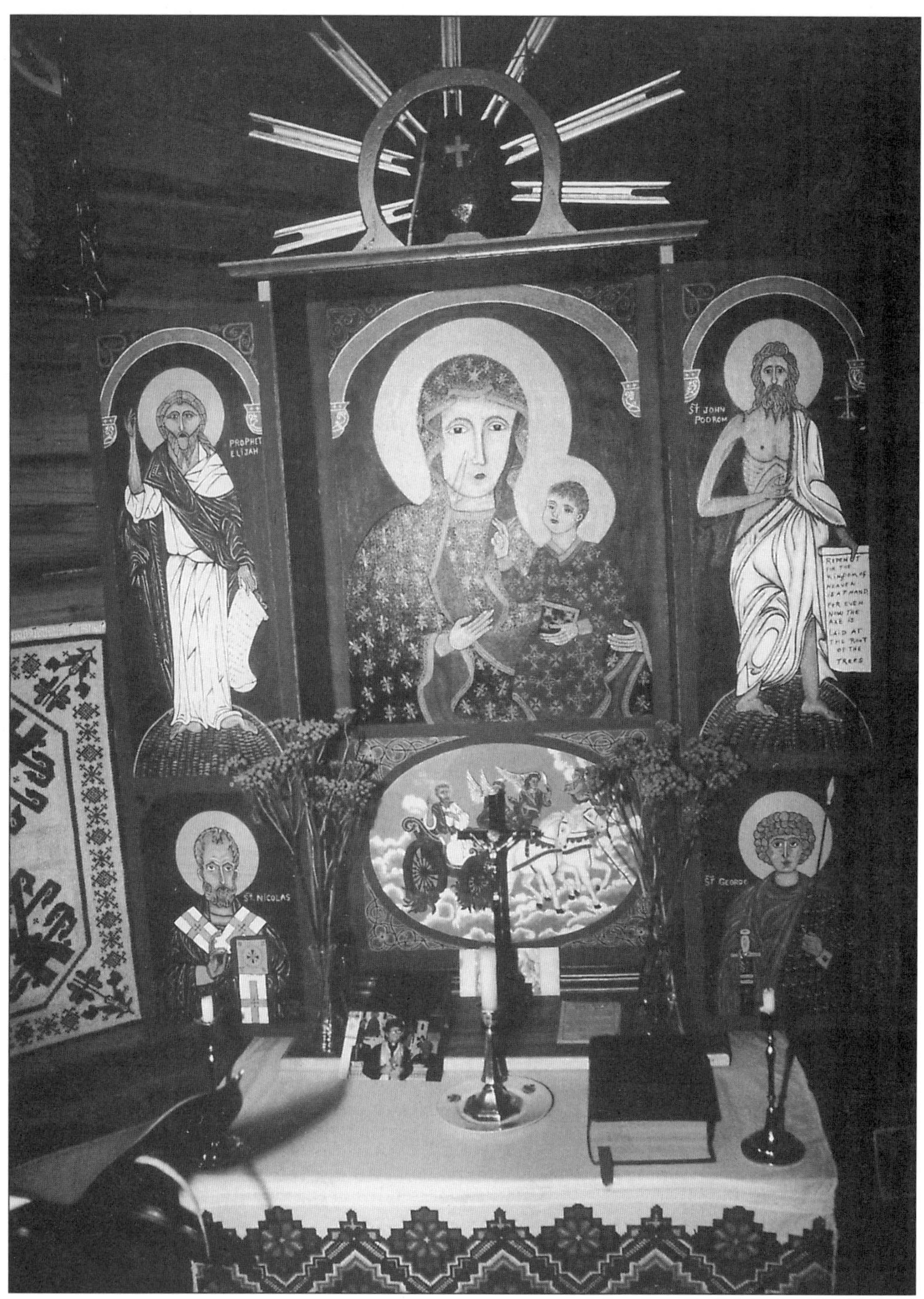

Gary Robertson's triptych, "Madonna, Mother of God of Czestochowa." Photo (1996): Michael Owen Jones

The tripych purchased by the Canadian Museum of Civilization in 1993 (the first icon he ever sold) typifies Robertson's style in painting, architecture, and interior decoration. It is visually "dense," even "cluttered," as well as "textured," every surface covered with designs or images. The back and sides of the box are painted medium blue with scallops and swirls in white and navy, giving the case a "marbled" effect. He painted a floral motif on the backs of the side panels in yellow, red, and green on dark background. The triptych is highly symmetrical, elements replicating or echoing each other and hence "balanced."

Robertson mentioned several times that he is self-taught as a builder and icon painter, although many years ago he purchased paints and received some instruction in iconography from Jacob Maydanyk (1891-1984) who had a church supply store from Winnipeg. Many of Gary's icons derive from images in calendars, newspaper clippings, and books as well as visits to churches in Manitoba. They represent different countries, cultures, eras, and styles. Some are his own combination of elements. He paints mostly in oil (often on masonite), but sometimes uses acrylic or even house paint. "I don't have access to a lot of paint," he said. He is vague about canons and procedures. "With no schooling I guess I just paint by my own method."

Talking about his way of doing things, such as the red floor in one room, fushia in another, and a mixture of Native American and Oriental rugs throughout, he said, "I'm a little outlandish in my colors. The house was actually a nice peach color, on the outside. The sun turned it pink. So I painted it yellow," although one section is unpainted wood and another is still pink. As he talked about the design of the house he said, "Balance is important, I guess. Like what a window will look like on the inside, it's got to look good outside: at night, with lights on. Everything has got to have a sense of balance."

When I noted that the house has a tactile quality inside and out, Robertson replied, "This is not just a house or a home, this is my own exterior from inside, my soul's exteriorizing with the building. Other people, I go in their houses, they have these new chipboard walls, I can't stand them, I'm totally uncomfortable in it. I could live in a 10 x 20 log shack. The fact that it's wood, it's logs, it's natural. Touching. So I guess when I'm sitting in the room everything is touching me, because in a sense everything in it is from within. Like some people, say, gee, like I've got so much clutter on the walls, but I can't stand bare walls. When I look at something, I might have the TV on but God knows where my mind is. So I need all these interesting things to look at."

In regard to the many indoor plants he said, "It's living too, like the house. I guess the house is living too, because it's all wood, it's all natural. . . . Without the plants the house is dead. I used to have less plants, used to put everything outside in summer, but frankly I could not stand looking —everything else in the room was fine but it was out of balance. That was the balance that was missing, the plants. Where I waited always for fall, put them back in again, it felt comfortable. And they're nice in the winter because you look out on snow, but there's all this green stuff."

Why construct the house, build the chapel, paint icons? "A hard question to answer," replied Robertson. After a pause he said, "I feel *directed* to have done this. That's the only way to describe it. There's no other motivation behind it. It's just something I had to do."

Slavko Protic

Born in 1947, Slavko Protic entered an art seminary in Belgrade, Yugoslavia, at age 13, the youngest student. He graduated with training in journalism, creative writing, photography, and illustration. In his 20s he wrote poetry, publishing three volumes for which he also did the illustrations. While in Paris in the 1980s he studied iconography of the Western Renaissance, which led him to seek instruction in Byzantine Orthodox art. According to Slavko's wife,

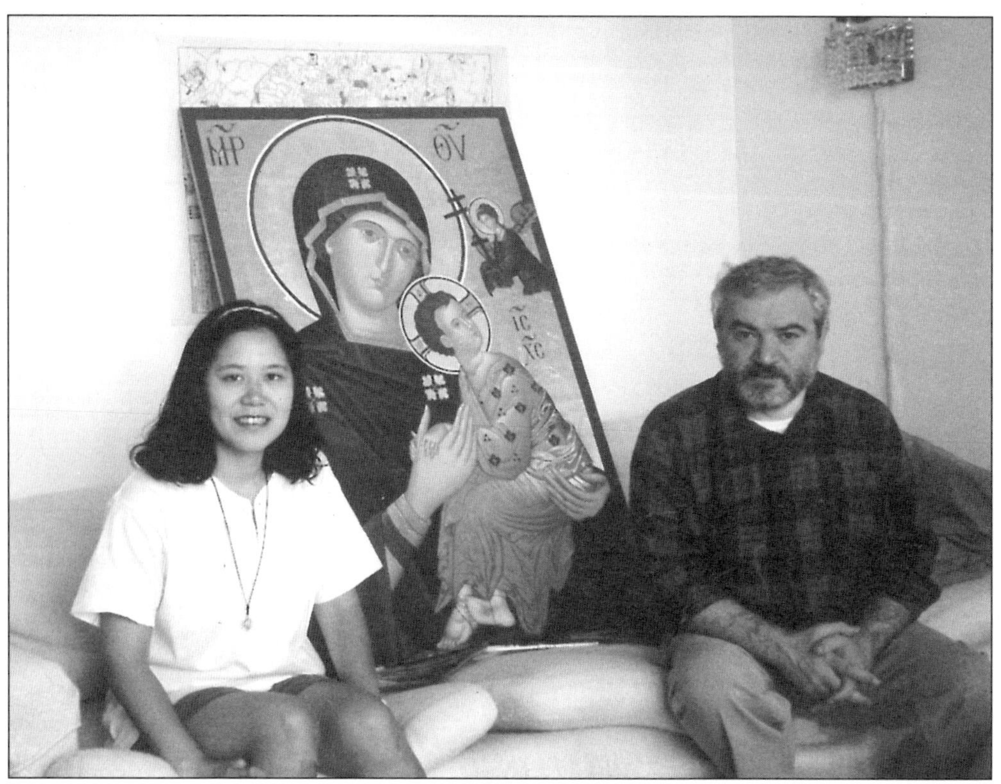

Regine and Slavko Protic with the latter's icon, *Mother of God of Canada*, acquired by the Canadian Museum of Civilization (cat. no. 94-86).

Regine, who describes his work in a letter (6 November 1993), "the greatest authority of iconography" — Bishop Daniel Krstich — "ordained Slavko as a deacon of iconography. Slavko is the first iconographer of the Eastern Orthodox Church to be ordained in over three hundred years." At first Slavko copied old icons but in 1988, when he travelled to North America where he finally settled in 1991, "he started painting new icons following the old canons." By now "Slavko has painted about thirty new icons, proto-types and they have a new heritage attached to the old tradition." He has created several images localized to Canada such as "The Joy of Canada," "The Eight Saints of North America", "St. Smirenkov the Aleut Elder," and "St. Peter the Aleut." Regine writes, "Plans for the future are to include the old native and Celtic art into iconography."

"Mother of God of Canada" exemplifies Protic's work. Painted with acrylics, it depicts the Virgin holding the Christ Child. A set of four maple leaves adorns the purple mantel on the Virgin's head and two other sets appear on her shoulders. Half a dozen leaves dangle from her right shoulder. Seven maple leaves appear on Christ's blue garment. The painting, purchased by the Museum in January, 1994, resembles "Joy of Canada" which graces the cover of *The Canadian Orthodox Missionary* (May/June, 1993). As Regine wrote (16 August 1993), "The Mother of God, herself symbolizes Canada in general. Her three stars are painted as Maple Leafs. The Infant Jesus garment is decorated with the Fleur de lis in the Maple Leaf. Symbolizing: Mother Canada, Keeping her child Quebec, sitting in her lap. This icon is 33 inches by 50 inches."

Because of general ignorance of Orthodoxy in Vancouver, said Protic, he could not find a church that would have the painting. There's also the issue of the maple leaves. "Nobody wanted it then. This is a 'satanic symbol '— the maple leaf. Can you imagine believing in this?" Asked why he painted it, he replied, "Because I discovered there is no Mother of God in Canada, and I came to live in Canada. And even if I want to go back [to Yugoslavia] I cannot. I'm banished forever. So, I live in this country, I'm supposed to do something for this country."

We had been discussing various matters including canons on the one hand, and "prototypes" on the other. Both concepts arose as he sorted through a pile of transfers: drawings on thin, transluscent paper — the back covered with graphite — that he uses to make multiple paintings of the same image. He knows the historical tradition of using aged oak or lime boards painted with homemade egg tempera composed of natural pigments. Such materials are not available to him, however, so he uses acrylics on masonite covered with skin glue and gesso, a choice for which he has been criticized. But he contends that there are no canons concerning materials, only colors (red for the Father, green for the Holy Spirit, purple for the world of God), the lack of three-dimensional perspective, the creation of a radiant inner light, and the avoidance of modeling the figures after particular individuals.

Protic also defends his creation of images and use of motifs for which there are no iconographic antecedents. These are his "prototypes," such as the "Mother of God of Canada" with its maple leaves. He insists that iconography should include some symbolism of the country in which it is painted. "This country does something for you and you are supposed to do something for this country. As much as you can. To settle down. Because you cannot live here — I mean sleep here, eat here — and to have your roots somewhere else. . . . You are in this country, and everything in iconography—there is a rule, and the rule is, you cannot take anything away. So you can add, but on the only one condition not to destroy the old way."

Protic has added to iconography by painting saints for which there are no known icons, creating images with symbols and design elements not previously included, and experimenting with subject matter and form (e.g., creating an "icon" of Gorbachev as a Black Knight slaying a dragon, and painting religious subject matter on the wide border of an arched mirror). Despite a desire to sustain himself financially through his art, he has found little market for icons, including his novel ones.

Varvara (Barbara) Rashid

Varvara Rashid was born in Bucharest, Romania, on 15 April 1961. Her mother was Orthodox; her father, a German, was neither Orthodox nor Catholic. In 1978 she received her high school diploma in architecture. According to an elaborate, four-color brochure listing her academic and artistic credentials, she has exhibited in Romania, West Berlin, Bulgaria, Yugoslavia, Hungary, Italy, and Canada. She later resided in Rome with her husband, Aldin (who has a doctorate in architectural history), where they collaborated to create, exhibit, and sell sacred art, particularly icons, and to restore and conserve art and antiquities. Presently they live in Vancouver where they opened a gallery of art, antiques, and restoration.

In an interview, Varvara said that she began making icons as a youth, at that time for family and local use. "I was painting icons out of the rules of iconography since child times. Just trying to imitate what I see in a book or what I have in my house collection." She was asked by people to paint icons that they could donate to the church. "So it was very much a kind of house thing with neighbors and friends," not with any thought of exhibiting her work. It was obvious, however, that she possessed great artistic talent.

She studied art and architecture in high school, turning to surrealism (as well as realism and photo realism) and leaving icon painting behind. It was Aldin who insisted that she return

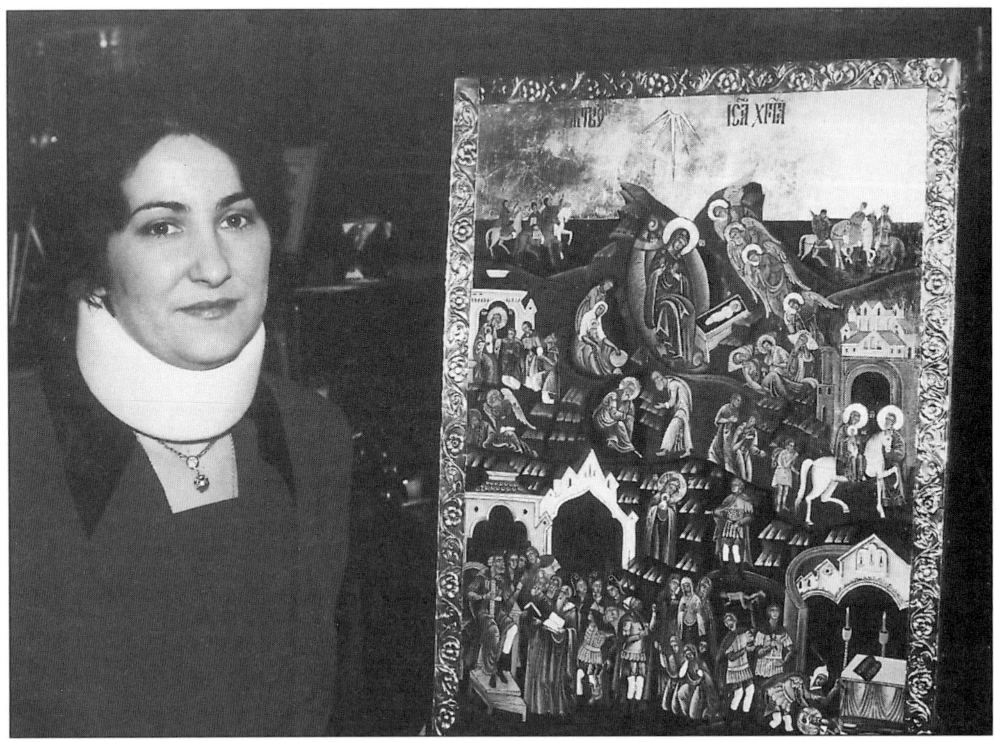

Varvara Rashid with one of her icon paintings. Photo (1995): Michael Owen Jones.

to tradition and take up icon painting again. "I learn academic art. Not just self taught. Seventeen to 20 years old, I didn't keep with the tradition; I was going very wild and surrealistic in my paintings. But then my husband said, 'Hey, you have to keep with your things. Nobody else is going to do it.' So he was more adult and mature than me [11 years separate them in age]. He was at that time a student in the architect school."

A newspaper article (Scott, 1992) mentions Varvara as a descendant "of one of Eastern Europe's greatest icon makers," Radu Munteanu. It also refers to some of the "rules" and "canons" of icon painting that Varvara follows. For example, the painting must receive the blessing of a priest before it is completed. Icons must be painted on wood using egg tempera: wood because Christ was crucified on a wood cross and Joseph was a carpenter, and egg because it symbolizes the cosmos. The gold leaf represents the divine light of God, blue and green are associated with human life, red indicates divinity; Christ's garments are blue and red, signifying his dual nature as human and divine. According to family tradition, she said, God may not be given corporeal representation. She insists on using mineral pigments in order to remain true to the traditional palette. Varvara has painted hundreds of icons, which now are priced at $1,000 to $30,000, many cloaked in embossed silver by Aldin. Monsignor Pietro Amato, the Vatican's icon expert, has certified that Varvara's icons are faithful to the old traditions.

Varvara painted realistic frescoes and surrealistic images to display in their Vancouver shop because so many people looking at her icons with their lack of three dimensional perspective and their simplified forms assume that she possesses limited artistic ability. "I tell you, I can paint as well as anyone else as an academic painter. . . . You don't choose to paint in this manner because you don't have the talent to do it realistically, it's just that that's the way it has to be done. It doesn't mean you don't have talent. And when I got in West, a lot of people didn't understand this thing: 'That's a limitation, that's the way she can paint, a little naive, not proportional, not the right shadow and light or something.' They didn't understand."

On hearing about other icon painters I had documented, such as Gary Robertson, Varvara said, "There's another person doing the same thing, in Vancouver, did you know that? He has a church on his house, real Orthodox and self-taught. Edward Hartley. He's a doctor."

"He looks just like a father," said her husband, Aldin.

"He looks like a priest but he's just a normal married man," continued Varvara. "Converted Orthodox. He built his chapel and painted all over, his church, his chapel in his own backyard. I, really, he may not have as much talent as many other iconographers but he's the first iconographer I've met that he's doing it with a full believing heart. You know what I mean? Probably like the man in Manitoba. I have some of his works at home? To me, I like them. They are so, I mean, you can feel the believe in it, not the artist so much, okay? It's really interesting."

Edward Hartley

Born in November, 1935, Edward Hartley is a semi-retired physician (general practitioner), self-taught icon painter, and an admitted "eccentric." Raised in Nova Scotia, he was brought up Anglican. "I started painting icons, let's see, married in '67, started painting in '68. It's just a hobby. We [his wife and he and their three children] became Orthodox in '71 and we joined the OCA, the Orthodox Church of America, daughter of the Russian church."

Why become Orthodox? "Because of the beauty and the truth, that's a good way to put it. We were led to Orthodoxy through the icons. And through our reading. And then we, in '70 we started attending an Orthodox church in Vancouver, the Holy Ressurection, the Russian one at 43rd and Quebec. And then we went there, would alternate one Sunday at the Anglican church and one Sunday at the Orthodox church, but we knew that our hearts were really Orthodox so eventually we were received."

With the help of a Greek immigrant, he built a chapel in 1976 in the backyard of his home in Surrey. Constructed of concrete blocks, it is painted silver. Laminated cedar beams support the omega-shaped roof. Wooden letters on the front chapel beam spell out in Greek a phrase from Psalm 68:26: "Bless God in the congregations." Hartley altered English characters to appear Greek, e.g., making the Greek "e" by reversing the direction of a number 3, turning the "v" upsidedown to form the lamda, and removing the bar from the "f" to transform the letter into a gamma while using the bar from the "f" to create a theta. In 1981 he added a porch on the north side of the west end, its shape emulating a cross. He built a raised, covered patio next to the chapel in 1991, the columns made from cardboard tubes—paper rolls—from the local paper mill. The Parthenon (or mini-Parthenon), as he calls it, as well as a shed next to it are light blue; the Hartley's house is white with blue trim.

Hartley prepared a 14-page booklet about his chapel. It describes the building, notable icons, and religious gifts from friends and acquaintances. It includes brief vignettes or short stories regarding what is depicted in some icons (he has painted nearly 500 most of which are in the chapel) along with scriptural passages and citations. It reads much like Hartley talked during a tour.

For instance, Hartley pointed to a mouse in the righthand corner above the door frame inside the porch, and a bird in the left corner. He said, "We have a church mouse, of course, and a little robin. It says in the Psalms the sparrow found herself a house and the swallow a nest where she lay her young. We didn't have a sparrow or a swallow so we came up with a robin." On page 5 of his booklet he writes, "Notice the mouse above the entrance door, and the robin,

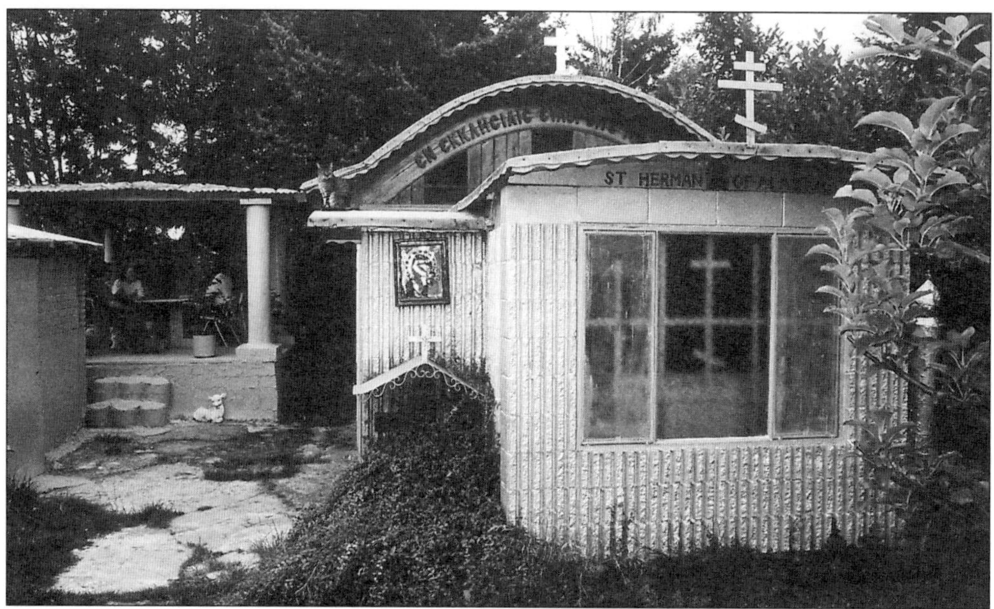

Edward Hartley's chapel and mini-Parthenon. Photo (1995): Michael Owen Jones.

given by Sheila Kirkwood. Yea, the sparrow hath found her an house, and the swallow a nest for herself, where she may lay her young, even thine altars, O Lord of hosts, my king and my God' (Psalm 84:3)."

The first page of his booklet states that "Saint Herman of Alaska Chapel was built in 1976 to the glory of Almighty God and in honour and memory of the newly-canonized Saint Herman the Wonderworker of Alaska, a Russian missionary and monk who came to Alaska in 1794; and in thanks to the Lord for their conversion to the Orthodox Faith of Edward and Vivian Hartley and their children James, Maria and Andrea in 1971." Pages two through six orient the reader to several architectural features, explaining what they are, who built them, where the materials came from. The remaining pages describe prominent icons, the iconostasis and altar, and donated items used in chapel services.

One inside wall of the porch boasts a stained glass window donated by Bill Manley whose mother brought it from England many years before. Filling the west end is a window with a cross in the center that was made, writes Hartley (p. 4), "by Allan Haggerty in memory of his daughter, Kathleen, who passed away at age five in 1979. May she be with those innocent ones 'which follow the Lamb withersoever He goeth' (Relevation 14:4)." When Hartley showed me the window, saying it was made by a man in Winnipeg in memory of his little girl, he concluded, "Everything [in the chapel] sort of has a little story."

Inside the chapel icons are everywhere. Large ones (perhaps three feet high) adorn the walls, their centers a little above eye level. Smaller icons hang above the larger ones. And above them is a frieze around the nave just below the ceiling; it consists of small, square paintings on thick glass blocks (e.g., on the north side are images of the serpent that tempted Eve, Noah's ark, the burnt offering, the burning bush, the seven-branched candleholder, King Solomon's temple, the symbols of Christ — the cross, the fish, the lamb of God — a dove representing the Holy Spirit, and wheat and grapes for Holy Communion). "And we have icons, of course, even

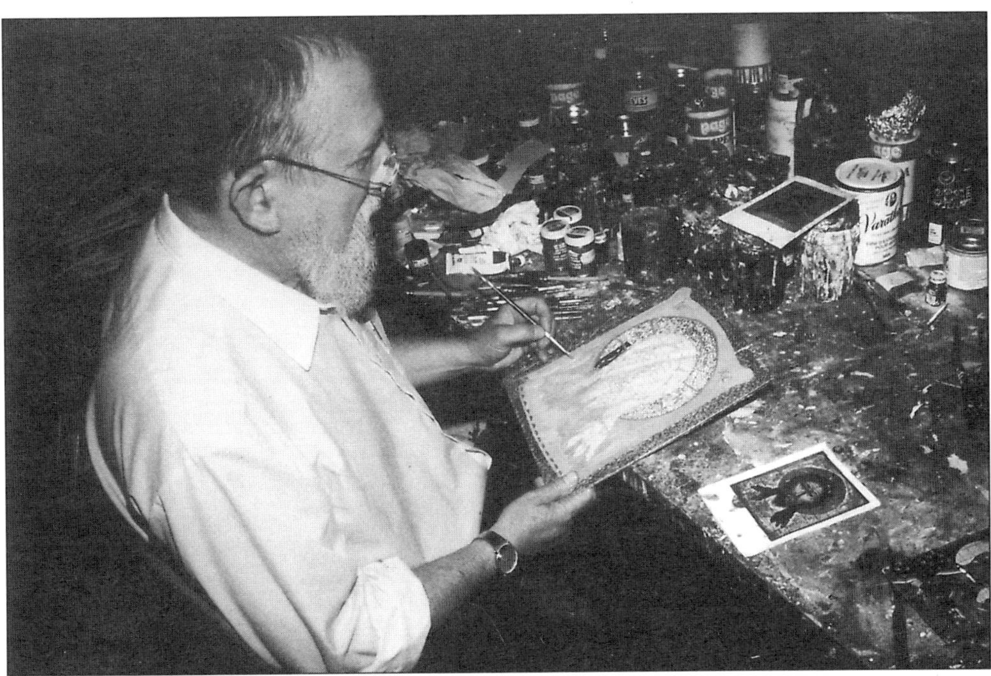

Edward Hartley painting an icon at his worktable. Photo (1995): Michael Owen Jones.

on the ceiling. We have more icons than any church in North America." Hartley laughed as he said this. He has stored many others in racks in the sanctuary.

Why do all this? "Uhhhh, a bit of uh, I hope, I hope a bit of healthy insanity, you have to be a little bit insane to, uh, uh, you have to be a little bit insane to be Christian in the first place, and a lot insane to be Orthodox." Hartley chuckled. "But we, I paint icons as a hobby, so we had the idea —there was a fellow in Victoria once had converted his backyard, uh, garage into a chapel. That's where I got the idea from. And then, I always had the idea of building one, but didn't have much carpentry ability. I built a bird house once and the birds wouldn't live in it!" he joked. "We met, uh, a Greek fellow we know for years that was out of work, Nick the Greek [Nicholas Fardoulis], so I told him my idea and a couple of days later he was over with the plans. So we took the plans to City Hall, didn't tell them we were buiding a chapel because I knew they would refuse it, wouldn't give us a permit, so we told them we were building a storage shed. So he said, 'That looks pretty fancy, what are you gonna store there?' So I said, 'I do a lot of painting, I want to store my paintings.' I think he figgered out I was a pretty conceited guy, so anyhow he gave us the permit. We went ahead."

In regard to painting, said Hartley, "I used to fiddle around a little bit with paints when I was a kid, you know, a few landscapes and such. And I'm self-taught, which is evident from the quality of the pictures, but we have fun." He chuckled. "I always say I enjoy my paintings even if nobody else does." For the most part he uses water tempera (Varvara Rashid recently introduced him to egg tempera which he has rarely used), often on cardboard, and varnishes the icon. A retired neighbor who haunts garage sales provides the frames.

A long table, paint splattered and covered with cans and brushes, fills the north wall of a room in the basement of his house. "I have a whole iconostasis and no place to put it," he said, chuckling; "and another small one in the furnace room!" He pointed to two small commercial prints on the righthand corner of the table, one the Black Madonna and the other a portrait of Christ. He had drawn lines across them horizontally and vertically. "I cheat when I draw them 'cause I square them off usually — get a more accurate drawing — and then make my squares bigger on the one I'm actually copying." When I took a photo, he posed, paintbrush in left hand, appearing to work on the copy of the Christ icon.

Later Hartley showed me an icon with orange background. It is the upper torso portrait of Christ in a red robe and green mantel, book in left hand, fingers of the right hand forming IC XC (the lower fingers stick straight out, symbolizing the two natures of Christ). The words "He Who Is" are in Christ's halo with "Ruler" to the left of the head and "of All" to the right. "This one is an egg tempera one. The colors . . . . the colors have more to them, there's more to them. Although some of the water, uh, tempera ones are quite nice too. But, but, because it's built up in the layers. The original has the 'He who is' or 'I am' in Greek. But I like to put some in English. . . . they're s'posed to be done on wood panels, of course — so purists get most upset when I do them on cardboard but I say, 'Cardboard is a processed wood.'" He has painted the back silver. "So if you have room in your luggage you can take an icon back, you see; then you can say you have an original Hartley icon. It won't be worth anything if it ever is for about 50 years until after I'm gone," he said, laughing, "but you can enjoy it." Later he remarked that by receiving an icon I will remember him. "And maybe some day we'll hop in the car and drive to California," he said, chuckling. "Somebody'll be knocking at your door. . . ."

COMPARISONS: CONTEXT, CONTENT, AND CONCERNS

The next step in considering who paints folk icons is to compare the four individuals in regard to context, content, and concerns. "Context" includes the circumstances in which they learned and manifested or displayed icon painting. "Content" comprises themes, materials, skill level, and degree of novelty. "Concerns" refers to why they paint icons and how they use them, what their personal aspirations are, and how icon painting relates to other aspects of their lives and experiences (for other treatments of such matters, see Bethke, 1996; Bronner, 1985; Feintuch, 1976; Flores-Peña and Evanchuk, 1994; Jones, 1989; Vlach, 1981; and Volkersz, 1989).

As icon painters all four are, to varying degrees, self-taught. Both Gary Robertson and Edward Hartley admitted to no formal training — other than the brief instruction of Robertson by Maydanyk and Hartley's general experiences in public school. Varvara Rashid taught herself in childhood to paint icons. Slavko Protic took up icon painting on his own after being trained as an illustrator. Rashid and Protic differ from the others, however, in that both have had extensive academic training and experience in illustration, painting, and/or architecture.

Besides differences in the circumstances of learning and degree of formalized training, the artists differ in regard to the situations in which or for which they paint. Robertson and Hartley create icons for viewing in their homes and chapels by themselves, family, friends, and guests. Robertson has refurbished banners and a wooden grave marker/altar for the Holy Cross Ukrainian Catholic Church in Elma where he serves as cantor and handiman, but his icons have not been substituted for or added to those in the church. He does not paint icons for sale, only personal use (the Museum's purchase of his first icon and a recent triptych was instigated by the institution for research purposes). Hartley intends to furnish his chapel and to have an icon for every day of the month (he apologized when I visited in August because the month's collection was incomplete; he had not yet painted an icon for the twelfth). His chapel offered regular services for 60 parishioners from 1978 to 1983, until a church was constructed in Langley, and still provides vespers and liturgies on special occasions. Like the donated items in his chapel, the icons that Hartley gives to others as gifts establish and reflect interpersonal relationships. By contrast, both Protic and Rashid seek to support themselves financially by the sale of icons to museums, churches, and private collectors. Both have exhibited in local galleries and sought publicity for their work. Paintings on display at home (Protic) or in a shop (Rashid), however personally meaningful, are for sale; they are commodities to be purchased by others, many of whom are not of the same religious background but who purchase the works for aesthetic and financial reasons.

In regard to content, different skill levels are obvious to the painters as well as viewers. Trained artists like Protic and Rashid have great control over color, brushwork, line, and mass. They are also masters of detail. Rashid is at work on an icon with 2,000 figures. Protic completed a painting of a battle in 1389 between Christian and Turkish armies (approximately five feet high by 12 feet wide) containing 3,000 portraits; it convinced Daniel Krstich, the Bishop of Buda, to empower Protic as a deacon of Orthodox iconography. Hartley and Robertson paint on whatever surface is at hand, often cardboard and masonite, and with available pigments, particularly water tempera (Hartley) and oils or house paint (Robertson). Rashid and Protic use specially prepared materials, the former insisting on egg tempera composed of natural pigments that she prepares herself. Hartley copies images, relying on the use of a grid technique. Both he and Robertson paint icons in varying styles from different eras and cultures. Protic and Rashid employ a consistent style. While adhering to certain conventions in representation, both Protic and Rashid paint novel images and formats. Rashid often creates icons that her husband can ornament with extensive silver embossing. Protic has painted an icon modeled after a totem pole, he incorporates unusual motifs such as primitive Celtic symbols and maple leaves, and he has produced numerous "prototypes" or icons lacking exact precedents or parallels.

The artists' concerns, self-image, and aspirations differ. Protic and Rashid clearly aspire to be identified as noted artists. They exhibit in galleries, seek publicity for their art, and hope to support themselves by selling icons to institutions and individuals. To the extent that their work is market driven, their art is separate from everyday life and greatly influenced by external factors, although as a youth Rashid painted icons for family and neighbors. By contrast, Hartley identifies himself as a semiretired physician and a devout convert to Orthodoxy, not principally an artist (a title he bears apologetically). He painted icons as a testament of his faith, built a chapel for fellow believers, and furnished the building with items donated by others as a means of connecting them to him as well as each other. Robertson views himself largely in terms of what he is not. He spurns city dwelling, a steady job, and urban life generally; his principal concessions to modernity consist of a telephone and antiquated TV set, refrigerator, and stove. He lives in a log house without running water furnished with antiquities salvaged from demolished buildings. He has reconstructed some of the older ethnic customs, rituals, language, and way of life rejected by his mother and her brother. His chapel and paintings testify to his conversion; they also construct a pleasing, sensuous, and spiritual environment integral to his daily life, proclaiming to his religious identity, his respect for the past, and his ability to live simply in the modern world without being enslaved to its technology or (misguided) values.

THE CONCEPTS OF ART, FOLKLORE, AND FOLK ART

Given the information about context and concerns along with content, one can readily guess which creations are least folk. But the inference is intuitive rather than articulated according to explicit criteria. Explaining why some works are examples of folk art and others are not requires a review of definitions and conceptions of folk and folk art. Five prevail.

"Modern Primitives" and "Outsider Art"

Usually associated with the art world rather than ethnography, one conception of folk art dwells on paintings and sculpture that are not part of the art "mainstream." They are said to be works by untutored, untrained, self-taught individuals ("naive primitives," "modern primitives"), usually not tied to cultural or ethnic traditions; alternatively, the creations of recluses or isolates, "outsiders," and "visionaries" (Hall and Metcalf, 1994; Volkersz, 1989).

This conception is rooted in the 1920s when a group of American painters attempting to break away from European models began to collect and emulate the simple, straightforward forms of eighteenth- and nineteenth-century nonacademics such as itinerant limners, sign painters, and carvers of duck decoys, carousel horses, or cigar store Indians and other figures (Metcalf, 1983, 1986; Metcalf and Weatherford, 1988; Rumford, 1980). It was elaborated by Cahill (1932), Janis (1942), Lipman and Winchester (1950, 1974), Bishop (1979), and others. In 1968 Blasdel introduced the term "grassroots artist" as an alternative to "primitive" and "naive" to distinguish the reclusive, isolated individual who creates large structures from found materials. In the 1950s, French artist Jean Dubuffet identified works by patients in mental asylums and self-taught visionaries as *Art brut* (translated to English as "raw art"). British critic Roger Cardinal (1972) popularized art brut with the term "outsider art," that is, art created by cultural outsiders.

According to this conception, none of the four iconographers has produced folk art and, simultaneously, all four have done so. None is a cultural outsider. Each represents a religious tradition, apparent in the way that Orthodox spirituality infuses the lives of Robertson and Hartley, on the one hand, and, on the other, the Bishop of Buda's proclaming Protic as a deacon of Orthodox iconography and the certification by the Vatican's icon expert that Rashid's icons are faithful to the old traditions. Although the artists are not cultural outsiders, neither do their icons exemplify work in the mainstream art world; Rashid has even felt compelled to paint in a photo realism style in order to gain a degree of artistic recognition and acceptance. The other element in this conception of folk art, that of being self-taught, applies to Robertson and Hartley as well as Rashid before she pursued art school, and to some extent Protic (who, although trained as an illustrator, took up icon painting on his own). In and of itself the criterion of self-taught, like the notion of being outside the art mainstream, is not sufficient to differentiate folk from nonfolk icons (regarding these and similar definitional problems, see Ames, 1977, 1980; Jones, 1975; Metcalf, 1983, 1986; and Vlach, 1980, 1986).

The other four conceptions are associated with ethnography. The first two emphasize "folk," the latter two the circumstances in which the "lore" is generated. Those that concern folk differ in regard to the nature of the group to which the term is applied. The two that focus on the lore and its context depart from each other in regard to whether the perspective is cultural or behavioral.

"The" Folk and "a" Folk

The oldest of the four ethnographic conceptions concerns the folk as a substratum of modern society or as a rural group cut off from the urban main-stream. It dates back 200 years in folkloristics (Jones and Georges, 1997). Sociologist Robert Redfield summarized basic ideas in "The Folk Society" (1947), writing that (p. 293) "Understanding of society may be gained through construction of an ideal type of primitive or folk society as contrasted with modern urbanized society. Such a society is small, isolated, nonliterate, and homogeneous, with a strong sense of group solidarity. The ways of living are conventionalized into that coherent system which we call 'a culture.' Behavior is traditional, spontaneous, uncritical and personal; there is no legislation or habit or experiment and reflection for intellectual ends." He refers to these and related traits as "folk mentality."

On the basis of this definition none of the icons can be labeled folk. All of the iconographers experiment, reflect, and think critically. None grew up in an isolated, nonliterate, homogeneous environment. All are products of modern urbanized society, although arguably Robertson has rejected some of the elements of that world. People today, who cannot by any stretch of the imagination be considered "the folk," produce traditional aesthetic forms (see, e.g., Burgess, 1996; Jones, 1987; Joseph-Witham, 1996; Pershing, 1995; Posey, 1996; Wojcik, 1995). Identifying these works as folk art requires an alternative conception (although vestiges of the Redfieldian ideas persist in folkloristics, and the notion of folk society seems dominate in some other fields; see, e.g., Smith and Stannard, 1989).

In 1952, Richard M. Dorson wrote (p. 6) that "A fuzzy and much abused term, it [folk] could nevertheless convey a sharp and lucid meaning. It needed the indefinite article: *a* folk, not *the* folk. Any homogeneous group, any group that was vitally integrated, made a folk. Such groups were formed by places of residence. . . ; by racial and national stocks with a common culture; by occupations. . . ." In contrast to the Redfieldian notion of folk society, or "the folk," Dorson proposed the idea of "a folk" as any homogeneous, integrated group. As Redfield before him, however, Dorson assumes that the group consists of like-minded members who participate in a distinctive culture.

In 1965, Alan Dundes took a less restrictive view, writing (p. 2) that "The term 'folk' can refer to *any group of people whatsoever* who share at least one common factor [emphasis in original]. It does not matter what the linking factor is — it could be a common occupation, language, or religion —but what is important is that a group formed for whatever reason will have some traditions it calls its own" (see also Dundes, 1966). For Dundes, the group need not have an elaborate, integrated culture but only "some" distinctive traditions.

A dozen years later Jan Harold Brunvand elaborated on the notion folk groups (1978:28-29), adding to the basic list of occupational, age, regional, and ethnic or national groups those set apart by religion, education, hobbies, neighborhood, and family. He also insisted on "some degree of conformity with group tastes and values." Therefore, "the first test of a folk group is the existence of shared folklore; then the background of this conformity can be investigated."

If we use the notion of folk art as products of "a folk," then the works of all four iconographers are examples of folk art because all four can be considered members of a group that share a common factor: religion. Further, all participate in some of the distinctive traditions of that group, exhibiting conformity to tastes and values by accepting certain canons in icon painting. Intuitively, however, we sense that differences between or among the four painters outweigh similarities. Information about context, content, and concern suggests that some individuals produce folk icons and others do not. Although the idea of folk groups continues to be popular in folkloristics (e.g., Oring, 1985, 1989), some basis other than labeling icon painters as members of a common group (a folk) is needed in order to differentiate their works.

Art or Lore as Culture and Behavior

In "What Is Folk Art? An Opinion on the Controversy" (1983), Robert Teske writes (p. 35) that "folk art must be defined in terms of: first, its acceptance of and dependence upon a communal aesthetic shared by a group of artists and their audience and shaped and reshaped by them over time; second, its traditional nature, with its conservative emphasis upon perfecting old forms instead of creating entirely new ones; and third, its transmission via apparently informal, yet often highly structured and systematic means. In other words, it is the social context in which an artifact is created and responded to, rather than the attributes of the artifact itself or the collector's intuitive response to these attributes, that provides the firmest basis for classifying the object as folk art."

By stressing communal aesthetic, conservatism, structured transmission, and social context, Teske directs attention to art or lore as a cultural phenomenon. To be considered folk, the art must originate in and reflect a group's common aesthetics and values, not idiosyncratic ones. On the one hand, this conception suggests that the later works of Rashid and Protic are nonfolk because (although it might argued that they accept a communal aesthetic in regard to what constitutes an icon) the artists emphasize novelty, and formality rather than informality characterizes the art's transmission (learning and display). On the other hand, the definition does not render the works of Robertson and Hartley folk. For Teske concludes with the statement (p. 38), *"In other words, the self-taught artist is virtually never a folk artist"* (emphasis added). As we have seen, Robertson, Hartley, and the early Rashid were, by their own admission, largely self-taught. They did not learn in an informal apprenticeship system. It is also debatable that Robertson and Hartley are part of "a group of artists and their audience," although Hartley has interacted with Rashid (who introduced him to egg tempera) and Vladimir Blagonadejdin (who gives classes in icon painting).

The cultural approach in Teske's definition of folk art informs the writings of other folklorists, such as Burrison (1983), Vlach (1980, 1986, 1988), and Zug (1994). Works that are not communal or conservative and that are done by self-taught artists or that are novel cannot be considered folk art conceived of as "the product of culturally cohesive communities" (Benedetti, 1987:3). None of the icons is folk according to this conception even though intuition suggests that there are significant differences between current works by Protic and Rashid and those by Robertson, Hartley, and the early Rashid.

Three ways of attempting to solve this apparent paradox come to mind. One is to try to distinguish, as Joan Benedetti proposes (1987), between "ethnic folk art" and "self-taught folk art." The former is the product of a "culturally cohesive group" and the latter is created by those who exist "largely as outsiders vis à vis their communities." Benedetti's examples of the first include Navajo rugs, Amish quilts, and Ukrainian Easter eggs; for the second she mentions the religious paintings of Howard Finster, Simon Rodia's towers, and the bottle village by Tressa Prisbrey. It appears that when individual authorship is not known, the works are folk in a cultural sense but they lose this distinction when their makers are identified. If so, then the distinction is not as useful in differentiating works by the four icon painters as might at first appear because all four are known. Given that the four are of varied ethnic and religious backgrounds as well, it is doubtful that any represent a culturally cohesive group (on problems regarding a cultural approach, see Chinn, 1993; Jones, 1976).

A second possibility is to follow the lead of John Vlach (1986, 1988) who refers to Edward Hicks, John Freake, Grandma Moses, and others as "plain painters" in contrast to "master artists." That is, "in the paintings generally labeled as folk the conventions of fine art are present but not fully deployed. The net result is a work like fine art but simpler, less ostentatious; it is a plain version of what potentially could have been quite elaborate or complex under different circumstances" (Vlach,

1988:xv). Initially this seems a good way to differentiate works by Robertson and Hartley, the "plain painters," from icons by master artists Rashid and Protic. However, Vlach was writing about portraiture and genre paintings, not icons. "These paintings, both the new and the old, represent not folk but popular culture. Because these paintings bespeak novelty or the need for modish imagery, they are best understood not in terms of the history of folk traditions — which at bottom consist of conservative motives aimed at the presevation of social norms — but in terms of the history of fashion, the enthusiasm for new styles of art, dress, and decoration" (Vlach, 1988:178-179; see also Emans, 1991). In other words, the paintings and circumstances are really not comparable to those of the Canadian iconographers dealt with here.

Finally, we can take more of a behavioral rather than strictly cultural approach to the study of folklore and folk art (Jones, 1993, 1994a, 1995c). A behavioral perspective seeks to discover how folklore relates to individuals' personal experiences including the events in which people create and utilize folklore examples (Jones, 1989). In *Folkloristics* (1995), Georges and Jones define folklore (p. 1) as "expressive forms, processes, and behaviors (1) that we customarily learn, teach, and utilize or display during face-to-face interactions, and (2) that we judge to be traditional (a) because they are based on known precedents or models, and (b) because they serve as evidence of continuities and consistencies through time and space in human knowledge, thought, belief, and feeling."

This definition of folklore and Teske's conception of folk art exhibit many correspondences, but emphases differ because one is more behavioral and the other cultural. Hence, Teske's second and third criteria of traditionality and informal transmission closely resemble Georges and Jones's first and second points concerning learning/display in face-to-face interactions and the existence of precedents/evidence of continuities and consistencies. Taking a cultural approach, Teske stresses communality and group identity (p. 36): "shared communal aesthetic," "shared identity," rejecting "individual or idiosyncratic departures from the canon that the community has developed and agreed upon." He dwells on conservatism as his conception of the traditional (p. 37): "Certainly folk artists do not seek innovation and change as ends in themselves in the way fine artists often do"; "Small changes. . .within the limits imposed by the traditon." And he emphasizes an apprenticeship model as his notion of face-to-face interaction and informal learning (p. 35): "In most instances, folk artists acquire their skills through an informal apprenticeship or association with one or more senior artists in their community."

None of the definitions of folklore or folk art mentions icon painting in contemporary society; the phenomenon probably was not even thought about when authors set forth their definitions. However, matters of context, content, and concern discussed earlier in regard to the four iconographers indicate that the behaviorally oriented definition of folklore helps explain why, as intuition suggests, works by Robertson, Hartley, and the early Rashid are examples of folk art whereas icons by Protic and the later Rashid are not folk. All the works are based on known models and serve as evidence of continuities and consistencies, but icons by Protic and the older Rashid are marked by greater departures from those precedents, even novelty and the creation of prototypes for their own sake. (In folk art, there may be innovation within tradition; by contrast, in the academic realm of icon painting artists aspire to maintain a degree of tradition within innovation.) The learning of art and iconography was far less formalized for Robertson, Hartley, and the youthful Rashid than for Protic and Rashid later in life (both call attention to their academic credentials). And Robertson and Hartley's use or display of icons occurs in situations of firsthand interaction rather than institutional settings; to stimulate interest in their icons as commodities in the art marketplace, Rashid and Protic publicize their gallery exhibitions and the purchase of their works by noted museums and collectors (for classification of other icon painters, see Jones, 1995a).

SUMMARY AND CONCLUSION

The question of who creates folk art, when, and why is but one of several issues regarding the classification of icon painters and their works in Western Canada. The artists themselves offer clues to ascertaining who does and does not produce folk icons when they explain that they are self-taught or dwell on their academic credentials and institutional exhibits and sales. Distinctions become more apparent with the collection of detailed information about the circumstances in which they learned and manifested or displayed icon painting (context); the themes, materials, skill level, and degree of novelty (content); and reasons why they paint icons and how they use them, what their personal aspirations are, and how icon painting relates to other aspects of their lives and experiences (concerns). One of the definitions of folklore (Georges and Jones, 1995:1) provides a basis for differentiating folk from nonfolk icons by pointing to the greater emphasis on tradition rather than novelty in folk art and the tendency for it to be learned, created, and displayed in informal settings of face-to-face interactions rather than in formal, institutionalized circumstances.

Classifying data as folklore as well as establishing generic and type sets of folklore forms and examples constitutes a fundamental aspect of folkloristic inquiry. One step in designating expressive behaviors as folklore entails assembling information not only about objects and texts but also the makers or performers as well as the circumstances in which the lore is generated. Another involves examining the assembled data in terms of a definition of folklore. Because there are multiple and competing conceptions of folklore, the analyst must evaluate not only the data but also the definitions to determine which seems the most defensible and appropriate. Such assessment may lead to modifications in conceptions in order to accommodate newly created or recently documented examples. A study of folk icons, their painting and particularly their use, suggests the need for different ways to think about art (Jones, 1989; 1995c).

For many, "art" denotes the "fine arts" and "decorative art," that is, nonutilitarian forms exemplified by painting and sculpture (Glassie, 1972; Jones, 1975; Pocius, 1995). Yet "all people engage in a wide range of creative acts that are judged by standards of excellence" (Pocius, 1995:414). Folklorists have documented a variety of traditional aesthetic behaviors (Jones, 1995b), from yard decoration (Burgess, 1996; Kitchener, 1994) and the personalization of living and work space (Jones, 1996: Pimple, 1986) to the costume art of Star Trek fans (Joseph-Witham, 1996), aesthetic recycling (Greenfield, 1986), house remodeling (Jones, 1980), rubberstamps (Posey, 1996), home canning (Martin, 1979), cooking (Goldman, 1981), eating (Adler, 1981), and even the arrangement of trash cans (Jones, 1987). Such studies reveal the integral role of tradition and aesthetic expression in people's everyday lives.

Research on folk icons in Western Canada extends the implications of these studies. For the painters, creating icons is not simply a pastime. Nor does it have the goal of producing commodities for sale or achieving one's place in the circle of art connoisseurship and annals of art history. Other motivations and rewards attend the painting of icons.

Iconography brought Hartley, the Episcopalian, to "the beauty and the truth" of Orthodoxy. As he said, "There's a lot of theology in one picture" and "you learn a lot painting icons, you read the stories. . . . The icons really make the saints *real*, you know, in a way. They *are* real, and they are here, but the icons bring it home." As he surveys his works on the walls of the chapel, in racks behind the iconostasis, and on shelves in the basement of his house, he becomes caught up in their sensory qualities. "It's quite, I think it's one of my better ones," he said in reference to his painting of Christ's burial which is carried in procession around the church on Good Friday. "It's hard to judge your own work but it's certainly a beautiful icon. It's the, uh, the colors are very rich."

Hartley has not only painted nearly 500 icons but also constructed a chapel to house them and serve the spiritual needs of himself, his family, and 60 other people. Holding their infant granddaughter, Vivian said, "Ed brings her in almost every day and talks to her about the church and the icons. You and Grandpa visit the church together, don't you?" Hartley displays items on window ledges, cabinet tops, door frames, and hanging from the ceiling that have been donated by friends and parish-ioners described by Hartley in his booklet and on tours. "Once you start something like this you'd be amazed what people bring you." Later, pointing to a star in the ceiling of the nave that someone had given him, he said, "Everything has a little, sort of a little story attached to it, a little memory." In sum, Hartley has created an environment that is at once a place of worship, a gallery of art, and a museum of memories. The space is both personal and communal, a place for private reflection and social interaction.

As in Edward Hartley's case, Gary Robertson's art consists not so much of the four dozen icons he painted but the lifestyle and environment he has created — the house he built and the way he furnishes it including chapel, altar in the dining room, plants, and assemblages of found and salvaged objects. Everywhere you see rich colors and textures, religious statuary, and antiques treated as sculptural forms. The logs of walls and ceilings are exposed, their earth tones a warm background for the reds, blues, and gold that dominate his icons. The green, carefully tended plants throughout the house add accent. Above windows, hanging from the ceiling, nailed to the walls, and resting in many nooks and crannies are old tools, equipment, and utensils such as snow shoes, drawing knives, a hand auger, crockery, a broad ax, bridle, and wash board. Oriental rugs cover the kitchen and living room floors. Antique chairs, cabinets, and cooking utensils furnish the kitchen. The room's walls are brick. A storage area in one corner above the wood stove and the old electric stove holds crockery pots, a huge copper tub, and tea kettles all of which rest on a beam into which he incised Polish designs in 1985. "These are from our Slavic past, too," he said. Designs carved into the upper wall in the dining room are of his own making. "I had no schooling" in art, architecture, and many other endeavors. "Just came out naturally. My old aunt says, 'You live the way people used to live.'"

Robertson has painted the living room floor deep red, the chapel floor black. The lower walls of the chapel are light blue, the upper wall light yellow, and the ceiling of the nave a medium blue. Chapel beams and other wood supports are exposed, their natural wood color and scalloped edges and other decorative elements framing the brightly painted walls and icons. "This is preaching. . . , but it's silent preaching. These, these icons stare out at you over, you know, time and into eternity. . . . They represent what's in another world. We don't worship them or anything, we just show them respect because of what they represent. . . .".

Like Hartley, Robertson has created a sanctuary, in this instance a refuge from the noise, pollution, and sources of stress and tension of city life of which he despairs. It is an environment that not only protects the body and nurtures the soul but also symbolizes an identity — a sense of self — that Robertson, like Hartley, has created. Their lives are their art.

References

Adler, Elizabeth Mosby. 1981. Creative Eating: The Oreo Syndrome. *Western Folklore* 40:4-10.

Ames, Kenneth L. 1977. *Beyond Necessity, Art in the Folk Tradition*. Winterthur, Del.: The Winterthur Museum.

______. 1980a. Folk Art: The Challenge and the Promise. in *Perspectives on American Folk Art,* ed. Ian M. G. Quimby and Scott T. Swank. New York: W. W. Norton. pp. 293-324.

Barasch, Moshe. 1992. *Icon: Studies in the History of an Idea*. New York: New York University Press.

Barida, Michael N. 1977. Iconography and Its Meaning. In *The Iconography of St. Nicholas' Church,* ed. The Ikon-Study Group, pp. 15-18. Toronto: St. Nicholas Ukrainian Catholic Parish.

Becker, Jane S. and Barbara Franco, ed. 1988. *Folk Roots, New Roots: Folklore in American Life*. Lexington, Mass.: Museum of Our National Heritage.

Beckham, Sue Bridwell. 1987. Death, Resurrection and Transfiguration: The Religious Folklore in Elvis Presley Shrines and Souvenirs. *International Folklore Review* 5:88-95.

Ben-Amos, Dan. 1984. The Seven Strands of Tradition: Varieties in Its Meaning in American Folklore Studies. *Journal of Folklore Research* 21:97-131.

Benedetti, Joan M. 1987. Who Are the Folk in Folk Art? Inside and Outside the Cultural Context. *Art Documentation* 6(Spring):3-8.

Bethke, Robert D. 1996. *Americana Crafted: Jehu Camper, Delaware Whittler.* Jackson: University Press of Mississippi.

Bilash, Radomir B. 1994. Peter Lipinski, Prairie Church Artist. *SSAC Bulletin* 1:88:3-14.

Bishop, Robert. 1979. *Folk Painters of America.* New York: Greenwich House, Distributed by Crown Publishers.

Blasdel, Gregg. 1968. The Grass-Roots Artist. *Art in America* 56 (Sept.-Oct.):21-41.

Bronner, Simon J. 1979. Concepts in the Study of Material Aspects of American Folk Culture. In *Approaches to the Study of Material Aspects of American Folk Culture*, ed. Simon J. Bronner and Stephen J. Poyser, pp. 132-172. Bloomington, Ind.: Folklore Forum, 12:2-3.

_______. 1985. *Chain Carvers: Old Men Crafting Meaning.* Lexington: The University Press of Kentucky.

Brunvand, Jan Harold. 1978. *The Study of American Folklore: An Introduction.* New York: W. W. Norton, 2nd ed.

Bulger, Peggy. 1980. Defining Folk Arts for the Working Folklorist. *Kentucky Folklore Record* 26:60-61.

Burgess, Karen E. 1996. *Home Is Where the Dog Is: Art in the Back Yard.* Jackson: University Press of Mississippi.

Burrison, John. 1983. *Brothers in Clay: The Story of Georgia Folk Pottery.* Athens: University of Georgia Press.

Cahill, Holger. 1932. *American Folk Art—The Art of the Common Man 1750-1900.* New York: Museum of Modern Art.

Cardinal, Roger. 1972. *Outsider Art.* New York: Praeger.

Chinn, Jennie A. 1983. The Problem of the Polyester Quilt: Defining Folk Arts in the Field. Unpublished paper presented at the American Folklore Society meeting.

_______. 1993. African American Quiltmaking Taditions: Some Assumptions Reviewed. In *Kansas Quilts & Quiltmakers*, ed. Barbara Brackman et al., pp. 157-175. Lawrence: University Press of Kansas.

Congdon, Kristin G. 1986. Finding the Tradition in Folk Art: An Art Educator's Perspective. *Journal of Aesthetic Education* 20:93-106.

Davies, Douglas. 1994. Christianity. In *Picturing God,* ed. Jean Holm, pp. 41-69. London, New York: Pinter Publishers.

Dorson, Richard M. 1952. *Bloodstoppers and Bearwalkers: Folk Traditions in the Upper Peninsula.* Cambridge, Mass.: Harvard University Press.

Dundes, Alan. 1965. *The Study of Folklore.* Englewood Cliffs, N. J.: Prentice-Hall.

_______. 1966. The American Concept of Folklore. *Journal of the Folklore Institute* 3:226-249.

Emans, Charlotte M. 1991. Review of *Plain Painters: Making Sense of American Folk Art,* John Michael Vlach. *Journal of American Folklore* 104: 218-221.

Faulds, Sara Selene and Amy Skillman. 1984. Biographies. In *American Folk Art: A Guide to Sources,* ed. Simon J. Bronner, pp. 99-116. New York: Garland Publishing, Inc.

Flores-Peña, Ysamur and Roberta J. Evanchuk. 1994. *Santeria Garments and Altars: "Speaking Without a Voice".* Jackson: University Press of Mississippi.

Feintuch, Burt. 1976. A Contextual and Cognitive Approach to Folk Art and Folk Craft. *New York Folklore* 1(1-2):69-78.

Georges, Robert A. and Michael Owen Jones. 1995. *Folkloristics: An Introduction.* Bloomington: Indiana University Press.

Glassie, Henry. 1972. Folk Art. In *Folklore and Folklife: An Introduction*, ed. Richard M. Dorson, pp. 253-280. Chicago: The University of Chicago Press.

Goa, David J. 1989. Three Urban Parishes: A Study of Sacred Space. *Material History Bulletin* 29(Spring):13-24.

Goldman, Judy Lael. 1981. A Moveable Feast: The Art of the Knish Maker. *Western Folklore* 40:11-18.

Greenfield, Verni. 1986. *Making Do or Making Art: A Study of American Recycling*. Ann Arbor: UMI Research Press.

Hall, Michael D. and Eugene W. Metcalf, Jr., eds. 1994. *The Artist Outsider: Creativity and the Boundaries of Culture*. Washington, D. C.: Smithsonian Institution Press.

Hartley, Edward. n. d. *St. Herman of Alaska Chapel*. Self Published.

Hemphill, Herbert W., Jr. and Julia Weissman. 1974. *Twentieth-Century American Folk Art and Artists*. New York: E. P. Dutton & Co.

Hordynsky, S. 1988. Icon. In *Encyclopedia of Ukraine*, ed. Volodymyr Kubijovyc, vol. II, pp. 294-297. Toronto: University of Toronto Press.

Isajiw, Wsevolod W. 1991. Ethnic Art and the Ukrainian-Canadian Experience. In *Art and Ethnicity: The Ukrainian Tradition in Canada*, ed. Robert B. Klymasz, pp. 29-37. Hull: Canadian Museum of Civilization.

Janis, Sidney. 1942. *They Taught Themselves: American Primitive Painters of the 20th Century*. New York: Dial Press.

Jones, Michael Owen. 1975. *The Hand Made Object and Its Maker*. Berkeley and Los Angeles: University of California Press.

______. 1976. The Study of Folk Art Study: Reflections on Images. In *Folklore Today*, ed. Linda Dégh, Henry Glassie, and Felix J. Oinas, pp. 291-304. Bloomington, Ind.: Center for Language and Semiotic Studies.

______. 1980. L. A. Add-ons and Re-dos: Renovation in Folk Art and Architectural Design. In *Perspectives on American Folk Art*, ed. Ian M. G. Quimby and Scott Swank, pp. 325-63. New York: W. W. Norton.

______. 1987. *Exploring Folk Art: Twenty Years of Thought on Craft, Work, and Aesthetics*. Ann Arbor: UMI Research Press. Logan: Utah State University Press, 2nd edition, 1993.

______. 1989. *Craftsman of the Cumberlands: Tradition and Creativity*. Lexington: The University Press of Kentucky.

______. 1991. A Folklorist's Viewpoint on Ukrainian-Canadian Art. In *Art and Ethnicity: The Ukrainian Tradition in Canada,* ed. Robert B. Klymasz, pp. 47-57. Hull: Canadian Museum of Civilization.

______. 1993. Why Take a Behavioral Approach to Folk Objects? In *History from Things: Essays on Material Culture*, ed. Steven Lubar and W. David Kingery, pp. 182-196. Washington, D. C.: Smithsonian Institution Press.

______. 1994a. How Do You Get Inside the Art of Outsiders? In *The Artist Outsider: Creativity and the Boundaries of Culture*, ed. Michael D. Hall and Eugene Metcalf, Jr., pp. 312-330. Washington, D. C.: Smithsonian Institution Press.

______. 1994b. Ukrainian Byzantine Icon Painters and Paintings in Canada: A Preliminary Report on Researching a Tradition. Unpublished report, Canadian Museum of Civilization.

______. 1995a. Folk and Academic Traditions Among Byzantine Icon Painters in Western Canada. Unpublished report, Canadian Museum of Civilization.

______. 1995b. The 1995 Archer Taylor Memorial Lecture: Why Make (Folk) Art? *Western Folklore* 54:253-276.

______. 1995c. Why Material *Behavior*? Paper presented at the American Folklore Society meeting, Lafayette, Louisiana.

______. 1996. *Studying Organizational Symbolism: What, How, Why?* Thousand Oaks, Calif.: Sage Publications.

Jones, Michael Owen and Robert A. Georges. 1997. Folklore. *Colier's Encyclopedia*, forthcoming.

Joseph-Witham, Heather R. 1996. *Star Trek Fans and Costume Art*. Jackson: University Press of Mississippi.

Keleher, Serge. 1989. Ukrainian Church Iconography in Canada: Models and Their Spiritual Significance. In *The Ukrainian Religious Experience: Tradition and the Canadian Cultural Context*, ed. David J. Goa, pp. 47-55. Edmonton: University of Alberta Canadian Institute of Ukrainian Studies.

Kirshenblatt-Gimblett, Barbara. 1989. Authoring Lives. *Journal of Folklore Research* 26:123-149.

Kitchener, Amy. 1994. *The Holiday Yards of Florencio Morales, "El hombre de las banderas"*. Jackson: University Press of Mississippi.

Klymasz, Robert B. 1989. Framing the Heritage: Towards an Understanding of the Ukrainian Arts in Canada. In *Millennium of Christianity in Ukraine, 988-1988*, ed. Oleh W. Gerus and Alexander Baran, pp. 293-295. Winnipeg: Ukrainian Academy of Arts and Sciences in Canada.

______, ed. 1991. *Art and Ethnicity: The Ukrainian Tradition in Canada*. Hull: Canadian Museum of Civilization.

Kostash, Myrna. 1993. *Bloodlines: A Journey into Eastern Europe*. Vancouver/Toronto: Douglas & McIntyre.

Kurelek, William. 1981. *The Polish Canadians*. Montreal: Tundra Books.

Lipman, Jean and Alice Winchester, eds. 1950. *Primitive Painters in America, 1750-1950*. New York: Dodd, Mead.

______. 1974. *The Flowering of American Folk Art (1776-1876)*. New York: Penguin Books, in cooperation with the Whitney Museum of American Art.

Lupul, Manoly R., ed. 1984. *Visible Symbols: Cultural Expression Among Canada's Ukrainians*. Edmonton: Canadian Institute of Ukrainian Studies, University of Alberta.

Martin, Katherine Rosser. 1979. Food Preparation and the Folk Aesthetic. *Kentucky Folklore Record* 25:1-5.

Mathewes-Green, Frederica. 1995. A Year in Orthodoxy: Preparing for Lent. *Image: A Journal of the Arts & Religion* 9 (Spring):113-125.

Metcalf, Eugene W., Jr. 1983. Black Art, Folk Art, and Social Control. *Winterthur Portfolio* 18: 271-289.

______. 1986. Confronting Contemporary Folk Art. In *Ties That Bind: Folk Art in Contemporary American Culture*, ed. Eugene W. Metcalf, Jr. and Michael Hall, pp. 10-28. Cincinnati: The Contemporary Arts Center.

Metcalf, Eugene W., Jr. and Claudine Weatherford. 1988. Modernism, Edith Halpert, Holger Cahill, and the Fine Art Meaning of American Folk Art. In *Folk Roots, New Roots: Folklore in American Life*, ed. Jane S. Becker and Barbara Franco, pp, 141-155. Lexington, Mass.: Museum of Our National Heritage.

Milspaw, Yvonne J. 1986. Protestant Home Shrines: Icon and Image. *New York Folklore* 12:119-136.

Murphy, Declan C. 1988. Cicero and the Icon Painters: The Transformation of Byzantine Image Theory in Medieval Muscovey. In *the Byzantine Legacy in Eastern Europe*, ed. Lowell Clucas, pp. 149-164. New York: East European Monographs, Boulder; Distributed by Columbia University Press.

Oring, Elliott. 1987. Generating Lives: The Construction of an Autobiography. *Journal of Folklore Research* 24:241-262.

Oring, Elliott, ed. 1985. *Folk Groups and Folklore Genres*. Logan: Utah State University Press.

______. 1989. *Folk Groups and Folklore Genres: A Reader*. Logan: Utah State University Press.

Pershing, Linda. 1995. *Sew to Speak: The Fabric Art of Mary Milne*. Jackson: University Press of Mississippi.

Pimple, Kenneth D. 1986. The Inmates of Eigenmann: A Look at Door Decoration in a Graduate Dormitory. *Folklore Forum* 19:5-35.

Pocius, Gerald L. 1995. Art. *Journal of American Folklore* 108:413-431.

Posey, Sandra Mizumoto. 1996. *Rubber Soul: Rubber Stamps and Correspondence Art*. Jackson: University Press of Mississippi.

Quenot, Michel. 1991. *The Ikon: Window on the Kingdom*. Trans. A Carthusian Monk. Crestwood, N.Y.: St. Vladimir's Seminary Press.

Rashid, Alden and Varara. n. d. *Comitato Romano "Messa Degli Artisti"* (exhibit catalogue; brief essays by Monsig. Pietro Amato and G. B. Gavani). n. p.

Redfield, Robert. 1947. The Folk Society. *Journal of American Sociology* 52:293-308.

Rumford, Beatrix T. 1980. Uncommon Art of the Common People: A Review of Trends in the Collecting and Exhibiting of American Folk Art. In *Perspectives on American Folk Art*, ed. Ian M. G. Quimby and Scott T. Swank, pp. 13-53. New York: W. W. Norton.

Schlieper, Heiko C. 1986. Icons and Art: An Icon Painter's View. In *Seasons of Celebration: Ritual in Eastern Christian Culture*, ed. David J. Goa, pp. 45-48. Edmonton: Provincial Museum of Alberta.

Scott, Michael. 1992. The Sacred Art: Putting Faith in Old Traditions and a New Life [Varvara Rashid]. *The Vancouver Sun Saturday Review* (April 18), Section D, pp. 4-5.

Sherrard, Philip. 1990. *The Sacred in Life and Art*. Ipswich, U. K.: Golgonooza Press.

Smart, Ninian. 1989. *The World's Religions*. Englewood Cliffs, N. J.: Prentice-Hall.

Smith, Robert J. and Jerry Stannard, eds. 1989. *The Folk: Identity, Landscapes and Lores*. Lawrence: University of Kansas Publications in Anthropology, 17.

Soloukin, Vladimir. 1971. *Searching for Icons in Russia*. Trans. P. S. Falla. New York: Harcourt Brace Jovanovich; a Helen and Kurt Wolff Book.

Stepovyk, Dmytro V. 1991. The Ukrainian Icon in Canada. In *Art and Ethnicity: The Ukrainian Tradition in Canada*, ed. Robert B. Klymasz, pp. 39-45. Hull: Canadian Museum of Civilization.

Teske, Robert Thomas. 1983. What Is Folk Art? An Opinion on the Controversy. *El Palacio* 88:34-38.

______. 1984. Ethnicity and Religion. In *American Folk Art: A Guide to Sources*, ed. Simon J. Bronner, pp. 139-168. New York: Garland.

Titon, Jeff Todd. 1980. The Life Story. *Journal of American Folklore* 93:276-292.

Vlach, John Michael. 1980. American Folk Art: Questions and Quandaries. *Winterthur Portfolio* 15:345-55.

______. 1981. *Charleston Blacksmith: The Work of Philip Simmons*. Athens: University of Georgia Press.

______. 1986. "Properly Speaking": The Need for Plain Talk about Folk Art. In *Folk Art and Art Worlds*, ed. John Michael Vlach and Simon J. Bronner, pp. 13-26. Ann Arbor: UMI Research Press.

______. 1988. *Plain Painters: Making Sense of American Folk Art*. Washington, D. C.: Smithsonian Institution Press.

Volkersz, Willem. 1989. Word and Image in American Folk Art. In *The Folk: Identity, Landscapes and Lores*, ed. Robert J. Smith and Jerry Stannard, pp. 91-120. Lawrence: University of Kansas Publications in Anthropology, 17.

Vryonis, Speros, Jr. 1988. Preface. In *the Byzantine Legacy in Eastern Europe*, ed. Lowell Clucas, pp. v-xiv. New York: East European Monographs, Boulder; Distributed by Columbia University Press.

Winchester, Alice. 1979. American Folk Art. *Encyclopedia Americana*. Danbury, Conn.: American Corp., vol. 11, p. 495.

Wojcik, Daniel. 1995. *Punk and Neo-Tribal Body Art*. Jackson: University Press of Mississippi.

Yelen, Alice Rae. 1993. Self-Taught Artists: Who They Are. In *Passonate Vissions of the American South: Self-Taught Artists from 1940 to the Present*, ed. Alice Rae Yelin, pp. 17-21. Jackson: New Orleans Museum of Art, distributed by University Press of Mississippi.

Yoder, Don. 1963. The Folklife Studies Movement. *Pennsylvania Folklife* 13:43-56.

Zug, Charles G., III. 1994. Folk Art and Outsider Art: A Folklorist's Perspective. In *The Outsider Artist: Creativity and the Boundaries of Culture*, ed. Michael D. Hall and Eugene W. Metcalf, Jr., pp. 144-160. Washington, D. C.: Smithsonian Institution Press.

TENDANCES DE L'ICONOGRAPHIE ACTUELLE DU SACRÉ AU QUÉBEC

par
Anne-Marie Poulin

TABLE DES MATIÈRES

PRÉSENTATION

La problématique

Au Québec, le sacré se porte fort bien. Tout comme son iconographie d'ailleurs qui connaît un regain inattendu grâce à l'implantation récente d'une forme d'imagerie millénaire, l'icône de l'Orient chrétien. L'important accueil accordé aux icônes est d'autant plus significatif qu'il signale la renaissance de l'imagerie sacrée, une renaissance qui vient pourtant à l'encontre des efforts de rationalisation déployés depuis le concile de Vatican II pour réduire, sinon éliminer, les signes sensibles de la piété comme l'imagerie de dévotion.

Face à cette tendance fondamentale, il y a lieu de se questionner sur le sens d'une renaissance de l'iconographie dans le contexte post-conciliaire, époque pourtant marquée au Québec par une situation aiguë de désaffection religieuse. Des

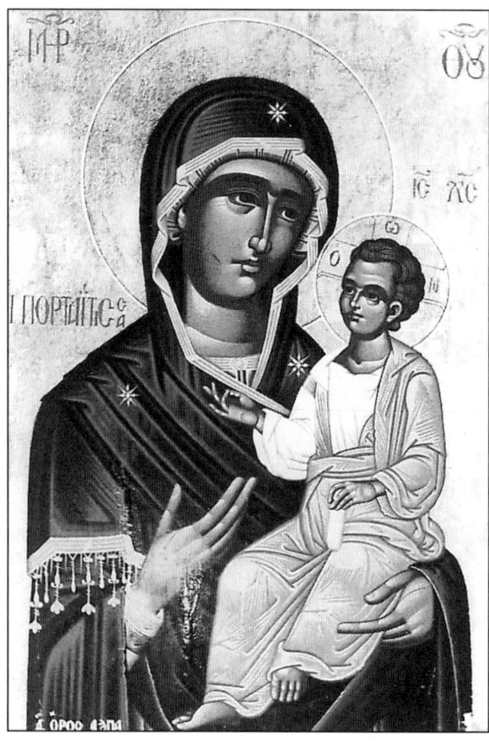

Prototype de la Portaïtissa de Montréal.
Photo attribuée à André Rostworoski,
Montréal.

interrogations se posent également sur le plan formel, quant à l'attrait de la nouvelle figuration, une forme d'art hiératique "étrangère" à la tradition plus que centenaire des "petites images saintes" au Québec, et que d'aucun considèrent "archaïque" par rapport aux critères de l'art moderne.

Le problème des tendances de l'iconographie actuelle du sacré est d'autant plus complexe qu'il engendre une série de dynamiques inusitées au Québec, telle la prise en charge du commerce de l'imagerie de la tradition byzantine par des religieux et laïcs québécois, la création indigène d'icônes et le développement d'un culte privé aux figurations de l'Orient chrétien et en particulier à la *Portaïtissa*, l'icône miraculeuse de Montréal.

Moins problématique mais non moins révélateur de tendances est le principal support matériel des icônes, les reproductions sur papier. Bien que l'intérêt scientifique pour ce genre de production non-exclusive et populaire trouve rarement preneur parmi les chercheurs[1], pour l'observateur du phénomène sur le vif comme l'ethnologue, l'imagerie produite actuellement et "*in situ*" constitue à la fois un *leitmotiv* et une source de premier ordre dans la quête du sens que l'on doit donner au phénomène de cette renaissance.

Pour assurer une meilleure appréhension de l'ensemble du problème de l'iconographie actuelle du sacré, un bref retour s'impose sur le contexte historique et les contours scientifiques l'ayant alimenté.

L'historique

Il est déjà reconnu que les bouleversements socio-culturels et religieux en Occident au cours des années 1960 ont eu un impact majeur au Québec. Parmi les plus importants, rappelons la rupture avec un mode de vie traditionnel et le balayage systématique de l'art sacré auquel s'est ardemment livré le clergé de la province suite au concile de Vatican II. Parallèlement à ces renversements, la société québécoise est confrontée à la nouvelle réalité multiethnique et pluraliste. Cette situation tous azimuts semble néanmoins avoir eu une certaine incidence sur l'éventuel accueil fait à l'imagerie de tradition byzantine. Ce qui fait dire qu'en dépit ou à cause des changements, la société québécoise de tradition catholique romaine demeure foncièrement liée aux expressions concrètes du sacré.

D'ailleurs, les premiers survols de la situation (une enquête exploratoire et une séminaire de 2e cycle en 1988 et 1989) présagent de la portée fondamentale et formelle des tendances iconographiques sur ce territoire[2]. Il ressort que les tendances les plus signifiantes se profilent autour de trois dynamiques: le commerce, la création et le culte aux icônes.

Suivant cet ordre, les tendances s'orientent vers la circulation universelle des reproductions de la *Portaïtissa*, l'icône miraculeuse de Montréal (sous forme de prototype enregistré) de même que la prise en charge de son commerce à partir de la métropole, l'émergence d'un noyau d'iconographes indigènes (entendons par là, Québécois de souche) tant classiques que post-modernistes et enfin, l'orientalisation accrue de l'imagerie de dévotion avec pour conséquence une mutation profonde sur le plan cultuel (pratiques et croyances).

L'évolution des dynamiques et de leurs tendances est remarquable du fait qu'elle s'effectue essentiellement dans l'*underground* et ce, depuis la fin des années 1970. Ayant précisé les contextes historique et scientifique du problème de même que son principal lieu d'évolution, il convient d'en préciser les principaux contours.

Les contours scientifiques

Vouloir saisir le fondement de l'iconographie actuelle du sacré et dégager ses tendances exigent une description, même sommaire, des contours classiques de la recherche sous-jacente au présent rapport. Elle comprend tout d'abord, l'hypothèse ayant orienté la quête du sens de la renaissance de l'imagerie sacrée, ensuite l'approche et les méthodes privilégiées, les sources utilisées, de même que le cadre spatio-temporel de sa réalisation.

La première vision systémique et intimiste du problème est élaborée à partir de l'hypothèse voulant que le commerce, la création et le culte des icônes émergent en réaction à la crise "iconoclaste" engendrée par Vatican II. À l'intérieur de ce paramètre, il s'agissait de découvrir si l'icône répondait à un renversement d'une conjoncture, signe que les chrétiens recherchent une religion plus sensible.

Vouloir appréhender le sens de la renaissance de l'imagerie sacrée au Québec, pouvoir d'autre part observer le phénomène *in situ*, commandaient de toute évidence une approche qualitative. D'où le recours à l'ethnologie. Bien que les moyens privilégiés ont été le contact direct et l'enquête orale, une juxtaposition de méthodes complète néanmoins l'approche sur le terrain. Par exemple, l'appréhension de la nature et de l'essence même de l'iconographie de l'Orient chrétien eut été impossible sans l'apport de la théologie, aussi bien orientale qu'occidentale, et de l'histoire de l'art.

Au niveau des enquêtes, deux types ont été retenus, l'un sommaire, l'autre élaboré. Le premier, emprunté à la sociologie, a le mérite d'avoir fourni une vision générale et quantitative du problème quoique distancié des participants. Le second, d'ordre qualitatif et relevant de méthodes ethnographiques personnalisées et éprouvées (rencontres, enquêtes orales, inventaires, relevés figurés ou photographiés, cueillette d'artefacts témoignant de l'implantation des icônes et de figurations inspirées de la tradition byzantine, etc.) permet quant à lui de dégager un sens au problème de fond. Pratiquement, les inventaires découlant de la recherche comblent de sérieuses lacunes documentaires dont sont souvent victimes des problématiques récentes et peu exploitées.

Réalisée entre septembre 1988 et mai 1991, l'étude rejoint un total de cent quatre individus, soit cinquante-cinq personne-ressources (prêtres, religieuses, commerçants, diffuseurs, imprimeurs et monteurs d'images, un prêtre melkite de Québec et quatre orthodoxes dont une historienne de l'art byzantin[3]) dix-neuf iconographes québécois de souche et trente participants (informateurs-clé) aux enquêtes orales élaborées.

L'enquête touche essentiellement le Québec et les populations francophones de l'est de l'Ontario et des états américains du nord-est. Signalons que le phénomène de renaissance de l'imagerie s'élabore à partir des trois grands centres urbains que sont Montréal, Québec et Trois-Rivières. Toutefois, pour ce qui est de la dynamique cultuelle, la recherche cible la région de la ville de Québec. Outre des motifs d'ordre pratique, le territoire renferme une population quasi homogène de souche française et de confession catholique romaine, et sa banlieue de Sillery est le premier endroit de la province où une reproduction de la *Portaïtissa*, l'icône miraculeuse de Montréal, a été exposé au public[4]. Sillery continue d'ailleurs à être un mini-lieu de pèlerinage à l'icône prodigieuse[5].

Les contours de la recherche étant fixés, il convient maintenant de décrire le contexte de réception des icônes dans un Québec qui est à ce moment en "diète figurative". Ce contexte particulier se constitue des efforts de maintien, de renouvellement et finalement du retour de l'imagerie de dévotion.

CONTEXTES

Réception des icônes dans un Québec en "diète figurative"

L'implantation récente des icônes au Québec tire partie d'un vide manifeste de figurations sacrées. Le vacuum esthétique religieux engendré par le concile de

Vatican II et auquel le clergé québécois a largement souscrit au début des années 1960 s'effectue sous le signe d'une foi que l'on dit plus adulte et éclairée. Ce virage soudain provoque, entre autres effets, l'évacuation rapide et quasi systématique des formes traditionnelles de la piété collective dont une des principales manifestations est le déclin subit de l'imagerie de dévotion. La "diète figurative[6]" qui s'ensuit est d'autant plus significative que l'imagerie de piété fut partie prenante du quotidien des croyants québécois pendant plus d'un siècle.

Disparition d'un siècle d'imagerie 1840-1960

À l'époque de la montée de l'ultramontanisme vers 1840, le Québec est littéralement inondé de "petites images saintes" en provenance de maisons d'éditions européennes. Imbue d'un réalisme éthéré, l'imagerie devient au Québec très populaire et fortement personnalisée[7]. Encore en 1960, on en importe dix millions pour une population de quatre millions de personnes[8]. Le paradoxe veut qu'au même moment la société traditionnellement catholique du Québec éclate[9], secouée à la fois par une révolution dite tranquille qui transforme toute sa structure socio-politique et culturelle, et par le mouvement oecuménique qui libéralise sans trop de direction l'ensemble de son héritage religieux.

En moins de dix ans, la société se sécularise, les églises se vident[10] en même temps qu'elles sont dépouillées de leurs principaux attributs figuratifs comme la statuaire et les tableaux. Dans la foulée, rites, manifestations et objets de la piété populaire, telle l'imagerie de dévotion, disparaissent ou perdent tout simplement leur signification d'origine. Rappelons qu'à l'époque, l'image dévote accompagne le croyant du berceau à la tombe, évoquant tout aussi bien les rites de passage que les événements du quotidien. À la fois convoitée et collectionnée, l'imagerie religieuse populaire trouvait place dans les albums-souvenirs au même titre que les photos de familles[11].

Parallèlement à la disparition des rites et signes sensibles de la piété, la société québécoise se voit confrontée au pluralisme naissant et à ses philosophies diverses, tels le bouddhisme, l'hindouisme, le taoïsme et le zen, de même que certaines pratiques nouvelles comme le yoga et la méditation transcendantale[12]. Visant surtout l'intériorisation et la maîtrise de soi, ces philosophies, orientales pour la plupart, comblent en quelque sorte le vide provoqué par les crises conciliaire et socio-culturelle du temps.

Vers 1970 et en réaction aux tendances séculaires, des groupes de catholiques cherchent à canaliser leurs propres aspirations pour la spiritualité intérieure à travers une nouvelle expérience religieuse[13] venant des pentecôtistes américains, soit le Renouveau charismatique. Force est d'admettre cependant que le mouvement axé sur l'Esprit-Saint et ses charismes s'appuie sur deux notions abstraites peu concilia-bles avec les représentations iconographiques existantes. Ainsi, la désaffection tout comme les nouvelles tendances religieuses émergeant à l'époque portent un dur coup à l'imagerie traditionnelle. Entre 1960 à 1978 par exemple, la demande pour l'imagerie de dévotion chute de façon significative, passant de dix à deux millions en moins de deux décennies[14]. Le déclin marqué pour cette forme d'art pictural inspire même la tenue d'un colloque en 1972[15], qu'aucune publication n'est d'ailleurs venue appuyer.

Échec du renouveau dans l'art sacré (1920-1950)

L'imagerie traditionnelle cède donc la place à de nouvelles représentations plus "laïcisantes". L'introduction d'une figuration plus moderne rappelle des efforts analogues qui se sont fait jour durant la première moitié du XXe siècle qui, en raison des forces ultramontaines et traditionalistes ainsi qu'une philosophie distanciée de la masse des croyants, avaient également échoué. Une rétrospective de la première poussée moderniste de l'art sacré au Québec montre qu'elle participe néanmoins, quoique de façon paradoxale, à l'éventuelle réception de l'art sacré de l'Orient.

Au Québec, les premières tentatives de renouvellement dans l'art sacré s'échelonnent de 1920 à 1950-55. Cependant, son historie reste à faire et seules les études récentes de Claude Bergeron et de Jean Simard[16], permettent d'y voir un peu de lumière. Bien qu'ayant une formation analogue en histoire de l'art, les auteurs abordent le problème selon des perspectives différentes, architecturale pour l'un, picturale pour l'autre.

L'aperçu historique des ouvrages montre qu'à partir des années 1920, des écoles d'art et d'architecture, des revues spécialisées et des groupes artistiques du Québec véhiculent une philosophie moderniste et réaliste inspirée de l'Europe[17]. Bon an mal an, le courant contemporain se maintient et se concrétise à Montréal en 1946 par la fondation du groupe *le Retable*. Son principal théoricien, le père André Lecoutey, peintre, sculpteur et verrier d'origine française confirme la pensée rationaliste du groupe à travers leur revue *Arts et Pensée*. L'analyse du cheminement du *Retable* et de leurs écrits amène Bergeron à conclure "qu'il ne peut être question [pour ces modernistes] d'imiter le style d'art ancien[18]".

En cela, *le Retable* se distingue nettement de son modèle parisien, l'*Art catholique*, établi par Maurice Denis en 1912. En cherchant à "réintroduire le bon goût dans l'imagerie de piété[19]" par exemple, le porte parole de l'*Art catholique* préconisait un art renouvelé à partir d'oeuvres classiques, c'est-à-dire européennes. Ainsi, ni au Québec, ni en France à l'époque est-il question de recourir aux sources communes de l'imagerie chrétienne, l'art byzantin. De plus, le classicisme renouvelé en Europe se heurte à la notion de modernisme de l'Amérique et plus spécifique-ment dans le cas qui nous intéresse, à la conception "canadienne[20]" du renouveau dans l'art sacré.

Au Québec, l'élan semble avoir porté fruit si l'on considère les propos de Jean-Marie Gauvreau alors directeur de l'École du meuble à Montréal. À l'occasion d'un expo-colloque sur l'art religieux contemporain tenu au Café du Parlement à Québec en 1952, il félicite quelques artistes dont Simone Hudon, Henri Beaulac et Rodolphe Duguay pour avoir réalisé "de beaux spécimens, encore trop rares parmi les platitudes offertes en vente dans nos comptoirs ou dans nos centres de pèlerinage[21]". Constatant une nette amélioration de l'art sacré depuis vingt ans, Gauvreau poursuit sa réflexion sur l'imagerie en indiquant qu'elle constitue "un domaine où nos écoles des Beaux-Arts et des arts graphiques pourraient se tailler une belle réputation[22]".

Ce souhait, d'ailleurs resté sans lendemain, semble référer uniquement à l'imagerie ornementale et non à celle sur papier. De là à conclure que la petite image de dévotion aurait été volontairement exclue dans l'effort du renouveau de l'art sacré amorcé à l'époque, il n'y a qu'un pas. L'analyse de Bergeron corrobore cette hypothèse en signalant que l'action du *Retable,* regroupant peintres, sculpteurs, verriers, céramistes et orfèvres (religieux pour la plupart) s'est surtout concentrée autour de l'architecture, de la décoration et de l'ornementation des églises[23]. Réservées presque exclusivement à l'enceinte officielle, les réalisations du *Retable* demeurent de ce fait élitistes et donc largement méconnues du grand public.

En contrepartie, Jean Simard observe que l'illustration sacrée connaît un meilleur sort en raison des publications de masse comme les almanachs[24]. Grâce à ce médium populaire, la population est exposée dès avant le milieu du XXe siècle à une imagerie moderne, abstraite et dépouillée qui tranche avec la figuration religieuse traditionnelle. Sans préjuger de l'impact de ces publications sur un changement d'attitude à long terme - l'étude reste à faire - la sensibilisation à une nouvelle forme d'art pictural s'inscrit néanmoins dans le courant moderne et international qui se fait de plus en plus insistant au Québec à partir des années 1950. À cet égard, nous risquons l'hypothèse voulant que la littérature religieuse populaire ait été le principal canal de sensibilisation à de nouvelles formes d'imagerie religieuse, posant ainsi les toutes premières conditions d'accueil à l'art sobre et abstrait de l'icône.

Quant à la transformation des oeuvres indigènes en imagerie de dévotion de petits formats, la possibilité semble assez mince ou tout au plus de courte durée. De fait, dans l'unique ouvrage sur l'imagerie religieuse au Québec, l'ethnologue Pierre Lessard indique sans plus élaborer, qu'entre 1950-1970 certains centres de dévotion ont tenté leur chance dans l'édition d'images[25]. Il est probable que la forte concurrence européenne à l'époque ait eu raison de ces efforts que nous connaissons encore trop peu[26]. Il est curieux par ailleurs que le mouvement de renouveau dans l'art sacré, qui a pourtant démontré une certaine originalité et indépendance face aux formes étrangères, ait lassé la petite imagerie sur papier entièrement libre de poursuivre ce que l'historien D. Lerch qualifie de "dépendance culturelle" du Québec vis-à-vis de l'Europe[27].

À la lumière de cette rétrospective il appert que les tenants du renouveau dans l'art sacré, plus portés vers l'exclusivité et l'aspect ornemental de l'art religieux, ont distancé l'oeuvre du récepteur contribuant ainsi à l'échec général de leurs efforts qui se concrétise entre 1950-1955[28]. Ce revers, joint à la conjoncture socio-religieuse et à la disparition d'une imagerie traditionnelle peu adaptée aux profonds changements de l'époque moderne, concourt à plonger le Québec dans un vide esthétique religieux quasi total.

Stagnation de l'imagerie de dévotion (1960-1976)

La période d'abstinence que le Québec s'impose durant les seize prochaines années, soit de 1960 à 1976, contribue en quelque sorte à libérer la voie pour l'imagerie byzantine. L'accueil qui lui est réservé met définitivement fin à la crise iconoclaste engendrée par Vatican II, en même temps qu'il signale une espèce de renouveau dans l'art sacré. Curieusement, la renaissance actuelle de l'art pictural religieux n'a presque rien en commun avec celui de la première moitié du XXe siècle. Ne répondant à aucune école de pensée, à aucun mouvement d'art organisé et encore moins à un effort du clergé du Québec, la renaissance de l'imagerie sacrée relève tout simplement de la base avide, il semble, de combler un vide religieux et esthétique évident.

Ainsi, après avoir tourné le dos au réalisme jadis prôné par le *Retable*, de même qu'à l'imagerie éthérée véhiculée pendant plus d'un siècle, les fidèles optent actuellement pour un art millénaire imbu de symbolisme qui semble mieux répondre à leurs nouvelles aspirations spirituelles. Certains, comme Nathalie Labrecque, auteure québécoise d'origine russe, croient que l'art des icônes répond "au goût contemporain éduqué par l'art moderne et abstrait[29]". D'où un certain rapprochement avec le mouvement original de renouveau dans l'art sacré paru dans la première moitié du XXe siècle et l'influence de la littérature populaire. Il est néanmoins paradoxal que le mouvement du *Retable* voué essentiellement à la modernité et au réalisme, ait influé sur l'éventuelle ouverture à un art millénaire abstrait axé sur le symbolisme et fondalement étranger à la culture occidentale chrétienne.

Bien que timides, des indices d'ouverture à l'égard des figurations byzantines apparaissent vers la fin des années 1960. En ces débuts, l'éveil à l'icône (de même qu'à l'orthodoxie) demeure en majeure partie exclusif aux élites. L'oecuménisme, la mise sur pied de centres d'étude et maisons de prière offrant bibliothèques et ateliers de spiritualité chrétienne orientale[30], la découverte d'iconographes québécois d'origine étrangère[31] et enfin la fondation à Montréal en 1975 du premier musée d'art byzantin en Amérique du Nord[32] contribuent à une première sensibilisation à l'art et à la spiritualité de l'Orient chrétien. Cependant, il appert que ces efforts demeurent l'apanage d'inités tant laïcs que religieux.

Par exemple, au début des années 1970, des communautés religieuses du Québec commencent à associer les icônes à leurs pratiques de prière et de médita-tion et à diffuser la liturgie orientale de l'icône, notamment les soeurs de Sainte-Anne de Lachine, les Carmélites déchaussées de Danville et les soeurs de la Présen-tation de Marie de Saint-Hilaire[33]. Celles-ci en particulier, vénèrent les icônes depuis 1973 après que leur supérieure à Rome, la Québécoise Soeur Jean Théo-phane Chagnon, en introduit la dévotion dans les maisons de sa communauté répartie dans seize pays. Conformément à la tradition de "dépendance culturelle" en vigueur au Québec depuis plus d'un siècle, la majorité des reproductions d'icônes ornant les chapelles des communautés religieuses proviennent d'Europe.

Ainsi, la disparition de l'imagerie traditionnelle du Québec, l'échec du renouveau de l'art sacré et le retour timide à l'imagerie sous forme d'icône concourent à renforcer la thèse sur le vide figuratif et la recherche d'une imagerie plus significative.

Au tournant des années 1980 la situation tourne. L'implantation discrète de l'icône et son apprivoisement initial en vase clos, font graduellement place à l'appropriation et au développement commercial, artistique et culturel des icônes. Trois dynamiques laissant poindre les nouvelles tendances iconographiques au Québec.

TENDANCES

Tendances issues de la dynamique commerciale

Le sens commun veut que le commerce soit "l'opération ayant pour objet l'achat ou la vente d'une marchandise ou d'une valeur après l'avoir transformée ou non". Compte tenu du rôle des acteurs et des lieux dans l'iconographie actuelle du sacré au Québec, une extension du terme s'impose pour inclure les notions de diffusion, de distribution et d'échange réalisés avec ou sans gain. Quant aux principales tendances issues de la dynamique commerciale soit la prise en charge du commerce d'une nouvelle imagerie sur papier et la circulation universelle des reproductions de l'icône miraculeuse de Montréal, leur genèse est perceptible dès la première implantation des icônes en 1976.

En terre québécoise, l'implantation de l'imagerie de tradition byzantine s'effectue en trois étapes successives mais fort distinctes l'une de l'autre. La première débute en 1976 et marque l'introduction médiatique à l'iconographie orientale chrétienne; la seconde, cible l'arrivée discrète de la *Portaïtissa*, l'icône miraculeuse de Montréal en 1981, et la dernière correspond à l'éclatement de ses prodiges à l'été 1984.

L'introduction générale aux icônes a lieu entre le 28 novembre 1976 et le 18 mai 1978 à travers une trentaine d'émissions conçues et réalisées par Roger Leclerc de Radio-Canada, dans le cadre de la série religieuse *Second Regard*. L'initiative, qui permet d'apprivoiser la théologie, la technique, la dévotion et la symbolique de l'icône de l'Orient chrétien, constitue le premier et seul effort connu à ce jour ayant sensibilisé le grand public à une nouvelle forme d'imagerie de piété.

En plus d'avoir familiarisé le public à l'iconographie byzantine, la série télévisée s'associe à la première diffusion de masse d'une reproduction de l'icône-thème, la *Trinité de Roublev*. C'est ainsi que 10 000 reproductions sont éditées pour le compte de Radio-Canada par le Centre André Roublev à Laprairie[34] et diffusées à titre gratuit par les soeurs de la Présentation de Marie de Saint-Hilaire.

L'émission suscite également une demande pour la nouvelle imagerie auprès de huit commerces spécialisés à Montréal (4), Québec (2), Sherbrooke et Trois-Rivières. De fait, la variété de reproductions d'icônes offerte passe, selon l'établissement, de huit à quatre-vingt entre 1976 et 1980. Outre le support simple sur papier, une tendance veut que les reproductions d'icônes les plus populaires soient celles sur plaquette de bois. C'est alors qu'apparaissent certains efforts de montage et de laminage de l'imagerie importée surtout par des institutions religieuses[35].

On perçoit dès lors l'embryon de plusieurs tendances liées à la dynamique commerciale. La prise en charge de l'édition d'imagerie au Québec, la transformation de l'iconographie en un art de masse, le rôle des religieux et des religieuses dans l'édition et la diffusion de la nouvelle imagerie et partant, l'émergence d'un commerce parallèle. Quant à la tendance figurative, aucun modèle particulier semble avoir retenu l'attention au cours de l'implantation initiale des icônes (1976-1980). Cependant à partir de l'été 1980, sous l'effet d'événements "mystiques", la situation de l'imagerie et de son commerce éclate.

Le virement correspond à l'enracinement graduel des icônes avec la différence qu'il vise essentiellement la *Portaïtissa*, véritable icône rapportée du Mont Athos (la Sainte Montagne) en Grèce à la fin de 1981. Pendant les trois premières années d'intégration, elle n'est l'objet d'aucune pratique commerciale et ce, malgré ses prodiges[36] ou du va-et-vient régulier entre un groupe restreint de catholiques romains de Montréal et l'Église orthodoxe russe hors-frontières[37]. Seule circule en milieu restreint de la métropole, une photo-couleur montrant la canalisation et l'ouate recueillant l'huile suintant de la surface de la *Portaïtissa*. Rumeurs de prodiges et de bienfaits aidant, plusieurs réclament un souvenir figuré de l'icône dite miraculeuse.

La photo prise à des fins de reproduction et de diffusion en juin 1984, se démarque dit-on par une tache indélébile que l'on croit être les traces d'un suintement en forme de chapelet à partir de la main droite de la Vierge. Ce cliché qui devient alors le prototype officiel de l'icône miraculeuse de Montréal[38] donne le véritable coup d'envoi à une production, une commercialisation et une diffusion éclatées. Confirmant et renforçant ainsi les tendances "commerciales" amorcées entre 1976 et 1980.

De fait, la production sérielle, la commercialisation et la diffusion à grand échelle de l'image prototype sont réalisées sous l'égide ou à l'instigation de religieux et de religieuses tant à Montréal qu'à Québec et Trois-Rivières. Notons que cette dynamique est soutenue par un fort contingent de laïcs engagés et bénévoles tout aussi voués à la dévotion et à la diffusion de la nouvelle "icône québécoise". D'où certaines pratiques commerciales plus ou moins structurées.

À ce chapitre, signalons qu'en dépit des droits de reproductions de la *Portaïtissa*, pas moins de sept versions - retouchées ou piratées - du prototype sont apparues peu après sa mise en circulation. Une pratique plus légitime consiste à valoriser le prodige local qui se serait manifesté sur le prototype montréalais, en créant une nouvelle image - relique pour le milieu témoin. Hormis ces exemples isolés, quatre modèles de la *Portaïtissa* circulent actuellement, dont trois en couleurs. En plus du prototype édité par la Société de Marie, Mère de Dieu à Montréal, deux répliques (l'une sombre, l'autre claire) et une en noir et blanc sont produites par les Services du renouveau charismatique de Sillery en banlieue de Québec.

Ajoutons que la dynamique de production de l'imagerie byzantine inclut également l'artisan-imprimeur et le lamineur (ou monteur d'images). De fait, à côté des commerces spécialisés dans l'impression et le laminage de la nouvelle *Portaïtissa*, on retrouve des institutions religieuses et des particuliers laïcs ou religieux, répartis ici et là au Québec, reproduisant et montant des "icônes" à titre privé. Dans la plupart des cas, ces efforts sont limités au rayonnement immédiat. Toutefois, certains étendent leurs activités à travers la francophonie nord-américaine par le biais de congrès religieux ou de milieux sensibilisés à l'icône miraculeuse comme celui des Haïtiens de New York.

À cette production laminée ou non se greffent des produits complémentaires dont l'épinglette (broche) et l'image aimantée pour véhicules réalisées en cuivre émaillée[39]. Cette dernière, appréciée par les camionneurs, remplace ou se pose à côté de celle de saint Christophe, patron des voyageurs. Introduits par la Fondation de Marie Immaculée de Sillery, ces nouveaux objets, fort prisés en Europe, reproduisent fidèlement le prototype montréalais qui demeure le mieux connu et le plus apprécié du grand public.

Une dernière tendance, non apparente lors de l'implantation initiale des icônes en 1976-78, est l'émergence de foyers de diffusion de l'iconographie byzantine et de la *Portaïtissa* miraculeuse en particulier. Dirigés par un personnel religieux ou des laïcs engagés, ces établissements à structure limitée s'élaborent sensiblement autour des mêmes services, soit un petit comptoir de ventes, un oratoire, des ateliers sur l'imagerie byzantine ou la mariologie, des dévotions ouvertes sur la spiritualité orientale chrétienne, le *counselling*, l'impression de circulaires sur l'historique de l'icône miraculeuse, ses prodiges et ses bienfaits, etc. La philosophie sous-jacente à ces modestes lieux explique le recours à la définition élargie du commerce signalée plus haut.

Parmi les vingt-trois établissements relevés entre 1973 et 1990, treize sont voués exclusivement à l'icône miraculeuse de Montréal. Dans l'ensemble, ces lieux favorisent nettement l'imagerie éditée au Québec, par opposition aux établissements spécialisés ou structurés, pourtant dépositaires d'une plus grande variété de reproductions d'icônes. C'est néanmoins à travers le petit commerce non-structuré et parallèle, c'est-à-dire dans l'*underground*, administré par des bénévoles que l'imagerie byzantine connaît son véritable essor. Un estimé très conservateur montre qu'il est responsable de la vente et de la distribution de plus de 6 000 000 de reproductions de la *Portaïtissa* entre 1984 et 1990.

Les prodiges de l'icône miraculeuse ne sauraient expliquer seuls le succès de distribution de l'imagerie byzantine. Le sens que donnent les établissements à structure limitée au commerce de l'objet sacré mérite également d'être considéré. Outre la tradition voulant qu'un article bénit ou consacré doit être donné et non vendu, la générosité du bénévole se comptabilise et se contrôle difficilement. Il n'est pas rare de remettre gratuitement à l'acheteur d'une reproduction laminée de grand format, une dizaine, une centaine, voire plusieurs centaines de petites images analogues sur papier!

Il est tout aussi difficile de calculer l'impact des dons de bienfaiteurs. Exaucés par l'icône miraculeuse, certains montrent leur reconnaissance en assumant le coût d'impression de plusieurs milliers d'images qu'ils diffusent personnellement ou par l'intermédiaire d'un centre de prière soit pour fins de vente ou de distribution gratuite. D'où les difficultés comptables et l'estimé conservateur!

Quoique cette façon de "commercer" nuise à l'évaluation quantitative du phénomène, il n'en demeure pas moins que les établissements à structure limitée font preuve d'une meilleure stabilité au niveau de la distribution générale des icônes que le commerce spécialisé. L'approche personnalisée et suivie des foyers de diffusion n'est certes pas étrangère à ce succès. Non plus que la filière missionnaire érigée et maintenue par le Québec depuis plus d'un siècle et qui est toujours active, ou encore ces mouvements religieux récents tels le Renouveau charismatique. Grâce à l'étendue et au dynamisme de ces réseaux, la *Portaïtissa* montréalaise est devenue un phénomène universel en peu de temps.

À la mondialisation de cette icône s'ajoute une dimension culturelle significative. En effet, l'abondante correspondance des principaux foyers de diffusion[40] de la *Portaïtissa* démontre que le commerce (tout comme le culte à l'icône) relève d'avantage de pays francophones. Par exemple, la France et la Belgique figurent parmi les meilleures "consommateurs" de l'icône miraculeuse après le Québec. Compte tenu de la longue tradition de "dépendance culturelle" du Québec envers l'imagerie européenne, la tendance iconographique actuelle constitue un virage intéressant.

Ainsi, depuis le dévoilement du phénomène miraculeux à Montréal, en 1984, des foyers de diffusion de même que des particuliers produisent, commercent et diffusent une imagerie nouvelle en parallèle aux commerces spécialisés. Pendant deux ans, cette dynamique connaît le succès grâce à une certaine transparence, une approche personnalisée et des réseaux établis.

La situation change radicalement à l'hiver 1986, alors qu'une crise largement médiatisée secoue l'implantation de l'imagerie byzantine et plus spécifiquement celle de l'icône miraculeuse[41]. Par conséquent, l'ensemble de l'activité commerciale - tant structurée, qu'artisanale - périclite, obligeant les fidèles à la *Portaïtissa* à se tapir à nouveau dans l'*underground*. Bien que cette crise ait lourdement hypothéqué la production sérielle de la *Portaïtissa*, d'autres événements lui permettent de recouvrer une certaine stabilité. L'année mariale en 1987-1988 et le millénaire de la Russie en 1988 concourent entre autres, à rétablir quelque peu la situation. Outre la médiatisation des événements Postes Canada procède à l'émission de quatre timbres illustrant des icônes de tradition russe.

Alors que diverses tendances issues de la dynamique commerciale semblent plafonner après 1986, un autre type de production - tout aussi significatif mais plus discret - évolue néanmoins en parallèle, sans brisure ni scandale, soit celle de la création originale des icônes au Québec.

Tendances issues de la dynamique artistique

La création d'icônes figure parmi les traits les plus marquants de l'histoire récente de la figuration byzantine au Québec. Évoluant discrètement mais sûrement, les tendances issues de la dynamique artistique tirent leur pleine signification du fait qu'elles posent les assises d'une nouvelle imagerie sacrée à partir du premier noyau d'iconographes québécois de souche. L'originalité du phénomène invite à examiner de plus près les créateurs d'abord et les particularités de leurs oeuvres ensuite.

L'émergence d'une génération d'iconographes indigènes, qui remonte à 1979, se veut une conséquence directe de la série télévisée sur l'imagerie byzantine. De fait, la majorité des dix-huit artistes recensés entre 1989 et 1991 admettent avoir été inspirés par la série d'émissions consacrée aux icônes réalisée par Radio-Canada de 1976 à 1978. Cette sensibilisation répondait selon eux, à une soif quasi généralisée pour une forme d'art plus significative. (Rejoignant par là une quête analogue en Europe).

En 1991, le profil sommaire du premier noyau d'iconographes québécois montre que l'artiste est généralement une femme en milieu urbain, le plus souvent une religieuse initiée à l'art et dont l'âge moyen est de 46,5 ans. Par exemple, parmi les dix-huit personnes recensées, quinze sont des femmes, neuf sont des religieuses. Quant aux trois hommes complétant le bilan, ils sont tous "frères religieux", portant ainsi le nombre d'artistes religieux à douze, soit deux tiers des iconographes connus jusque là.

La tendance récente (automne 1994) indique que le nombre d'artistes indigènes augmente de façon substantielle, de 18 à 31 en moins de quatre ans et que cette poussée demeure essentiellement féminine. De fait, sur un total de 31 artistes on retrouve 29 femmes. Par contre la présence religieuse connaît un certain recul malgré 6 nouvelles recrues. Le tableau de comparaison ci-dessous illustre la diminution qui s'établit maintenant à 50% par rapport à 66% en 1991. L'écart peut être attribuable à l'organisme créé en novembre 1993 pour rassembler iconographes et iconophiles dans le but de parfaire leurs connaissances fondamentales (spirituelles) et formelles liées à l'art de la tradition byzantine.

Tableau de comparaison des recensements
d'iconographes québécois de souche

	Sexe		Statut		Régions		
	Femme	Homme	Marié	Religieux	Montréal	Québec	Autres
1991	15	3	6	2	7	7	4
1994	29	2	15	16	10	8	13

Pour ce qui est de la répartition géographique des iconographes, on note un déplacement assez important vers les régions périphériques. Alors qu'en 1991 la majorité (14 sur 18) provient des grandes régions de Montréal et de Québec, celles-ci ne recrutent actuellement qu'un peu plus de la moitié des artistes. Une tendance non perceptible au tableau veut en outre que le Québec soit perçu comme une terre d'initiation à l'iconographie auprès d'anciens résidents, étendant de ce fait l'intérêt pour la réalisation d'icônes au Canada français.

L'intérêt manifeste pour l'iconographie est d'autant plus étonnant que les artistes doivent confronter leurs concepts "innés" de l'art de l'Occident avec un art millénaire de l'Orient pourtant soumis à de stricts canons formels et fondamentaux. Le recours à des maîtres étrangers, soit du Québec, de la France ou des États-Unis, s'est donc avéré indispensable aux premiers intéressés à cette forme d'art au début de 1980. Ce sont maintenant les "pionniers" et "pionnières" qui initient les aspirants iconographes. Conscients de la "jeunesse" de cet art sacré au Québec, maîtres et élèves participent régulièrement à des stages de perfectionnement auprès d'icono-graphes reconnus à Montréal, à New York ou en Europe.

Au-delà de la maîtrise formelle de l'iconographie, l'artiste québécois cherche à approfondir ses connaissances fondamentales des icônes en fréquentant des maisons de prières ouvertes à la spiritualité orientale chrétienne[42]. L'on sait déjà qu'il débute son travail en récitant la prière de l'iconographe et réalise son oeuvre dans le silence et le recueillement en présence d'une icône consacrée et de la traditionnelle bougie. Selon les iconographes "*in via*", le ressourcement périodique constitue une démarche essentielle permettant de renforcer le climat recherché pour l'"écriture" exigeante des icônes.

Tout en se soumettant aux règles et modèles traditionnels de l'iconographie de l'Orient chrétien, l'artiste québécois n'hésite pas à recourir aux médiums et supports modernes, à puiser dans l'hagiographie occidentale ou à créer ses propres modèles. Ce faisant, il participe au courant "post-moderniste" prôné par des orthodoxes influents[43] - du Québec comme de l'Europe - en même temps qu'il se situe à l'origine d'une iconographie nouvelle et complexe.

De fait, le corpus actuel des iconographes québécois, que l'on estime à environ 1 000 icônes, s'imprègne également de "couleur locale". Par exemple, des modèles traditionnels comme le Christ, la Vierge, la Trinité ou les anges font valoir leur contexte de réalisation par des inscriptions en français. D'autres illustrent des notions fondamentales de la liturgie occidentale (ex. la Transubstantiation), prennent vie sur des matières aussi diverses que le cuir et la soie, intègrent des commémorations et des éléments décoratifs ou, fait assez exceptionnel, incluent le paysage indigène. Innovatrice ou choquante, force est d'admettre que l'icône québécoise n'est pas une copie conforme de l'art byzantin.

Là où le corpus québécois se démarque le plus, c'est quand il s'inspire de l'hagiographie occidentale. Les principaux thèmes retenant la faveur des artistes du Québec sont les patrons et fondateurs de communautés religieuses (masculines ou féminines), et l'hagiographie populaire. Qu'il vise des sujets traditionnels ou modernes, reconnus ou non par l'Église de l'Occident ou de l'Orient, le corpus ne peut laisser indifférent. Alors que certaines icônes soulèvent des critiques (ex. la Sainte Famille), d'autres font l'objet de reconnaissance internationale chez l'initié tant orthodoxe que catholique romain.

La création québécoise demeure par contre fort méconnue du grand public. Exclusive, limitée en nombre, produite en "circuit fermé" et correspondant davantage à une expression de la foi, son commerce ne saura en être le but ultime. En général, les oeuvres sont commandées par des paroisses, communautés et monastère religieux ou par des collectionneurs avertis. Cependant, grâce aux techniques modernes cette production originale commence à rayonner hors du milieu des seuls initiés.

C'est ainsi que des répliques d'icônes québécoises sont présentées sous forme d'images de piété, cartes de souhaits et affiches d'exposition ou illustrant des dépliants de dévotions, revues, feuillets dominicaux ou calendriers. Bien que la majorité des oeuvres sont éditées au Québec, certaines trouvent preneurs en Europe. Des expositions de groupe ou en solo, des reportages, des articles et des conférences contribuent également à mieux faire connaître l'iconographe québécois et son oeuvre. Notons qu'en général les iconographes cherchent peu la publicité, se laissant plutôt découvrir au fil du temps.

Il est d'ailleurs significatif qu'en moins de 15 ans, ces artistes discrets aient réussi à poser les premier jalons d'une iconographie originale tant au Québec que sur le plan international. En effet, les prototypes distinctifs issus de la symbiose est-ouest ou post-moderniste, font que l'icône québécoise soit, malgré ou à cause de son originalité, de plus en plus reconnue et appréciée en Amérique comme en Europe.

Bien que la production artistique demeure marginale tout comme celle du commerce décrite plus haut, elle s'en distingue par la créativité, l'originalité du corpus, son rayonnement de même que par son apport féminin.

Sur le fond, les deux formes d'art - exclusif et populaire - expriment un besoin analogue, celui de combler le vide figuratif religieux au Québec. Constat d'ailleurs renforcé par l'émergence d'un culte nouveau et particulier aux icônes.

Tendances issues de la dynamique cultuelle

À l'instar du commerce et de la création originale des icônes, la dynamique cultuelle origine de la base et évolue essentiellement dans l'*underground*. Considérant que la notion de culte réfère à des pratiques et croyances réglées par la religion, force est d'admettre que la dévotion aux icônes et à la *Portaïtissa* en particulier, manifeste un glissement important par rapport au passé religieux du Québec. Plus privé que communautaire, plus intériorisé et mystique qu'actif, le nouveau culte marial s'éloigne en effet des canons romains pour se rapprocher de la spiritualité orientale chrétienne où l'icône joue d'ailleurs un rôle de premier plan.

Une autre tendance fondamentale veut que le culte à la *Portaïtissa* soit en marge des dévotions reconnues à la Vierge. La situation s'explique par le problème des manifestations miraculeuses, par la prudence traditionnelle des autorités religieuses catholiques romaines face à ce type de phénomène et enfin, du fait que la dévotion origine de la base et continue à évoluer à travers elle. Ce sont d'ailleurs les tendances au niveau des nouvelles pratiques et croyances émergeant de la base qui donnent un sens à la dévotion aux icônes et partant, un sens à la renaissance de l'imagerie sacrée au Québec.

Dans le cadre de ce rapport, nous n'abordons pas l'ensemble des pratiques et croyances qui alimentent la dynamique cultuelle actuelle. Nous ciblons plutôt les aspects concrets de la dévotion pour mieux cerner le rôle de la figuration byzantine dans l'élaboration du nouveau culte d'une part, et évaluer ensuite son impact sur l'imagerie qui a proliféré au Québec entre 1840 et 1960.

D'emblée, le culte à l'icône miraculeuse de la *Portaïtissa* passe par l'aménagement d'oratoires domestiques, à la fois supports et témoins de nouvelles pratiques et croyances. S'éloignant du "coin de prière" traditionnel[44], la forme et le contenu de l'oratoire actuel reflètent les profonds changements qui affectent les gestes et paroles des utilisateurs[45].

Très en vue dans les diverses aires familiales, la majorité des nouveaux oratoires occupent une superficie assez imposante. Certains fidèles prévoient même leur emplacement lors de l'achat d'une nouvelle maison ou dans leur plan de construction, alors que d'autres lui réservent une pièce entière. La forme d'oratoire la plus courante s'élabore autour d'une bibliothèque murale.

En plus des reproductions d'icônes, une variété d'objets sacrés, de livres de piété, parfois même de matériel audiovisuel contenant des conférences religieuses et de la cassette de musique sacrée, se greffent aux oratoires domestiques. Suivant la tradition du "coin de beauté" chez les orthodoxes, on retrouve une source de lumière, sous forme de bougie ou de lampe, de même que des fleurs fraîches ou séchées destinées à mettre l'icône ou l'ensemble d'icônes en valeur.

Le relevé des oratoires dans la région de Québec montre que les reproductions de la *Portaïtissa* dominent largement l'imagerie religieuse[46]. Parmi les 76 images répertoriées, on retrouve une vingtaine de figurations modernes, traditionnelles et byzantines. De ce nombre, onze représentent des icônes de l'Orient chrétien et font l'objet de plus de cinquante-cinq reproductions, soit 74% de l'ensemble.

La popularité de la nouvelle imagerie de dévotion permet de dégager trois tendances formelles fort significatives. Outre l'ouverture marquée sur les figurations byzantines, on remarque une pénurie de l'hagiographie traditionnelle occidentale (6%) et l'absence quasi-totale de la statuaire religieuse pourtant très populaire jusqu'au tournant des années 1970.

Fait assez étonnant, c'est sans hésitation que les informateurs-clé troquent dévotions et imageries traditionnelles contre la nouvelle icône miraculeuse. C'est ainsi que la Vierge sous ses diverses formes occidentales (4), le Sacré-Coeur (2), sainte Anne (1) et un crucifix cèdent leur place à l'immigrante de l'Orient chrétien. Et, comme tout immigrant qui se respecte, la nouvelle arrivée facilite l'entrée d'autres membres de sa famille iconique, comme le *Pantocrator*, les *Vierges* de *Vladimir*, de *Korsun*, de *Czestochowa*, la *Trinité de Roublev* etc.

Le culte à l'icône maintient néanmoins certains parallèles avec la dévotion et l'utilisation traditionnelles des images dévotes au Québec. À l'instar du culte à la thaumaturge de Sainte-Anne-de-Beaupré, celui à l'icône miraculeuse de Montréal fait l'objet de pèlerinage à lettres[47]. Les principaux centres de dévotion à la *Portaïtissa* situés à Montréal, Québec et Trois-Rivières en font foi et l'analyse du contenu des messages à la Vierge souligne l'importance de la pratique, notamment pour le croyant en détresse[48]. D'autres rapprochements avec les usages traditionnels montrent que l'icône peut être utilisée comme symbole de protection ou comme talisman. En dépit de ces liens avec le passé religieux du Québec, la nouvelle dévotion montre une différence fondamentale sur le plan perceptuel. Une différence, qui permet de saisir l'attrait particulier de l'icône et qui va au-delà des formes.

La grande distinction réside dans l'évocation d'une présence particulière qui accompagne l'iconographie orientale, une présence qui transcende l'image. Cette caractéristique inhérente à l'iconographie orientale est corroborée depuis des millénaires par érudits, iconographes et ecclésiastiques de l'orthodoxie comme de la catholicité romaine.

De fait, le mystère et le symbolisme liés à cette forme ancienne de l'art chrétien donnent un sens nouveau aux dévotions en mutations depuis Vatican II, incitant de plus en plus de croyants à l'intégrer comme support concret à leurs pratiques de piété et à développer un culte personnalisé et privé. À la lumière de ces tendances, il appert que le symbolisme "transcendant" de l'icône répond à une sensibilité que le réalisme éthéré de l'imagerie moderne ou traditionnelle ne pas su combler jusqu'ici. À tel point que le croyant québécois choisit de ne pas renouer avec sa tradition d'imagerie.

D'ailleurs faut-il se surprendre que le Québécois, lui-même forgé au symbole et au sacré depuis plus de trois siècles, soit sensible à une coutume figurée imbue de symbolisme? Sans oublier que l'icône est non imposée, produite au

Québec, et que la *Portaïtissa*, principal objet du culte, prend racine et choisit de se manifester sur son territoire.

Les tendances issues de la dynamique culturelle témoignent de changement majeurs depuis Vatican II. Outre le déplacement d'un culte privé qui se développe en marge de l'Église-institution et l'orientalisation des pratiques cultuelles, les tendances démontrent l'importance des signes sensibles dans le recueillement et la piété. Éléments qui ont été écartés lors du renouveau dans l'Église du Québec à compter des années 1960.

CONCLUSION

Le survol des tendances de l'iconographie actuelle du sacré contribue à élucider, du moins qualitativement, le sens de la renaissance d'une imagerie pieuse au Québec et la contribution des diverses dynamiques dont elles sont issues.

Marquées du sceau de l'individualisme et de l'originalité, les tendances reflètent l'esprit autonomiste et spontané généré par les contextes socio-culturel et religieux des années 1960-70. Formellement, elles signalent une orientalisation de l'imagerie sacrée qui se manifeste dans des pratiques commerciales, artistiques et cultuelles. Au-delà du concret, les tendances font valoir le mouvement de fond qui se profile sinon dans l'Église-institution, du moins auprès de la base. Un mouvement qui se traduit par la recherche d'une religion plus sensible et qui pour cela recourt aux sources de l'imagerie chrétienne, l'icône de l'Orient chrétien.

Enfin, l'histoire de l'image dévote du Québec, longtemps intégrée à la culture religieuse traditionnelle et que d'aucuns croyaient disparue, effectue par cette renaissance un virage majeur. Un virage à être observé et consigné dans toute son actualité en raison de la "révolution" formelle et fondamentale qui la sous-tend et aussi parce qu'elle se poursuit toujours sans bruit dans l'*underground*.

BIBLIOGRAPHIE SOMMAIRE

Documents imprimés

A.-M. Poulin et J.A. Harries. (dir.) *Culture et tradition*. Québec/Terre-Neuve. Université Laval/Memorial University. vol. 13, 1989. pp. 9-53.

Anne-Marie Poulin. *L'iconographie actuelle du sacré au Québec: le cas de l'icône miraculeuse de Montréal*. Mémoire de maîtrise. Québec, Université Laval, 1992. xvi-134 p. ill.

Documents archivistes

Archives de folklore de l'Université Laval (AFUL), Sainte-Foy, Québec.

Fonds Larouche-Villeneuve, boîtes 6-I; 9; 12 et 28.

Fonds Icône, collection A.-M. Poulin, J. Simard. Dossier exploratoire sur l'icône miraculeuse, Marie, Mère de Dieu, Porte du Ciel. Classeurs I et II, novembre 1988.

NOTES

1. Le seul ouvrage ayant abordé le problème de l'imagerie sacrée sur papier est celui de l'ethnologue Pierre Lessard dans un mémoire ciblant la figuration traditionnelle au Québec depuis 1840 à 1960. *Les petites images dévotes. Leur utilisation traditionnelle au Québec*. Québec, Presses de l'université Laval, 1981. 175 p., ill.

2. Déposée aux Archives de folklore de l'université Laval, l'enquête exploratoire réalisée par l'auteure comprend 4 volets: historique, symbolique, esthétique et religieux. Le séminaire a eu lieu sous la direction de Jean Simard avec le concours de six étudiants, dont moi-même. Une partie des résultats a fait l'objet de trois articles dans la revue *Culture et tradition*, vol. 13, 1989, p. 9 à 53.

3. Nathalie Labrecque (Pervouchine), Montréalaise d'origine russe et auteure de la thèse *L'Iconostase: une évolution historique en Russie*. Montréal, Bellarmin, 1982. 294 p. ill.

4. Aux Services du renouveau charismatique, rue Cardinal Bégin à Sillery.

5. À l'église Saint-Michel, rue Persico, où se trouve en plus la Fondation Marie-Immaculé dédiée à la diffusion et à la dévotion de l'icône miraculeuse. En 1991, la Fondation comptait plus de 90 000 membres.

6. Expression du dominicain français Frannçois Boespflug. Elle s'inspire d'un souhait du père Alain Couturier qui voyait la nécessité d'éliminer les "bondieuseries" de la rue Saint-Sulpice à Paris pour place à des images plus significatives (1945-1950).

7. Dominique Lerch, "Un cas de dépendance culturelle". *Le vieux papier*, fascicule 277, 1980, p. 79.

8. Lerch, *ibid.*, p. 76 et P. Lessard, *op. cit.*

9. Cette affirmation demeure hypothétique compte tenu de l'absence de statistiques précises sur les importations d'images. Toutefois, importateurs, grossistes, distributeurs et marchands d'images sacrées s'entendent sur le fait que le marché de l'imagerie sacrée au Québec français a suivi la courbe de la désaffection religieuse.

10. Situation évoquée au niveau de la pratique religieuse et dans les publications. Dans le premier cas, rappelons que depuis la fin des années 1960, la pratique religieuse en milieu urbain est estimée entre 10% et 15%; celle en milieu périphérique autour de 20%. Les ouvrages quant à eux renvoient à des titres évocateurs de la situation: Guy Bourgeault, Jean Caron et Jean Duclos. *L'Église s'en va chez l'Diable*. Montréal, Les Éditions de l'Homme, 1968. 174 p. Colette Moreux. *Fin d'une religion. Monographie d'une paroisse canadienne-française*. Montréal, Presses de l'Université de Montréal, 1969. 485 p.; Guy Bourgeault *et al. Quand les églises se vident: vers une théologie de la pratique*. Paris, Desclée de Brouwer/Montréal, Bellarmin, 1974. 160 p.; Jean Simard, Jocelyne Milot, René Bouchard. *Un patrimoine méprisé. La religion populaire des Québécois*. Montréal, Hurtubise HMH, 1979. 309 p.

11. P. Lessard, *op. cit,* p. 25 et C. Moreux, *ibid*.

12. Guy Laperriere, "L'Adaptation à de nouveaux modes de vie". *Le Grand héritage. L'Église catholique et la société du Québec*. Québec, Musée du Québec, 1984. pp. 129-169.

13. Une des rares études sur l'adaptation aux changements religieux de l'époque est celle du sociologue Roland Chagnon, *Les charismatiques au Québec*, Montréal, Québec-Amérique, 1979. 211 p. Voir également l'article de Laperriere, *op. cit.* p. 153.

14. Lerch, *op. cit.*, p. 79.

15. Organisé à l'Université du Québec à Trois-Rivières par Benoit Lacroix o.p. 1970 à 1982.

16. Jean Simard, *Les Arts sacrés au Québec*. Boucherville, Éditions de Mortagne, 1989. 319 p.; Claude Bergeron. *L'architecture des églises du Québec 1940-1955*. Québec, Presses de l'Université Laval, 1987. 384 p.

17. Bergeron, *ibid.* Introduction et Simard, *ibid.*, p. 276.

18. Bergeron, *ibid.*, p. 54.

19. Simard, *ibid.*, p. 276.

20. Jusqu'aux années 1960, le terme "canadien ou canadienne" désignait plus spécifique-ment le Canadien d'expression française.

21. Collectif. *L'art religieux contemporain au Canada*. Québec, 1952. p. 60.

22. *Ibid*.

23. Bergeron, *op. cit.*, pp. 53-54.

24. Simard, *op. cit.*, p. 276. Par exemple l'artiste Rodolphe Duguay destine une partie de ses images à l'*Almanach de Saint-François* des franciscains de Trois-Rivières et conçoit une image originale de la Vierge pour le Centre marial canadien. Ces mêmes images servent à illustrer les écrits poétiques que sa femme Jeanne L'Archevêque consacre à Marie: *Mater* (1946), *Cantilènes* (1947), *Épouse et mère avec Marie* (1947). L'auteur signale par

ailleurs le rôle de Mgr Albert Tessier qui conçoit l'idée de diffuser les oeuvres de
Duguay à travers [...] les cartes de voeux.

25. Lessard, *op.cit.*, p. 6.

26. Dominique Lerch fait allusion à cette lacune dans son article "Un cas de dépendance
culturelle, l'imagerie au Québec", *Le Vieux Papier*, Paris, fascicule 277, pp. 69-79.
Malheureusement, l'article n'inclut pas deux autres aspects de son rapport
inédit,"Imprimer, lithographier et vendre au Québec", portant sur les éléments d'identi-
té régionale transmis soit par l'imagerie populaire, soit par la presse populaire aux XIXe
et XXe siècles (*Ibid*, p. 69).

27. *Ibid*.

28. D'autres facteurs qui ne peuvent être traités dans le présent article contribuent évidem-
ment à l'échec du *Retable*, tels le régionalisme des années 1930, l'impact du courant
international après la deuxième grande guerre, ou encore les effets du *Refus global* en
1948, etc.

29. *L'iconostase. Une évolution historique en Russie*. Montréal, Bellarmin, 1982. p. 25.

30. Notamment l'Académie Saint-Cyrille et Saint-Méthode greffée à l'Église russe catholique La Présentation de Marie ainsi que la Maison de prière Emmaüs fondée et dirigée
par le père Lucien Coutu s.j. Les deux centres de piété sont jumelés quant à la diffusion
de la spiritualité orientale chrétienne. Signalons également l'émergence de maisons de
prière comme la Communauté du désert à Nicolet, ouverte aux religieux et laïcs
souhaitant modeler leur vécu sur celui des premiers chrétiens.

31. Par exemple, Marie Desderian, Goerge Gorgis, Jualinan Kolozar, Nathalie
Pervouchine-Labrecque, Iona Manelosco, Rosetta Mociornitza, José Munoz, Steban
Papa, le père Papazian (ermite), Goerges Schelevow et son fils Alexandor, Irène
Stawinska, le père Patrick Tibérinien, le couple Magdalena et Sigmund Stygar.

32. Fondé par l'iconographe montréalaise d'origine roumaine Rosetta Mociornitza.

33. N. Pervouchine-Labrecque, *op. cit.*, (pp. 24-25). L'auteure souligne également l'apport
indéniable du père J. Ledit s.j., du Collège Russicum de l'Institut oriental de Rome et
curé de la paroisse russe orthodoxe, La Présentation de Marie à Montréal.

34. Établie en 1976 sous l'instigation du père Naveau, alors recherchiste à Radio-Canada
pour les émissions sur les icônes, la maison d'édition ferme ses portes après deux ans
d'activité.

35. Anne-Marie Poulin. *L'iconographie actuelle du sacré au Québec: le cas de l'icône miraculeuse de
Montréal*. Mémoire de maîtrise. Québec, Université Laval, 1992. XVI - 134 p., ill. Voir p.
42 pour la liste nominative.

36.   Les prodiges se manifestent sous trois formes: le suintement d'une huile, le parfum et la poussière d'or ou d'argent. Seules ou combinées, les manifestations apparaissent autant sur l'icône originale que sur des reproductions et des photos.

37.   Église en exil depuis la révolution bolchévique en 1903 et en rupture totale avec toutes les autres branches de l'orthodoxie. Cette institution de droite, militant en faveur du retour de la monarchie en Russie est, de plus, farouchement opposée à toutes formes d'unité entre les chrétiens.

38.   Cette icône qui possède une nomenclature assez impressionnante répond à 16 différentes appellations au Québec. Les deux plus populaires étant Notre-Dame de la Porte (terme qui correspond davantage à son inscription) ou encore Marie, Mère de Dieu, Porte du Ciel popularisée par sa maison d'édition de Montréal, la Société de Marie, Mère de Dieu. Plusieurs l'identifient tout simplement comme l'icône miraculeuse de Montréal.

39.   Réalisations de D. Bérubé, joallier de Québec.

40.   La Société de Marie, Mère de Dieu à Montréal, la Fondation Marie-Immaculée et les Services du Renouveau charismatique, situés tous deux à Sillery.

41.   La crise réfère au "scandale de Sainte-Marthe-sur-le-Lac" qui a fait la manchette dans les journaux du 9 au 15 février 1986 autour d'une statue truquée de la Vierge "pleurant du sang". Le rapprochement entre la supercherie et l'icône miraculeuse relève du fait que les reproductions d'icônes figurent parmi les 90 objets de piété impliqués dans la fraude. Cf. au pages 43-46 du mémoire de maîtrise pour plus de détails.

42.   Dont la Maison Emmaüs à Montréal et la Villa Manrèse à Sainte-Foy.

43.   Notamment Olivier Clément s.j. de l'Institut Saint-Serge de Paris et le père Popusco, curé de l'église de la Présentation de la Vierge à Montréal.

44.   Jusqu'au début des années 1960, le coin de prière s'organise généralement autour d'un crucifix flanqué d'images du Sacré-Coeur de Jésus et du Sacré-Coeur de Marie ou d'une statue éclairée d'un lampion, posée sur une tablette murale.

45.   Notons que les pratiques gestuelles et linguistiques élaborées dans la thèse originale sont exclues du présent rapport.

46.   Cette observation est également valable pour Montréal, Trois-Rivières, Chicoutimi, etc.

47.   Anne Doran. *Le pèlerinage à Sainte-Anne-de-Beaupré. L'Actuel, 1958-1973*. Thèse de doctorat. Paris, Écoles des hautes études en sciences sociales, 1979. 814 p.

48.   Marcelle Cinq-Mars, "La Vierge Marie dans l'imaginaire des croyants: analyse des prières déposées à l'icône de Marie, Mère de Dieu, Porte du Ciel". *Culture et Tradition*, vol. 13, 1989, p. 42-53.

RÉFLEXIONS SUR LE CONCEPT D'EXPOSITION
« *ICÔNE-EIKONA* »

par
Claire Labrecque

L'art de l'icône, qui a près de 1500 ans d'existence, trouve ses origines à Constantinople, l'ancienne Byzance. Forme d'art sacré depuis longtemps défendue par les orthodoxes grecs et russes, l'icône trouve son expression dans la représentation personnifiée de l'âme, de la foi. Malgré des siècles d'histoire, cette forme d'art n'a pas connu d'évolution stylistique et iconographique comparable aux autres formes d'art. Et encore, l'art de l'icône ne s'insère plus depuis un siècle dans les mouvements de l'art, non pas à cause de son abandon par les artistes, mais plutôt en raison de la fidélité des artistes iconographes aux règles de cet art. N'ayant pas connu un renouvellement complet de ses fondements, l'art de l'icône est depuis longtemps mis à l'index, dans une catégorie à part, particulièrement dans les ouvrages de synthèse en histoire de l'art. Pourtant, l'art de l'icône est loin de s'éteindre. Bien au contraire, il s'est sans cesse maintenu sur le continent européen, particulièrement en Grèce et dans les pays d'Europe de l'Est, et cela malgré les chambardements politiques, sociaux et idéologiques qui ont touché ces pays à différents moments de l'histoire. Encore de nos jours, les peintres iconographes européens respectent assez fidèlement les dogmes anciens prescrits dans le Livre du Mont Athos pour la réalisation d'une icône; c'est encore plus manifeste chez les artistes de conviction orthodoxe.

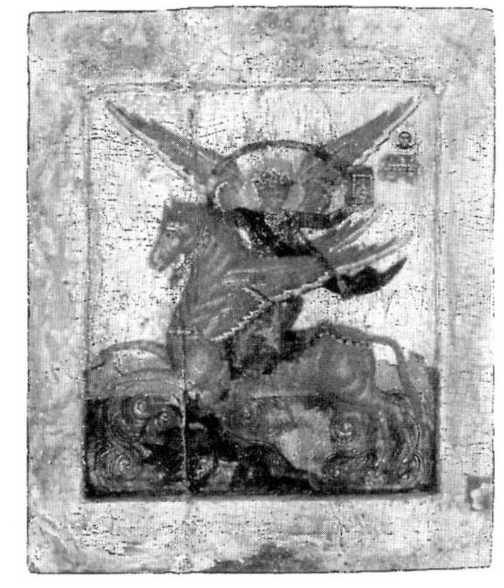

Si on note un conservatisme persistant dans la production européenne, qu'en est-il de la production d'icônes à l'extérieur de ces frontières? L'art de l'icône connaît une popularité grandissante en Amérique depuis une quinzaine d'années, particulièrement aux États-Unis et dans le milieu artistique québécois. Mais comment se traduit *« l'expression iconique »*[1] loin des vieux continents? Quelles sont les bases ou les origines de la production d'icônes au Québec? Observe t-on des distinctions dans les notions d'iconicité, dans le style ou dans les thématiques? Ayant eu à concevoir un concept d'exposition sur l'art de l'icône, à l'été 1995, j'ai redécouvert cette forme d'art qui ne s'est jamais éteinte et j'ai dû répondre à ces multiples questionnements[2]. Cette exposition avait pour objectif de dégager les principes fondamentaux de cette forme d'art en confrontant des icônes anciennes aux icônes actuelles. Non seulement j'ai eu l'occasion de constater la richesse des collections d'icônes anciennes conservées dans les institutions canadiennes[3], mais aussi l'originalité de la production d'icônes actuelles, particulièrement au Québec.

L'ART DE L'ICÔNE DANS NOS COLLECTIONS

Les collections publiques canadiennes renferment plusieurs centaines d'icônes anciennes provenant de différentes sources. Il s'agit d'icônes de différents types, à partir d'icônes traditionnellement peintes sur bois jusqu'aux petites icônes de type «médaillon de pèlerin»[4]. Ce nombre important d'icônes dans les collections canadiennes est redevable en partie aux communautés ethniques de religions orthodoxes qui vécurent sur le sol canadien depuis le siècle dernier[5]. La présence de ces groupes venus d'Europe de l'Est (ukrainiens, roumains et autres) a permis la circulation d'un grand nombre d'icônes au Canada et l'enrichissement des collections publiques. Autrement, on ne doit pas oublier les nombreuses donations d'icônes provenant de différents pays aux musées.

Si nos institutions muséales possèdent d'intéressantes collections d'icônes anciennes, on oublie trop souvent les icônes conservées dans «l'anonymat» des institutions religieuses. Pourtant, les icônes aux mains des communautés religieuses constituent sans doute près de la moitié de la collection totale d'icônes au Québec. Leur possession par les communautés religieuses s'explique facilement. D'une part, les maisons-mères ont longtemps enrichi les institutions religieuses «coloniales» en leur transférant des objets de culte des plus variés. En raison des nombreuses donations par les maisons-mères au cours des siècles derniers, les collections de nos communautés religieuses se sont largement enrichies d'objets d'art sacré d'une valeur indéniable, dont plusieurs icônes anciennes. D'autre part, en raison de leur usage sacré, il n'est pas étonnant de retrouver autant d'icônes ... dans les communautés religieuses.

Or, malgré ces transferts d'oeuvres importants vers les communautés religieuses, la fabrication d'icônes par les membres de ces communautés débuta plus particulièrement à partir de la deuxième moitié du 19e siècle. Cela s'explique peut-être du fait de la diminution des échanges avec les maisons-mères, mais cela s'explique surtout en raison d'un certain besoin d'identification aux cultes davantage nord-américains. Ainsi, on voit se multiplier au 19ᵉ siècle les icônes à la Vierge du Sacré Coeur ou au Sacré Coeur de Jésus. À cette époque, on ne peint pas une icône précisément selon les règles du Mont Athos. On représente les figures que l'on vénère plutôt à la façon d'une icône[6]. Aussi, il n'est pas rare de voir des icônes « québécoises » du 19ᵉ siècle peintes à partir d'une variété de matériaux des plus divers[7]. Ce phénomène n'est pas unique aux icônes dites québécoises, puisqu'on observe l'usage de procédés techniques similaires dans des icônes produites partout au Canada et qui furent réalisées souvent par les milieux orthodoxes de différentes ethnies[8].

Mes recherches m'ont peu à peu forcée à m'éloigner du secteur public pour découvrir une quantité incroyable d'icônes anciennes chez les collectionneurs privés. Si ce « réseau» n'est pas facilement accessible, en raison de l'isolement des collectionneurs, il mérite notre intérêt. Ces pièces de collection proviennent soit d'un héritage familial, ou bien elles furent acquises lors de voyages dans les pays d'Europe. Il s'agit dans bien des cas d'icônes de grande valeur, tant du point de vue de leur état de conservation, qui est souvent exceptionnel, que de leur datation. L'âge d'une icône ancienne est souvent inconnu du collectionneur privé qui sait uniquement qu'il s'agit d'un objet ancien... pour avoir passé de main en main, de génération en génération. J'ai cependant réussi à préciser la datation d'icônes anciennes appartenant à des collectionneurs privés aux alentours du 16ᵉ et du 17ᵉ siècle. La précision de ces datations fut basée sur les détails techniques, sur les types de revêtements (basma) et sur les particularités iconographiques[9].

Les collections privées constituent donc une source importante d'oeuvres méconnues du large public, qu'il s'agisse d'icônes anciennes que d'icônes actuelles. C'est en effet en visitant les collections privées que j'ai pris contact non seulement avec le monde ancien, mais avec la production actuelle d'icônes. Ainsi, s'il est relativement facile de retracer des icônes anciennes, j'ai découvert qu'il est encore plus facile de découvrir l'art « iconique » actuel , puisque sa production va bon train en raison du nombre croissant d'artistes qui font revivre cet art.

QUÉBEC À LA CARTE: L'ART DE L'ICÔNE DEPUIS LES 20 DERNIÈRES ANNÉES

Malgré une période d'obscurité de près d'un siècle, l'art de l'icône ne s'est toutefois pas éteint avec le temps. Encore aujourd'hui, de nombreux artistes icono-graphes perpétuent, avec la même conviction, les gestes des tout premiers "imagiers de Dieu". Peut-on qualifier leur geste de créateur, alors que l'idée même de la création a toujours été rejetée, dans le passé, par les orthodoxes? Sans rompre totalement avec les règles orthodoxes, la plupart des iconographes actuels ne se limitent plus au "geste de reproduction" de l'icône. Certains innovent par les thèmes, d'autres par la forme ou par la technique. Art à la portée de tous, il connaît une large diffusion principalement dans les églises orthodoxes, mais aussi auprès d'un grand nombre de personnes en tant qu'objet de dévotion.

L'exposition *Icône-Eikona* permit de faire le pont entre le passé et le présent en regroupant une trentaine d'oeuvres anciennes et actuelles (du 16ᵉ au 20ᵉ siècle). Les iconographes qui participèrent à cet événement résident pour la plupart au Québec. Le choix des participants fut établi de façon à représenter les différentes cultures orthodoxe et non-orthodoxe. Parmi les artistes québécois, on retrouvait Marthe Bélanger, Céline Boucher, Joana Cirstea-Taurand, Titu Dragutescu, Rosette Mociornitza, Lise Ouellet, Petit Frère Sylvain, Denise Rioux, Jeanne Vanasse et Svetla Velikova. Les oeuvres de deux artistes européens, Nikolas Karim (Liban) et Mercourios Dimopoulos (Grèce) faisaient partie de l'exposition. Les oeuvres de ces artistes ont été présentées de façon à côtoyer des icônes anciennes.

La juxtaposition d'icônes anciennes et récentes avait pour objet de faire voir les constantes dans la fabrication de l'icône et les transformations qui se sont opérées avec le temps. Les oeuvres de l'artiste d'origine bulgare Svetla Velikova se distinguaient remarquablement par la force du dessin, l'énergie de la ligne, par l'éclat des couleurs et la chaleur des dorures cuivrées qui se doivent d'être symboliques. On pouvait reconnaître rapidement le style très allongé et à la fois puissant des figures marquées de traits noirs, traitement à la manière bulgare des modèles russes de l'école de Roublev.

Les icônes des artistes d'origine roumaine Titu Dragutescu et Joana Cirstea-Taurand se différenciaient par un traitement plus ornemental des thèmes, par la mise en valeur esthétique des éléments de l'image et de la bordure, cadre fictif de l'icône. Le spectateur a pu constater la subtilité des jeux de couleurs dans ces oeuvres, qui procèdent d'une variété incroyable de teintes et de leur saturation, nécessitant une grande maîtrise technique. Deux oeuvres de Rosette Mociornitza, aussi d'origine roumaine, furent présentées au public en raison de leur traitement fort particulier, alliant le traitement en aplat et le bas-relief résultant de l'application de touches de plâtre peint. Le type des figures, tout à fait propre à cette artiste, se reconnaissait par les traits étirés mais expressifs d'une certaine dignité. C'est d'ailleurs particulièrement le traitement des visages avec de très grands yeux, découpés sur un fond souvent complètement noir, qui captiva le spectateur.

Du côté des artistes européens, le peintre grecque Mercourios Dimopoulos présenta une icône fort éloquente du style intimiste et «classique» de l'artiste. La pose frontale et statique d'un saint Philippe sur un fond abstrait, divisé en trois zones contrastées, demeure tout à fait fidèle au style byzantin. À cet égard, les oeuvres de cet artiste, qui s'éloignent très peu des modèles premiers, ne cherchent nullement à renouveler le langage iconique, mais plutôt à intensifier les qualités iconiques héritées du passé. Le public a pu observer un peu le même phénomène avec les oeuvres de l'iconographe libanais Nikolas Majdalani, lequel peint des icônes dans le plus grand respect des canons dits classiques. À la différence, les oeuvres de ce dernier se démarquaient par le format beaucoup plus grand des oeuvres et par le recouvrement important de la dorure, produisant un effet à la fois totalement abstrait et très décoratif. La dorure « orangée » qui recouvre ses icônes semble avoir

été chauffée pour en modifier la teinte. L'artiste a su jouer contraster les couleurs
« forme-fond » pour amplifier le caractère surnaturel des figures. Ainsi, son audace
va jusqu'à juxtaposer bleu turquoise, jaune doré et rouge terre de Sienne.

Parmi les iconographes d'origine québécoise, six artistes ont participé à
l'événement. Les icônes de Marthe Bélanger, Céline Boucher, Petit Frère Sylvain,
Lise Ouellet et Denise Rioux ont su rappeler que la peinture d'icônes est un geste
empreint de dignité, mais aussi qu'elle est le fruit d'une longue méditation. L'artiste
Jeanne Vanasse présenta une version tout à fait moderne du thème de *Saint Georges
terrassant le dragon*, tout aussi empreint de dignité. Mais son interprétation fit en sorte
que l'icône semblait investie d'une puissance d'expression totalement nouvelle. On
peut relever des caractères particuliers aux oeuvres des peintres d'icônes québé-
cois(s), comme le traitement très méticuleux des oeuvres, mais surtout la préférence
pour les représentations semi-narratives, c'est-à-dire des représentations d'un saint à
un moment de sa vie. Ce type de représentation, que je qualifierais «d'Occidental»,
est en effet plus fréquemment retenu que les représentations de personnages
inanimés, en posture frontale et revêtus de vêtements avec plis à l'Antique. Dans
l'ensemble du corpus québécois, on a pu remarquer cette tendance au naturalisme
des poses et des éléments de l'image. Enfin, le public a pu sentir un certain besoin
d'identification des artistes à leur culture. Lise Ouellet et Denise Rioux n'ont pas
hésité à représenter sous forme d'icône des thèmes plus près des croyances locales,
une Vierge du Sacré Coeur et saint Ignace de Loyola.

ICÔNE-EIKONA: UNE EXPOSITION EN HOMMAGE À LA MÉMOIRE ET AU PRÉSENT

L'exposition *ICÔNE - EIKONA* visait à montrer d'une part les caractères
permanents de cet art millénaire et, d'autre part, toute la diversité d'approche et
d'interprétation de l'image sainte en cette fin du 20ᵉ siècle. Pour ce faire, l'exposition
fut établie en fonction de deux grands axes: la présentation d'icônes anciennes (du
16ᵉ au 19ᵉ siècle) et la présentation d'oeuvres actuelles. Agissant à titre de conserva-
trice de l'exposition, j'ai voulu présenter la production actuelle comme un art
"rafraîchi" puisque la production actuelle laisse place à divers types d'interprétation
de l'icône, voire même à un mouvement de création chez certains iconographes. Par
interprétation, j'entends soit l'interprétation des thèmes ou celle du rendu formel
(volumes, poses et traits du visage). Par création, j'entends la réalisation d'icônes sur
de nouveaux thèmes religieux jusqu'ici jamais représentés, ou encore la réalisation
de thèmes classiques transformés au moyen de la technique, de la matière ou des
coloris. Du point de vue technique, on a pu observer la richesse des pigments, la
somptuosité des textures et la translucidité de la matière d'une icône qui vient d'être
réalisée.

La mise en salle fut prévue de façon à respecter les thèmes majeurs, mais
aussi de façon à rappeler la nature fondamentale et les origines de l'icône. Ainsi, la
couleur des salles, l'éclairage et la disposition des oeuvres devaient d'une part

s'inspirer des intérieurs d'églises orthodoxes, et d'autre part, mettre en valeur les oeuvres en fonction des différents matériaux, des couleurs diverses et des formats des plus variés. Les surfaces murales des salles furent peintes de couleur ocre et rouge «scarlett», qui sont les couleurs le plus fréquemment associées aux décors d'églises orthodoxes, mais que l'on retrouve aussi souvent dans les icônes. D'autres sections murales furent peintes de couleur grise pour s'harmoniser avec les recouvrements d'argent. De grands personnages tirés de la *Déésis*, peints sur de longues tentures de toile par l'artiste Paul Ivanovich Voevodine, furent placés dans les salles comme éléments décoratifs et afin de signaler la direction des thèmes. L'éclairage des oeuvres a été voulu très intimiste, pour rappeler la contemplation de ces oeuvres sacrées.

Les oeuvres anciennes furent présentées pour leur valeur intrinsèque, historique et artistique, mais aussi comme éléments de comparaison. La sélection de ces oeuvres fut réalisée en fonction des différents lieux de production de l'icône (Roumanie, Russie, Grèce, Bulgarie...) et en fonction de la grande variété des thèmes représentés. Il était important de présenter des icônes anciennes pour souligner les constantes dans la fabrication de l'icône et les transformations qui se sont opérées jusqu'à nos jours. Il était tout aussi important de souligner ces autres constantes présentes dans le geste de réalisation de tous les iconographes: le désir de traduire la vérité, de combler un vide et le besoin de revenir aux sources. La réalisation d'une icône demeure, encore aujourd'hui, une profession de foi de l'artiste.

Le circuit de l'exposition était divisé en cinq regroupements d'icônes venant rappeler les thèmes majeurs de cet art. La première salle, intitulée *Images saintes*, contenait un groupe de cinq icônes représentant des personnages saints. La définition première de l'icône étant "image sainte", le thème des saint(e)s était le plus approprié pour occuper ce lieu introductif. On y retrouvait une oeuvre ancienne du 19ᵉ siècle représentant *saint Nicolas*, un saint majeur de l'histoire de l'Église orthodoxe et sans aucun doute le saint le plus représenté dans l'histoire de l'icône. Les autres icônes étaient des oeuvres récentes, réalisées par des artistes de différentes cultures, grecque, québécoise et roumaine; elles représentaient saint Philippe, saint Ignace de Loyola, saint Élie et le Christ.

Dans la seconde salle, intitulée *Variations sur le thème de la Vierge*, on pouvait voir un groupe d'icônes composé essentiellement d'oeuvres sur le thème de la Vierge. Étant donné la popularité de ce thème, de tout temps, nous avions réservé un espace à ce type de représentation. Cet espace contenait donc deux icônes anciennes, l'une du 18ᵉ siècle et l'autre du 19ᵉ siècle, ainsi que deux icônes récentes. L'icône du 18ᵉ siècle était ornée du fameux recouvrement d'argent que l'on nomme *riza*, lequel ne laisse voir que la figure et les mains peintes sous le recouvrement métallique.

La troisième salle, intitulée *Passages de la vie du Christ*, faisait référence à quelques étapes de la vie du Christ. Sept icônes occupaient l'espace de cette salle, dont deux icônes anciennes prêtées par le Musée d'art de Joliette. Il s'agissait de pièces exceptionnelles, soit une *Crucifixion* du 16ᵉ siècle ainsi qu'une Résurrection du 19ᵉ siècle, de format "triptyque". Ces icônes, comme les autres oeuvres plus récentes, furent placées selon l'ordre chronologique événementiel de la vie du Christ.

Dans la quatrième salle, intitulée *La Déisis,* nous avions fait une place particulière à ce thème majeur. La *Déisis* fut recréée de façon suggestive en partant d'une sélection partielle des icônes de ce thème et par leur disposition dans un ordre logique correspondant aux structures du thème à l'intérieur de l'iconostase. La Déisis étant la composition illustrant la hiérarchie céleste rassemblée autour du Christ, elle demeure l'élément principal occupant l'iconostase au centre de l'église orthodoxe. C'est pourquoi ce thème devait être bien illustré dans le parcours.

La cinquième et dernière salle, intitulée *Les anges ou les gardiens,* terminait le circuit thématique par des thèmes "puissants", soit les anges et les gardiens de la foi. Cette salle fut réservée aux archanges saints Michel et Gabriel, aux anges de l'Ancien Testament ainsi qu'à saint Georges terrassant le dragon. Une oeuvre ancienne du Musée de Winnipeg (16ᵉ siècle) était la pièce la plus remarquable de cette salle. Il s'agissait d'un *Archange Michel* livrant un combat contre les forces du mal. Les autres icônes de cette salle étaient des réalisations récentes et elles furent placées de manière à créer une sorte "d'écho" visuel et de bien faire voir les différences d'inter-prétation de ces thèmes par les peintres d'icônes.

Enfin, dans le couloir de la Maison Hamel-Bruneau étaient présentées des icônes plus particulières, se distinguant du reste de la production soit par leur forme ou par leur technique. Cet espace était donc réservé à la présentation d'icônes de type "médaille de pèlerins", à la présentation d'un triptyque à la Vierge à l'Enfant de l'artiste Rosette Mociornitza et d'une icône russe de style *italianisant,* datée de la fin du 17ᵉ siècle, début du 18ᵉ siècle.

La rencontre d'icônes anciennes et récentes dans une même exposition permit d'en connaître davantage sur les transformations de cet art, mais surtout d'apprécier les qualités iconiques et picturales très particulières de la production actuelle. Cette rencontre fut aussi une occasion de réhabiliter cet art longtemps considéré comme un art de copiste. Il est vrai que certains modèles originels ont servi à toutes époques de base aux peintres iconographes. Il est tout aussi vrai qu'il existe un mouvement perpétuel, dans le processus de réalisation de l'icône, qui s'explique en partie par le respect du dogme par les peintres d'icônes. Il ne faut cependant pas oublier que l'art de l'icône ne peut être étudié sur les bases dont on se sert pour analyser toute autre forme d'art.

J'oserais comparer le caractère à la fois perpétuel et relativement variable de l'icône à celui de l'art théâtral. On peut par exemple jouer plusieurs centaines de représentations d'une même pièce de théâtre dans le respect du texte originel, mais avec toute une gamme d'émotions, de variations, d'interprétations différentes qui ne feront que rappeler tout le potentiel créatif et expressif des interprètes reprenant un même thème et se jouant de ses limites. Comme dans le jeu de l'interprète, le peintre d'icône laisse passer ses émotions, une part de son vécu, de ses expériences humaines ou spirituelles et de sa sensibilité. S'il reprend un thème connu, il lui donne une autre dimension redevable à sa culture, à sa perception du modèle ou du message que lui livre le modèle, le texte.

NOTES

1. Pour une définition des principes iconiques, nous suggérons l'ouvrage d'Egon Sendler, *L'icône. Image de l'invisible*, Paris, Desclée de Brouwer, 1981.

2. L'exposition *« Icône-Eikona »* fut présentée du 11 avril au 16 juin 1995 à la Maison Hamel-Bruneau, centre de diffusion culturelle de la ville de Sainte-Foy, Québec.

3. Le Provincial Museum of Alberta et le Musée canadien des civilisations possèdent chacun plus d'une cinquantaine d'icônes (19e et 20e siècles) alors que le Musée d'art de Joliette possède une collection d'une dizaine d'icônes anciennes (16e - 19e siècle).

4. Le New Brunswick Museum possède une collection intéressante d'icônes de type « médaillon de pèlerin ». No d'accession: 983.48.41 à 50, 983.14.24.1 et 2.

5. Plus particulièrement en Saskatchewan et en Alberta.

6. La rareté des matières premières typiques pour la fabrication de l'icône peut expliquer ce choix; on pense ici aux pigments végétaux à la base de la tempera ou à la poudre d'albâtre, élément de translucidité.

7. Comme base de fabrication des icônes, on retrouve aussi bien des plaques de cuivre ou de laiton émaillé que du bois, matériau plus conventionel.

8. L'Art Gallery of Greater Victoria et le Saskatchewn Western Development Museums possèdent des pièces de ce type; no accession: a)77.317, b) WDM-93-S-87, WDM-93-S-88.2.A.B.

9. Je tiens à remercier le professeur George Galavaris de l'Université McGill pour ses conseils judicieux sur les principes de datation des icônes.

ON THE ICONOGRAPHY IN
ST. ONUPHRIUS CHURCH

by
Radomir Bilash

In 1996, St. Onuphrius Ukrainian Catholic Church was relocated to the Canadian Museum of Civilization from a rural community once called Barich, north of Smoky Lake, Alberta. Commemorating the Ukrainian-Canadian presence in the early development of the Canadian Prairies, the church has been restored to its 1952 appearance. Typical of many other Ukrainian churches, St. Onuphrius also reflects the various trends and historical events that influenced the religious life of Canada's Ukrainian communities. As outlined below, many of these factors predate Ukrainian immigration to Canada.

The information presented here is drawn from a variety of sources including the press kit prepared by the Museum for the official opening of the church on June 26, 1996, and CMC archival files identified as "Module 23. St. Onuphrius Church (Ukrainian Church)", part of the Canada Hall History file series. Also, Steve Prystupa, CMC's Curator in charge of this exhibition project, provided additional data.

SOME HISTORICAL NOTES

Most Ukrainians who settled in Canada before World War I came from Galicia, a sector of present-day western Ukraine. Others came from an adjacent territory known as Bukovyna. The Galicians were primarily members of the Ukrainian (Greek) Catholic church, while the Bukovynians were mostly Orthodox. Although both of these churches trace their origins to the official acceptance in Ukraine-Rus' of Christianity in its Byzantine Greek ("Orthodox") form in 988 A.D., the organization of a Ukrainian Catholic Church was largely the product of events in Polish-ruled Galicia at the end of the 16th century. The supremacy of Rome (rather than of Constantinople) was officially recognized by Ukrainian church authorities based in Poland although many Byzantine characteristics, traditions and practices were retained. The dissension and polemics caused by this arrangement still surface today. Consequently, in St. Onuphrius, the display of both Romanist statues and Byzantine icons is a synchronic reflection of east/west traditions linked to these historical developments.

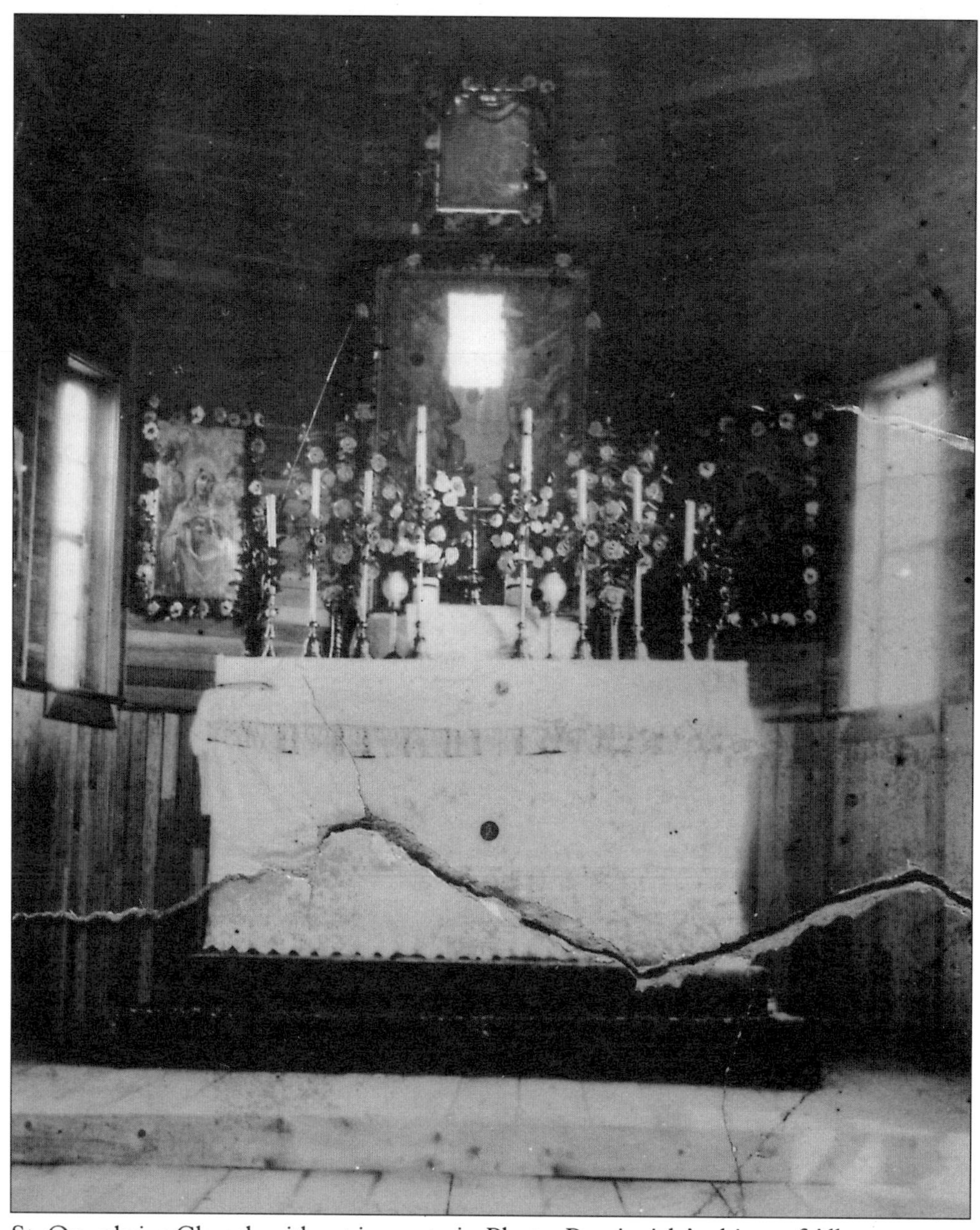

St. Onuphrius Church without iconostasis. Photo: Provincial Archives of Alberta.

As can be expected, the most elaborate forms of churches in western Ukraine were found in urban areas. Rooted in Byzantine iconography and architecture these came to form a distinct Ukrainian style. However, it is the peasant tradition of village folk architecture that was transferred to Canada when, after 1890, large numbers of Ukrainians began immigrating to Canada. Their construction of churches might be termed mimicry. Few were versed in any forms of construction, let alone the skilled craftsmanship required to build the multi-storeyed domed churches back in the Old Country. Virtually none of them was a skilled church painter. Yet invariably they felt obligated to build a structure that was worthy of being a temple of worship, one that surpassed their own homes in materials, workmanship, and decoration.[1] Some were able to contribute the painted or paper icons to the church that they had intended for their own homes. Others resorted to the best available alternative: store-bought paper icons and religious objects that could be adapted to an eastern rite liturgy and reminded them, either in content or style, of the ones that they had left behind in the Old Country. Wall finishes were often left unpainted, or else they were painted in some neutral light color. It wasn't until a year or two before the start of World War I that church walls were being painted in Byzantine styles by painters who were formally trained in this field, or by settlers who were talented and self-confident enough to mimic the motifs that they recalled from their past.

For almost a decade, the construction and ornamentation of Ukrainian churches was undertaken at the initiative of immigrants. The absence of clergy representing their traditional denominations made their work vulnerable to the canons of alien religious groups and authorities already based in Canada. And thus, many Roman Catholic and Russian Orthodox features were incorporated into these early efforts. The first official guidelines for Canada's Ukrainian Catholic communities were published in 1914.[2] These decried the inappropriate developments that surfaced during the early years of Ukrainian settlement in Canada and specified that Ukrainian church architecture in Canada along with the style and placement of icons and liturgical objects should follow certain rules and aesthetic standards.

THE TRADITION AND ST. ONUPHRIUS

In the church painting tradition common to Ukrainian churches, the heads of saints are depicted with a golden aura encircling their heads (indicating glory in heaven). Gold, considered the most important of all colors, represents divine energy and conveys magnificence. As well, the deities are presented in specific poses and clothed in specific ways. For example, the Mother of God is depicted as Immaculate, dressed in a white garment, representing her innocence, and a blue cloak, representing her constant devotion to heaven. She is represented in more than one location in the church and often in more than one of several distinct and regulated poses. In some cases, she is depicted with the baby Jesus on her left arm, while in others she is viewed as the Queen of Heaven, with a crown on her head and holding a sceptre in her right hand. Another version reminds worshippers of her role as the Suffering Mother, and shows her with up to seven spears imbedded in her heart. In another instance, the Mother of God appears standing on a globe of the Earth enwrapped by a serpent, symbolizing her victory over Evil through her Immaculate Conception. In this pose, she wears a wreath of stars and lifts her eyes upward to Heaven, hands folded on her chest (indicating her constant praying for mankind). Icons of the Holy Trinity, often found dominating the area of the main dome, also show God the Father with His feet resting on the globe, as a reminder of His authority over Heaven and Earth.

The placement and juxtaposition of icons are organized both horizontally and vertically. The arrangement of beings in horizontal layers throughout the structure in specific juxtapositions helped worshippers infer the importance of specific patriarchs, saints, martyrs, prophets, angels and the apostles in the overall organization of the church. The highest point of the structure, often painted blue with gold stars to represent the heavens and connote contemplation, was reserved for a representation of God.

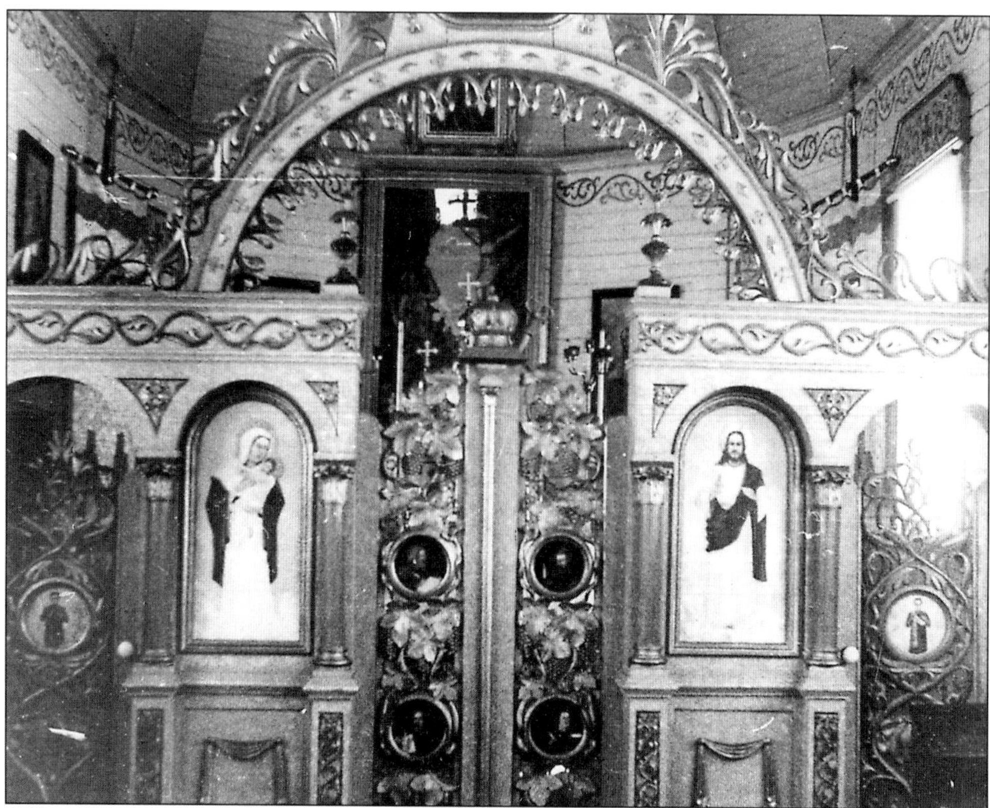

St. Onuphrius Church after 1934. Photo: Provincial Archives of Alberta.

The schemata of church painting also reflect differences in the assigned use of space. Most churches are built with their altars facing east, a reminder to worshippers facing that direction that the Paradise of their ancestors, lost through the sin of Adam, was located in the East.[3] It also reminds them that Jesus Christ, whose sacrificial death made Paradise available to Christians once again, was born in the East. As well, churches are subdivided into three main chambers, from west to east: narthex, nave, and sanctuary. From north to south, the spatial organization of the church is further organized into female and male sectors. As a result, icons reflecting the life of Jesus are usually located in the southern half of churches, while those based on the life of the Mother of God are located in the northern half.

The iconography is most concentrated and varied on the *ikonostas*, the Ukrainian word for the wall or partition that separates the sanctuary from the nave. The *ikonostas* in St. Onuphrius dates from 1934, and in keeping with tradition it summarizes the hierarchic vertical/horizontal approach to the placement of icons. A set of double doors in the middle of the *ikonostas* opens to the altar. "Tsar's/king's doors/gates", "holy doors", or simply "great doors" are common designations for this set of doors. They occupy a commanding position and show images of the Four Evangelists (Saints Matthew, Mark, Luke and John) that, in St. Onuphrius, are painted on canvas. The Mother of God (holding the infant Jesus) and Christ are depicted independently on either side of the central doors; these are the main, mandatory ("*namisni*") icons. Single, lesser doors (often called "the deacons' doors") flank opposite ends of the *ikonostas*; used by those who assist at the liturgy or sometimes by the priest himself, each door shows a single full-figure commemorating the deacons St. Stephen and St. Lawrence.

The earliest forms of the *ikonostas* were low and usually had only one level of icons. Later, more rows were added. A full *ikonostas* could have as many as fifty icons! To top the *ikonostas*, tradition requires the placement of an icon of the Last Supper that in St. Onuphrius is crowned by a gilt cross. The *ikonostas* in St. Onuphrius was carved by Harry Holowaychuk, one of a family of craftspeople who came to Canada from Ukraine. The entire *ikonostas* (including the icons) was painted by Leo Snaychuk, an Edmonton artist who earned his living painting Ukrainian community halls and buildings. His specialty was decorative painting, including backdrops, stage scenery and stage curtains.

Peter Lipinsky (1888-1975), another prominent church artist of the time, created the painting of St. Onuphrius, the church's patron saint, that hangs in its special place of honour and prominence, -- in the sanctuary behind the altar. (It is speculated that the church may also have received its name from a certain Onufry Kulchisky, one of the founding members of this parish who lived near the original church site.) Lipinski is also credited with iconography that appears on two movable liturgical objects that form part of the St. Onuphrius complex -- an Easter shroud and a processional icon.

In 1952, Ivan Keywan (1907-1992) was hired to paint the church's interior. He was a professionally trained artist who had emigrated to Canada from Europe after World War Two. In addition to various decorative touches, Keywan painted several distinctive symbols inside the church, including the dramatically positioned eye within a triangle that appears overhead on the ceiling of the nave. The three sides of the triangle represent the Trinity: its three persons, Father, Son and Holy Spirit in one; the eye symbolizes the all-knowing, all-seeing presence of God. Other significant iconographic motifs include the dove (a familiar representation of the Holy Spirit) on the ceiling above the altar, the harp on the railing of the choir loft (symbolizing all music that glorifies God), and the Cyrillic inscription in Old Church Slavic on the arch over the *ikonostas* that, in English translation, reads "Holy, Holy, Holy, Lord God of Hosts!", an exclamatory refrain of glorification extracted from the Divine Liturgy.

Of the four artisan-iconographers cited above, only Peter Lipinsky and Ivan Keywan are adequately documented.

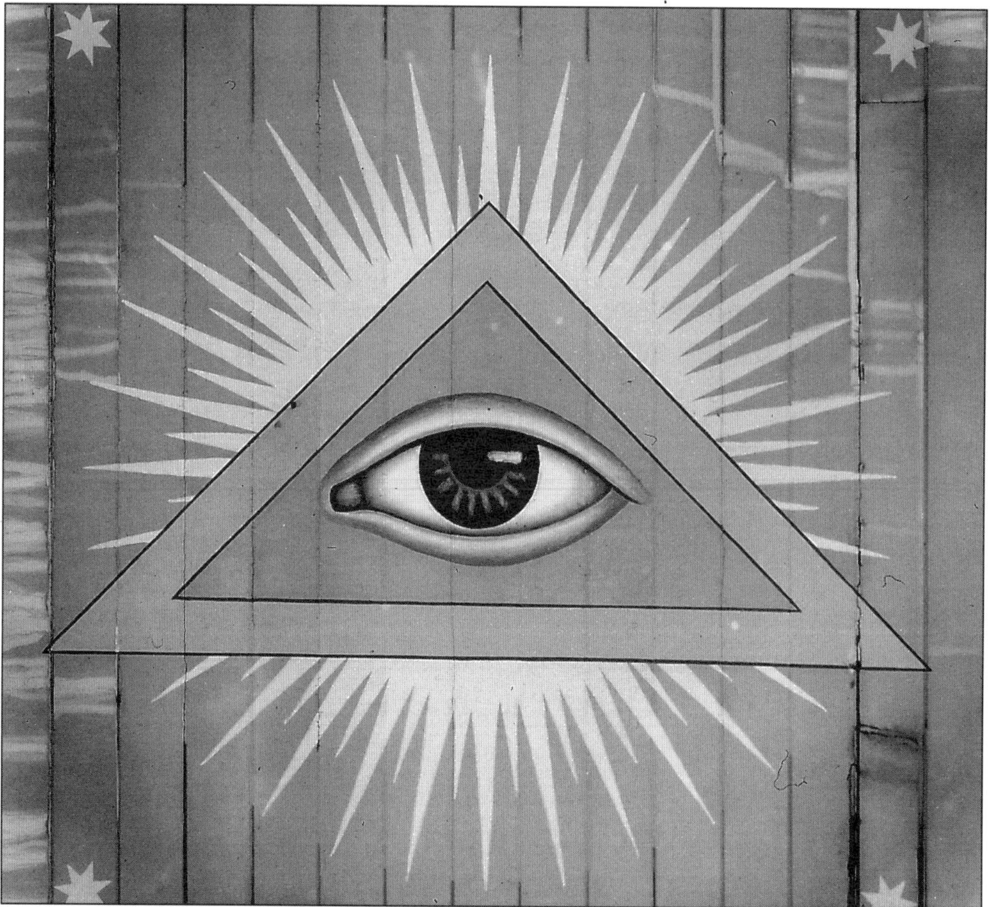

The "eye of God" painted by Ivan Keywan on the ceiling of St. Onuphrius Church. Photo: R.van Schaik.

Notes

1. See, for example, Andrij Makuch, *Hlus' Church: A Narrative History of the Ukrainian Catholic Church at Buczacz, Alberta,* Edmonton: Alberta Culture and Multiculturalism, 1989.

2. For details see Bohdan Kazymyra, "Slidamy Ispovidnyka Iepyskopa Nykyty Budky: pravyla Ukrains'ko-katolyts'koi tserkvy v Kanadi", in Oleh. B. Gerus et al, eds., *The Ukrainian Experience in Canada: Reflections*, Winnipeg: the Ukrainian Academy of Arts and Sciences, 1994, pp. 173-197.

3. See Julian Katrij, *Nasha khrystians'ka tradytsiia* [=Our Christian Tradition], New York-Rome, Vydavnytstvo Oo.Vasyliian, 1988, pp. 223-225.

NOTES ON THE UKRAINIAN ICON
TRADITION IN CANADA

by

Lesya Granger

This article explores, from an art historical perspective, aspects concerning form, content and context as they pertain to the Ukrainian icon tradition in Canada. Topics touched upon include origins, factors that account for the Ukrainian Canadian community's on-going interest in icons, and contemporary manifestations of this phenomenon in Canada. Most of the iconographers and artists cited in the course of the discussion are represented in the East European collections of the Canadian Museum of Civilization in Hull, Quebec.

The Icon in Ukraine. The icon tradition was officially recognized in 988 A.D. when Christianity became the country's religion of state. As the affairs of church and state became closely connected, icons came to serve a variety of functions. For divine protection and social identification, icons were taken to war, hung on city gates and traded among ancient city-states. For centuries they served as diplomatic gifts and provided booty when cities were sacked. Though rooted in Byzantine iconography, the icon tradition in Ukraine was never immune to influences from Western Europe. It was also influenced by folk artists who always drew upon local styles and popular traditions. In the seventeenth, eighteenth and nineteenth centuries engravings and lithographs of religious subjects, many from Western Europe, also affected the Ukrainian icon. To a large extent, then, in addition to its being a vehicle for spiritual contemplation and religious devotion, the icon in Ukraine constituted a pictorial reflection of the country's cultural dynamics.

Materials. Materials used in the creation of traditional icons were governed by Church canons and by the availability of materials. The earliest portable icons in Ukraine were painted with egg tempera on gessoed linen glued to wooden panels, a process developed in the Byzantine era. The background, halos, highlighted depiction of cloth, and inscriptions were generally rendered in gold leaf. Figures, architecture and objects were depicted by an application of layers of local colour, progressing from dark to light hues.[1] The nature of the tempera and the gold leaf, and the style which emerged from this technique, have strong graphic qualities. This is why many texts refer to the "writing" of icons.[2]

In the fifteenth century, western renaissance art had introduced oil paints to artists around Europe. Beginning with the sixteenth century, oil paints were occasionally used in Ukraine to paint new icons or to restore old ones. This and the preference for oil paints in the eighteenth and nineteenth centuries changed the nature of icons. Unlike egg tempera, oil paints enable the artist to create subtle changes in the tonal scale. Icon painters of the 16-19th centuries used this ability to render skin tones in a naturalistic fashion, and they transformed the linear and graphic qualities of Byzantine icons into modelled representations.

In Canada, immigrant painters such as Peter Lipinsky (Edmonton), Julian Bucmaniuk (Edmonton), Wadym Dobrolige (Edmonton) and Theodore Baran (Saskatoon) used oil paints to produce "faux-murals" for churches by painting on canvas which they pasted to the walls. Many artists also created individual oil paintings depicting saints and biblical scenes in a naturalistic, albeit sometimes stylized, fashion. Such canvases are larger than the traditional portable icons which, at the time, were replaced by framed lithographs and other reproductions of icons or holy pictures.

Currently, Ukrainian iconography in Canada shows a return to the ancient egg tempera technique. Marianna Savaryn (Edmonton), Juvenalij Mokryckyj (Woodstock, Ontario), Emil Telizyn (Toronto), Ihor Andriyiv (Ottawa), and Heiko Schlieper (Ottawa) follow this technique when painting portable icons for the Ukrainian community.

Canadian iconographers have taken advantage of various new materials that have been developed in the past fifty years. Some of these have been used to replace egg tempera, while maintaining its qualities. For example, gouache, an opaque water-based paint, has the ability to be layered or applied in fields of local colour. For example, *Madonna of the Sun* (1989) by Sophia Lada (Toronto) is painted with gouache paints . Lada paints in local colours and adds shading by hatching lines in a manner similar to egg tempera.

Synthetics such as acrylic paints are very popular among contemporary Canadian icon painters. These paints are durable, quick-drying and waterproof when dry. Acrylic paints are not as malleable as oils and therefore are more suitable for the graphic style of the icon. In addition, they possess the ability to be layered quickly. Acrylic paints can be mixed with other synthetic materials such as gels to achieve layered and textured surfaces. In some of her icons of the Virgin and Child, Christine Granger (Ottawa) uses thick layers of acrylic gel and acrylic paint to create highly textured and tactile surfaces. Taras Snihurowycz (Winnipeg) has experimented and created his own materials. This retired dentist combines chemicals and compounds used in dentistry to build up modelled surfaces on his icons and to create a patina on them. He uses dental drills and other tools to carve forms into his works.

Some artists use a combination of materials and techniques. A *Pantocrator* by Halyna Mordowanec-Regenbogen (Windsor) is painted with oil paints on canvas glued to a wooden panel with a background of gold leaf. This artist combines the oil painting technique with wood and gold. In her icon of Saint Andrew, Vera Senchuk (Winnipeg) uses acrylic paint for the image, gold leaf for the background, egg tempera for the inscription, and acrylic varnish to fix the image. Instead of egg tempera, oil or acrylic paint, Montreal artist Adrianna Lysak burns lines into a wooden panel, parts of which she covers with 24 carat gold leaf. The use of new materials enables artists to articulate line, colour and the surface of the icons in various novel ways.

Since its beginnings the icon tradition included works fashioned from other materials; enamelled medallions, embroidered tapestries, relief carvings, and paintings on glass are examples of this phenomenon. Several Canadian iconographers emulate these artistic traditions. The embroidered icons created by Ivanna Petrowska (Ottawa) resemble ancient embroidered icons and tapestries from Ukraine from the sixteenth and seventeenth centuries. Petrowska uses stitching that is similar to an ancient Ukrainian embroidery technique called *hlad'*, and she sews pearl beads around the image. T. Snihurowycz creates copper enamelled icons similar to medallions and jewellery created in the Princely Era of twelfth century Ukraine. He also creates carved icons that echo traditional wood carvings from Western Ukraine. The beeswax icons by Roger Desilets (Oakburn, Manitoba) resemble copper and other cast metal icons. Beeswax candles are very popular in the east Christian rite, and beeswax is the key element in the creation of Ukrainian Easter eggs. By casting his images in beeswax Desilets underlines their links with traditional and religious aspects of Ukrainian culture. Icons created by these artists are hybrids of old and new materials, local techniques, and folk traditions.

Popular taste and mechanical reproductions have influenced the material and medium of the icon tradition for centuries. In seventeenth century Ukraine, images of icons were reproduced in engravings. In the nineteenth century, icons were depicted on ceramic tiles and plates.[3] In the late nineteenth century, icons were rendered on banners, using cross-stitch embroidery. Most recently, in Canada, the decal technique has been employed by artisans such as Elsie Yarmol (Toronto) to create commemorative icon plates.

Popular western art and mainstream culture continue to influence the icon tradition by broadening and changing its material repertoire. Roman Catholic artistic traditions such as stained glass windows and religious statues have been incorporated into Ukrainian eastern rite church decor. For example, Leo Mol, an established artist from Winnipeg, is known especially for his monumental stained glass windows in Sts. Vladimir and Olga Ukrainian Catholic Cathedral in Winnipeg. Similarly, to mark the centenary of Ukrainian settlement in Canada Gary Robertson (Elma/Janow, Manitoba) created an outdoor shrine consisting of a glass box in which stands a Sacred Heart statue of Christ; a three-barred Orthodox cross appears on the pedestal of the shine.

Themes. In Ukraine the most popular theme portrayed on portable icons was the Virgin and Child, of which there exists numerous prototypes. The *Hodeghitria* type, an icon of Mary gesturing toward Christ: "pointing the way", was especially popular.[4] This thematic preference has continued in Canada. Icons of Mary and Christ are given as gifts for almost any occasion. This theme is versatile because it is essentially a condensed form of the visual vocabulary and theological or symbolic substance of Eastern icons.

Other popular icons in Ukraine were those depicting guardian saints such as Saint Nicholas the Wonder Worker, Saint George the Warrior, and Saints Michael and Gabriel the Archangels. In Canada these icons are also popular sacramental gifts, though preference for specific saints depends on the area from where devotees immigrated, as well as family traditions, personal devotion, and taste.

In Canada, the incorporation of historical themes in icons was especially pronounced when in 1988 the Ukrainian community celebrated the millennium of Christianity in Kyivan-Rus'. These icons celebrate figures and events surrounding this event. In Ukraine, the tradition of turning to history for inspiration is evident in portable icons of Saints Borys and Hlib, the first canonized saints of Kyivan-Rus', and in the fresco of the children of Grand Prince Yaroslav the Wise in the central nave of Saint Sophia Cathedral in Kyiv.

Among early Ukrainian immigrant painters in Canada, the process of referring to history began with the insertion of the trident, Ukraine's national symbol, into icons and church decor. Ukrainian Catholic and Orthodox churches in the diaspora signified the freedom of religious, national and cultural expression, and this prompted professional artists such as Ivan and Wolodymyr Denysenko and Ivan Dyky to paint tridents and other nationalistic emblems in churches. Artists such as Stanislaw Konash-Konashewsky (Montreal) also painted these symbols on portable icons, and G. Robertson depicted the trident on the walls of the chapel-home which he completed in 1992. E. Telizyn, too, has incorporated modern and ancient versions of the trident, and the city-emblems of Kyiv and Lviv into his designs for stained glass windows representing the union of eastern and western Ukraine .

Several historically significant figures emerge in many Ukrainian icons. Church leaders such as Andrey Sheptytsky (1865-1944) have been depicted on murals, window designs and portable icons; Saints Ol'ha and Volodymyr the Great are depicted on several iconostases in Ukrainian churches in Canada and on portable icons commemorating the millennium. Some compositions are complex constructs based on historical accounts, artifacts, as well as myths and legends. Many depict elaborately embroidered costumes, symbols, and recreations of scenes from Ukraine's Princely Era. The conglomeration of symbols, figures, architecture and costumes creates an epic grandeur and a monumental style.

Themes that are selected and typified by artists and devotees reveal that icons are seen as symbols of freedom and cultural tradition. They become condensed cultural formulations — visible symbols that are easily identified. Indeed, traditional "visual themes appear to have been reduced in number, simplified, and consolidated."[5]

Styles. Currently, elements of the Byzantine style are preferred by contemporary Canadian icon painters.[6] Through a combination of certain pictorial devices (such as linear, stylized forms and a symbolic use of colour) the Byzantine style evolved to represent incarnated Divinity and the junction between physical and spiritual realms. As in Ukraine, so too in Canada, the distinct Byzantine style of icons has been affected by academic art. This influence has resulted in various combinations of styles, much diversity, and many hybrids.[7]

The transformation of style builds on a tradition that has been subject to change and innovation for many centuries. During the western European renaissance and the baroque era, an increase of naturalistic, decorative and expressionistic elements enhanced the pictorial realism which artists in Ukraine sought to incorporate into icons. In the late eighteenth-century, classicism, which entailed simplicity of composition and greater naturalism, also affected the visual style of the icon tradition. As a result, the linear and graphic qualities of the Byzantine style were subverted.

During the first few decades of the twentieth century, the revival of the Galician icon and the Byzantine style in western Ukraine resulted in a renewed interest in the compositions of ancient icons. Moreover, at this time throughout Europe, modern art's emphasis on formal elements led to the abstraction of the image. Among Ukrainian modernist artists this interest led to adaptations of the Byzantine style and techniques; they formed what is often referred to as the *neo-Byzantine style*. This style frequently incorporated elements drawn from other styles — classicism, cubism and rayonism.

Today, Canadian icon artists exhibit the full spectrum of styles and various combinations of them. Consequently, no single style dominates. Rather, there is a plurality of stylistic elements that remains grounded in the Byzantine style.

Ornamentation. During Ukraine's Kyivan-Rus' era ornamentation, comprised of decorative colours, lines and patterns, was subtle. Gold, the major ornamental element, adorned backgrounds and halos and was sometimes replaced by colours such as yellow ochre to symbolize heavenly light. Gilded lines highlighting depictions of drapery were often arranged into patterns that were repeated throughout the image. The few portable icons that have survived from this era reflect this subtle use of ornamental colour, line and pattern.

After the fourteenth century, line and pattern were more pronounced. Hatching lines, to denote tonal gradation of skin were applied and patterned in a decorative fashion. At the end of the fifteenth century, artists began to insert specific folk designs into the depiction of cloth in their icons. In the sixteenth century, gilded backgrounds regained popularity and were often adorned with incised, carved or moulded patterns. During the baroque era, ornamentation evolved into ornate embellishments consisting of complex and expressionistic floral motifs and cloud shapes which were often carved into backgrounds, frames and iconostases. This was followed by classicism in the eighteenth century in which subtle gold patterning covered the entire surfaces of the backgrounds. Icons of the nineteenth century consisted of a combination of ornamental elements from each of the preceding styles.

Today, Canadian artists work with each of these types of ornamentation, yet two significant trends emerge. "Neo-Byzantine" ornamentation draws strongly on the earliest icons and on those which have survived in Greece. Other artists produce icons rooted in the Byzantine tradition but bearing idiosyncratic ornamentation comprised of a personal selection of ornamental elements drawn from various other artistic styles.

Backgrounds and halos depicted in neo-Byzantine icons are not profusely ornamented nor are they adorned with pattern or motif. Canadian Ukrainian iconographers such as V.Senchuk, M.Savaryn, and Ju.Mokryckyj add a minimum of ornament to the backgrounds or halos in their icons by gilding them. Chrystyna Mykytiuk (Toronto) gilded only the halos of the figures in her icon depicting the Holy Family. Artists such as E.Telizyn and G.Robertson paint backgrounds and halos with a solid colour, such as yellow ochre, to emulate the gold leaf. Ornamental line is also used sparingly by these artists. C.Mykytiuk outlines her figures and their halos with thick, dark lines. Some painters represent realistic patterns on their depiction of cloth and clothing. Traditional Ukrainian embroidery with its links to Ukrainian folk culture is especially popular: E. Telizyn's *Oranta*, for example, shows a typical black and red embroidery pattern on her cloth kerchief.

Artists who incorporate western art styles into their icons tend to use ornament more freely than the neo-Byzantine icon painters. C. Granger paints a variety of patterns onto backgrounds, halos and garments in her icons. Irene Nosyk (Toronto) painted a loosely-rendered monochromatic floral motif on the background of her icon. Some of these artists also incorporate three-dimensional ornamentation into their icons. I. Nosyk and A.Lysak gouge and burn the wooden backgrounds of their icons, Snihurowycz carves and moulds ornamental figures and objects into and around his icons, and Granger builds up patterned surfaces on her icons.

Although the return to the Byzantine style has curbed the tendency for profuse ornamentation, Ukrainian-Canadian icon artists continue to use ornament in their icons. Linear ornamentation creates an interesting tension between the concepts of 'writing' and painting icons: gilding, linear ornament and patterning also emphasize the decorative function of the icon. These elements reflect the artists' personal tastes: specific ornamental elements and the amount of ornamentation used are closely linked to the style with which artists choose to work. Moreover, ornamental patterns can affect the content and meaning of the work because some patterns are recognizable to the viewers. For example, since traditional embroidery patterns signify ethnicity, patriotism is subtly inserted into the icon to make it "Ukrainian."

Frames. Some of the ornamentation on icons made by Canadian artists is found on the frame or decorative border around the image. Many of the geometric patterns and floral motifs depicted on historical-theme icons refer directly to the ornamental mosaics and frescoes found in certain landmark churches from the Princely era in Ukraine's history, such as Saint Sophia or Saint Cyril's in Kyiv.

Originally, ordinary picture frames were not part of the iconographic composition in portable icons in Ukraine. As in other icon traditions, Ukrainian icons were painted on wooden panels with a hollowed-out interior surface, called the *kovcheh*, which leaves a frame-like edge around the image. This protruding border often contains images and inscriptions. It is symbolic of the icon's fluctuation between the physical realm and the spiritual one because the image often crosses over from the *kovcheh* onto its border. It also emphasizes the icon's function as a window into the spiritual world, and is an inherent aspect of its iconographic composition. Some contemporary artists, like H. Mordowanec-Regenbogen of Windsor, emphasize the *kovcheh* with patterns or geometric motifs.

In seventeenth century Ukraine the *kovcheh* was often replaced by a painted border or a separate frame. In Canada some artists refer to the *kovcheh* in a purely pictorial fashion: they do not hollow out the wood-surface to produce a *kovcheh* but rather paint a border around the icon to resemble it. M.Savaryn paints the border on her neo-Byzantine icons, as does S.Lada on her icon-like painting. C.Granger paints a multiplicity of thick and thin lines that help frame her icons. I. Andriyiv painted a thin white outline around his icon of St. Dimitrij Solunsky.

The frames of icons by T.Snihurowycz are very elaborate. He adorns some of his frames with mini-icons and secondary panels in a manner reminiscent of icons that appear on the sixteenth-century iconostasis of tha Church of the Holy Spirit in Rohatyn, western Ukraine. These Rohatyn icons are surrounded by three-dimensional archivolts containing small panels of mini-icons. Some of Snihurowyzc's frames are three-dimensional and suggest the influence of Western architectural sculpture. The figures on either side of his *Lady of the Sign* and *Pantocrator* look like caryatids or the carved figures on the jambs of Romanesque churches.

Initially, large icons in Ukraine were placed into elaborately carved holders, such as iconostases, which resembled frames. Later, ordinary picture frames were introduced into the tradition because they offered protection to the icon during transportation. Frames also helped bring icons into mainstream culture. Contemporary icon artists such as C.Granger, T.Snihurowycz, G.Robertson and A.Lysak continue to place some of their icons into ordinary picture frames. Conservative iconographers who wish to keep to the Byzantine tradition more closely generally do not use frames at all. However, occasionally one can find examples of Byzantine-like icons encased in frames.

A separate frame, however, re-orients the icon as an "image-object" because it turns the icon into an art object, elevating it to the level of "fine art". Through framing, the icon may cease to function as a ritual object and is sometimes made into an "objet d'art" or an ordinary furnishing incorporated into a contemporary Western setting. Perhaps this transformation makes the icon more accessible and understandable to people.

Conclusion. The migration of Ukrainians to Canada and their integration into Canadian society prompted them to find meaning in their cultural heritage. Icons have been an important catalyst in this search for an identity and its preservation. The freedom to work with new forms and materials broadened the icon tradition and eased its recontextualization into Canadian culture To continue the tradition in a meaningful way creators and devotees turned to traditional thematic and stylistic qualities — to the most ancient forms of Ukrainian icons and their Byzantine prototypes. Some may see this phenomenon as simply a reversion to an archaic style, an infatuation, or a utopian search for a pure and seemingly authentic form. Nonetheless, this focus on antecedents has opened up the tradition, addressed its meaning, reaffirmed the content of the icon, and confirmed its spiritual significance. The essence of the icon has been revisited and understood anew. The dialogue has allowed artists to explore the realm of sacred art and to take the tradition in a new direction.

NOTES

1.	Further details and explanations concerning these techniques are found in Egon Sendler's *The Icon: Image, Elements of Theology* (Redono Beach, California: Oakwood Publications, 1988), pp. 187-198, 202-203, 205, and 210-214.

2.	In the Slavic and East European traditions icons are often described as being "written."

3.	See, for example, plate nos. 81 and 82 in Ol'ha Kratiuk et al., Kolomyis'kyi muzei narodn'oho mystetstva Hutsul'shchyny [= The Kolomiya Museum of Hutsul Folk Art] (Kyiv: Mystetstvo, 1991). The first plate depicts Saints Peter and Paul and the second, the Madonna and Child, on glazed ceramic bowls made in Western Ukraine during the end of, and middle of, the nineteenth century respectively.

4.	Sviatoslav Hordynsky, *The Ukrainian Icon of the XIIth to XVIIIth Centuries* (Philadelphia: Providence Association, 1973), p.15.

5.	Robert Klymasz, "Searching for Icons in Canada: A Brief Report" (Hull, Quebec: Canadian Museum of Civilization, 1994), p. 3.

6.	Dmytro Stepovyk, ."The Ukrainian Icon in Canada," in Robert B. Klymasz, ed., *Art and Ethnicity: The Ukrainian Tradition in Canada* (Hull, Quebec: Canadian Museum of Civilization, 1991), p.42.

7.	Cf. Klymasz , *op. cit.,* p. 4.

THE PORTUGUESE *AZULEJOS* IN TORONTO[*]

by
Pauline Greenhill

After the southern part of the Iberian peninsula was invaded by Arabs in 711, it came under the artistic and technical influence of the Near and Middle East, and the Mediterranean. These were the sources from which ceramic tiles *(azulejos)* were introduced to Spain and Portugal.

"Of all European countries, Portugal was the one in which walls were by far the most often decorated with tiles, and is the one in which the greatest number may still be seen today" (Berendsen 1967, 69). Churches, chapels, monasteries, old mansions, pleasure houses and facades were decorated with *azulejos*. They were also part of garden decoration in flowerbeds, orange groves and fountains. "Foreign travellers, in the seventeenth century failing to understand this ceramic craze, went as far as recording that Portuguese houses are made of glazed clay" (Simoes 1956, 16).

It was perhaps not surprising, however, that *azulejos*, unlike traditional gardens, made their way to Canada, sometimes even in a literal sense, with the immigrants. Although tiles lost some of their instrumental qualities in a colder climate, their decorative value was certainly not diminished.

Examples of all the historically documented colour styles of *azulejos* were found. The most popular type were totally polychromatic.

Since they possessed valuable and culturally appreciated objects, second generation *azulejos* owners, those who had inherited the tiles with the house, generally expressed a positive attitude toward having them. It was possible to speculate that these tiles had belonged to older people who had sold their houses or died. A few examples of *azulejos* which had been taken off the front of the house when the family moved away have been seen elsewhere. These were valuable objects which would not normally be left behind if they could be taken.

Many people mentioned that *azulejos* were something which was owned only by rich people in Portugal, and which they could not afford until they came to Canada. It seems that the prices would vary from about four to five dollars per tile for the more plain outside sections, to around twenty dollars for the central elaborate portions. Thus, such a picture in total would probably now cost between 120 and 150 dollars for the twelve tile pictures (fifteen examples), ninety to 120 dollars

---

[*] Excerpts from Greenhill's "Study of Outdoor Household Shrines in Toronto", a report on her field research undertaken in 1981 for the Museum's Canadian Centre for Folk Culture Studies. (See annotated bibliography included elsewhere in this volume for full citation.)

for nine tile pictures (five examples), sixty to ninety for the six tile pictures (three examples), and considerably less for the two single tile examples.

Although the backing for the tiles is machine-made in most cases, the tile pictures were not mass produced. Most of the tiles bear the manufacturer's name, usually Aleluia Aveiro, but it seems that these pictures must be specially commissioned.

The ceramic importer in Montreal from whom the information was obtained did not as a general rule import tile pictures of saints, and I could not find anyone in Toronto who did so. Most owners of *azulejos* got them on visits to Portugal, or had friends or relatives bring them over.

Despite the difficulty of obtaining these pictures, they continued to be very popular. In the sample for this study, several had been erected within the last few years, and a recent walk through another area revealed *azulejos* which were put up no more than a few weeks before this writing. This was not a dying tradition, although in a few cases I encountered some opposition to the idea of putting up such a display from members of the younger generation. At least one informant disagreed entirely with her parents that their religion should be made public and seemed somewhat embarrassed about it.

Azulejos are the objects, but religion is definitely the subject of these pictures.

Symbolically in keeping with the church's attitude toward veneration of saints, the type of image found in most of the *azulejos* pictures was iconic in style; frontal, laconic, and lacking in shadows. There tended to be a standard form and image for each figure, perhaps because "a conventional form better preserves the distance which separates the holy [from the secular] than does the individual vision of the artist" (Van Der Leeuw 1963, 164). Iconolatrous art, by releasing the figure from action and placing it in relation to the spectator, full face and inert, made it part not of the past, but of the present (Della Seta 1914, 352). As a representation of the saint, the icon shared the sanctity and glory of its prototype, to whom its likeness was understood (Ouspensky 1967, 324). Perhaps significant to this was the fact that I was usually given the name of the figure depicted when I pointed to the shrine and said "What is that called?"

It was not surprising that the Holy Family was quite popular in this sample. The family as an institution was supremely important to the Portuguese immigrants, forming, among other things, the links by which immigration to Canada was possible. As many parents did not speak English and wished to maintain their ties with Portugal, and their children attempted to adapt to the new culture, the family was also one of the first levels on which the impact of immigration was felt. Family breakdown was more common in Canada than in the old country (Report n.d., 2-3) and it was a struggle to maintain traditional connections between family members. Several informants mentioned that the Holy Family not only set a good example, but represented the togetherness of Portuguese families in comparison with those of other Canadians. The Holy Family was to be emulated as well as revered.

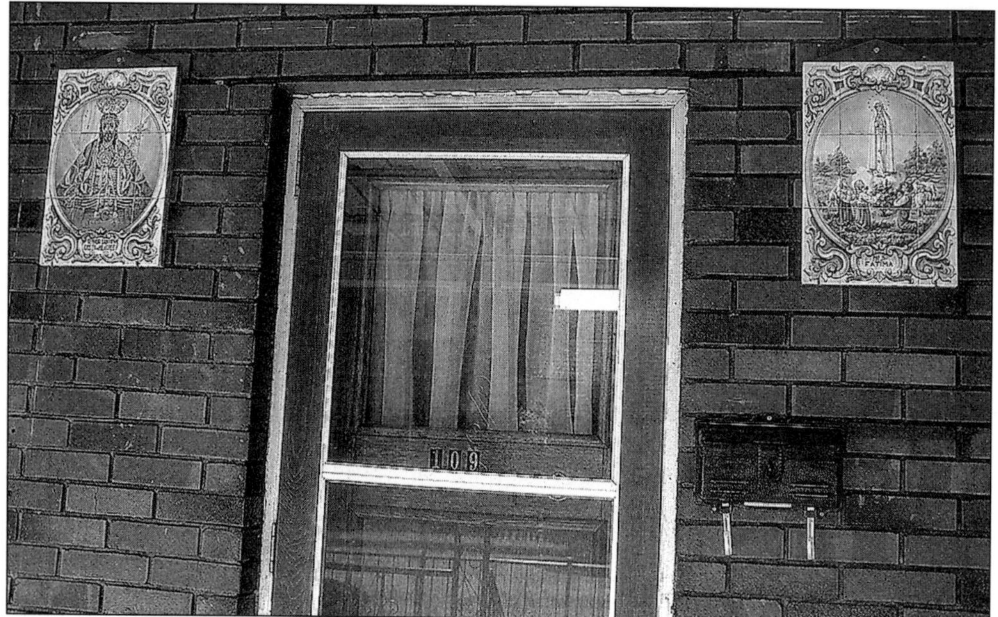

Doorway flanked by religious *azulejos*, Toronto, 1981. Photo: John Junson.
CMC S81-3451.

The Holy Family was usually portrayed with Jesus as a boy or a child since St. Joseph died when Christ was young (Broderick 1976, 267), but apart from this, the *azulejos* representing the Holy Family exhibited more variation than those of any of the other figures. One very unusual example deviated from the iconic norm in that it showed a scene; Joseph was seen planing a board with his tools and products scattered in front of him. (This was a traditional way of showing St. Joseph.) (Drake and Drake 1916, 69) The work was being done out of doors; tree and hills could be seen in the background. Mary was seated, feeding a number of white doves. Only the Christ child struck a conventional iconic pose.

Not surprisingly, we can safely say that the residents of this area put up *azulejos* because they were Portuguese, and that most of these were to religious figures because the owners were Catholic. This was ethnoscientifically confirmed by the informants' comments. However, it was the fact that the display took place outside which was particularly interesting.

It has been stated above that strong ties were maintained with Portugal. In practical terms this was seen in the fact that most of the shrine objects were brought from the old country, but it was symbolised by the placement of these objects, which were so strongly identified with Portuguese culture, outside the home.

One might wonder why such a display of Portuguese nationality would be necessary in an area where other evidence of cultural association was so abundant. Certainly, it seemed unlikely, given the latter factor, that it was a xenophobic reaction. More, it was a celebration of being Portuguese and Catholic. Often this was an in-group feeling, since the average Toronto resident was ignorant of, or indifferent to Portugal and Portuguese culture.

Although the immigrants chose to import shrine materials and *azulejos*, other components of traditional wealthy Portuguese life, such as gardens, were not brought to Canada. Practical considerations, such as the small size of house lots and variable weather conditions limited the amount of gardening possible, although certainly within the limitations which existed, a great deal of care was spent on the total appearance of the front of the house. *Azulejos*, on the other hand, could be successfully included in a Canadian house as decoration, although their main instrumental qualities, that they were cool in hot weather and easier to clean than other outside building materials, were not transported. In fact, cold, and especially extremes of weather, could be very problematic for tin glazed earthenware, causing cracking and crazing in the surface.

The saints and religious figures chosen for veneration were extremely significant to Portuguese culture. Not only were the most important figures of overt Catholic devotion, Christ and Mary, the most popular in this sample, but the Holy Family as a group was also frequently venerated. It seemed that the choices for devotion reflected an attempt to come to terms both with traditional culture and the new situation in which the immigrant was found. This was seen especially in devotion to the Holy Family which represented a model to be emulated, an example of the traditional status-quo, and a glorification of it. Significantly, the 'togetherness' of the Holy Family and of their own families was emphasized by my informants, whereas the traditional family was most often cited as the first casualty of immigration to Canada.

The devotions found in Toronto seemed to be more family-oriented than nationality-oriented, partly because Acoreans seemed to have strong local affinities and separate identities from those of the mainland Portuguese. In addition, this association, as well as the constant display, indicated that this was a year-round [rather than seasonal/calendric] devotion.

It was not surprising, then, that Portuguese immigrants to Canada should choose to maintain such an attractive and distinctive tradition. To them, being in Canada was synonymous with material success. Economic considerations were the most significant in the choice to move to Canada and thus a positive attitude to the Old Country could be maintained. Since *azulejos* were associated in Portugal with wealthy houses (as well as churches, monasteries, etc.), they came, in Canada, to symbolize success and material goods achieved in the New Country. That they celebrated what was for the immigrants some of the best of traditional life and culture was a happy coincidence which will probably confirm their survival in Portuguese Canadian communities.

Bibliography

Berendsen, Anne, *et al*
    1967   *Tiles: A General History*. London: Faber and Faber

Broderick, Robert C.
    1976   *The Catholic Encyclopaedia*. New York: Thomas Nelson.

Della Seta, Alessandro
    1914   *Religion and Art: A Study in the Evolution of Sculpture, Painting and Architecture*.
    London: T. Fisher Unwin.

Drake, Maurice and Wilfred Drake
    1916   *Saints and their Emblems*. London: T. Werner Laurie Ltd.

Ouspensky, L
    1967   "Icon," in *New Catholic Encyclopedia*. New York: McGraw-Hill.

(?)
    n.d.   "Report on the Portuguese Seminar," in *Papers on the Portuguese Community*.
    Toronto, Ontario. Ministry of Culture and Recreation, Multicultural Development
    Branch.

Simoes, J.M. dos Santos
    1956   "*Azulejos* in a Land of Many Colours." *Connoisseur*, 137: 15-27.

Van Der Leeuw, Gerardus
    1963   *Sacred and Profane Beauty: The Holy in Art*. New York: Holt, Rinehart and
    Winston.

ROMANIAN RELIGIOUS ICONOGRAPHY AND ICONOGRAPHERS IN CANADA[*]

by
Paula Vachon

INTRODUCTORY NOTES

In the Romanian tradition, two kinds of icons are prevalent: one painted on wood, the other on glass. In general, the former conforms to the canonical rules and standards while the latter draws its inspiration from Romanian folk art. The great majority of Romanian icons are executed in tempera on wood or glass. Other icon techniques are the mosaic, encaustic painting, paint on bone or ivory, engraved metal, repoussé, and hand embroidery.[1]

The iconostasis in the Byzantine tradition of the Romanian orthodox church is an authentic architectonic creation, divided in three tiered registers. It is composed mainly of precious sculptures of carved wood covered by coloured and gold plated stucco, a technique which ties it directly to icon. The traditional iconostasis generally consists of at least forty-one icons, including the larger ones, called "imperials". These are distributed on the lower level and always depict, on the right side of the "imperial" doors (central doors of the altar), Jesus Christ and the vocational icon of that particular church and, on the left side, Mary with Child and a Saint Hierarch of the Orthodox Church. The central register is illustrated with the twelve Apostles and the highest one with the Prophets. The lateral doors are ornamented with the images of the Archangels Michael and Gabriel. On top of the imperial doors, is always seen the Last Supper crowned with the Crucifixion Cross.[2] Interesting examples of iconostasis can be found in some Romanian Orthodox Churches across Canada.

Frescoes are relatively scarce in the Romanian Orthodox Churches of Canada. This can be explained by a number of factors: lack of specialised iconographers, production costs, etc. Still, several examples are worthy of note. Very representative are those painted in 1970 in the Saint George Romanian Orthodox Cathedral at Windsor, Ontario,[3] those painted in 1989 in the Holy Resurrection Romanian Orthodox Church at Hamilton, Ontario[4] and those painted in the Saints Constantine and Helen Romanian Orthodox Church at Edmonton, Alberta, all by Father Felix Dubneac. Interestingly, the paintings on the walls of the New Annunciation Church in Montreal, Quebec, are the work of two Russian painters from the

---

[*] This report is largely an excerpt from the author's longer survey dated December 1995 and listed in the annotated bibliography found elsewhere in the present publication.

Jordanville Holy Trinity Monastery and of two Romanian iconographers, Viorica Velescu and Constantin Florea. The paintings are on detachable panels.

The following are general observations regarding the interior ornamentation of Romanian churches in Canada:

1. In the early days of Romanian settlement in Canada (a rural phenomenon confined mostly to the prairie provinces) when the faithful were mostly peasant farmers from Transylvania and Bucovina, the iconostasis tended to be made *in situ* from local materials and decorated with photomechanical prints of icons produced by the Biblical Institutes of Bucharest or Cernăuţi as in the Boian example[5] or the iconostasis in the Shell Valley, Manitoba Romanian Orthodox Church, made by a local parishioner, Metro Sopka and decorated with printed icons[6].

2. Churches built in urban environments after 1915 generally ordered their iconostasis, with their respective icons, from the motherland. The first Romanian church in Montreal presents an interesting case, its carvings being made in Bucovina in 1917, and the icons of the iconostasis being painted in oil on canvas by a professional Bukovinian painter, Matei[7]. Iconostasis were sometimes made and painted by itinerant artists. Such is the case of the first Orthodox church in Hamilton where George Siniuk, an artist from Bucovina, carved and painted a small iconostasis in 1917[8].

3. Many iconostases in churches built or rebuilt in the second half of this century were made in North or even South America whether the churches belonged to the Romanian Orthodox Episcopate of America, the Romanian Orthodox Episcopate in America and Canada or to the Independent Romanian Orthodox Church in Montreal which is a separate entity. Cases in point are the iconostasis of the New Annunciation Church of Montreal which is made of exotic South American wood and carved by a Colombian sculptor[9] and the iconostasis of Saint George Church in Toronto, made to fit an Anglican type of building. We also note that the icons on the iconostasis were commissioned from artists of ethnic origins other than Romanian: Russian monks in the case of the New Annunciation Church in Montreal, a Bulgarian iconographer, I. Tomev, in the case of Saint George Church in Toronto, Ukrainian iconographers J. Gaspar in the case of St. Elijah the Prophet Church in Lennard, Manitoba, D. Bartoshuk in the case of Saint George Church in Winnipeg and Greek painters in the case of Saint Mary's Church in Calgary.

4. Some of the new churches were originally buildings of other denominations renovated or refurbished to accommodate the orthodox religious service. For example, Saint George Church in Toronto and Saint John the Baptist Romanian Orthodox Church in Montreal were originally Anglican churches and Saint Demetrius Romanian Orthodox Church in Winnipeg was originally Greek Orthodox[10].

5.   In the 1950s and 1960s, Romanian churches commissioned their iconostasis from the Ukrainian school of carving promoted by Providence Church Goods Company in Winnipeg. Examples of this school's work are found in the churches of Hamilton and Timmins (Ontario[11]), Lennard (Manitoba) and MacNutt (Saskatchewan[12]). From the 1970s, churches in Windsor, Edmonton, Winnipeg, Montreal, commissioned their iconostasis from the carving workshops of monasteries in Romania, particularly from the Plumbuita Monastery near Bucharest. These iconostases came to Canada in pieces to be mounted and painted here:(1) by an iconographer established in Canada, the Archimandrite Father Felix Dubneac in the case of Windsor, Hamilton and Edmonton[13]; (2) by invited Romanian guest-painters, the Moroşan brothers in the case of Saint Demetrius Romanian Orthodox Church in Winnipeg, Manitoba[14]. Other iconostases came directly from Romania completely assembled and painted (for example that of Saint John the Baptist Romanian Orthodox Church in Montreal[15]).

ARTISTS' PROFILES

ALEXE, RUXANDRA DIDI

Personal data Born in Galaţi, Romania, Ruxandra Didi Alexe holds a master's degree in fine arts from the Nicolae Grigorescu University Institute of Fine Arts and a diploma from the "Byzantine Church Painting School of the Romanian Patriarchate" in Bucharest, Romania. She and her husband George Alexe, a theologian and writer, immigrated to Canada in 1969 and to the United States in 1971. She presently lives in Detroit, Michigan.

Artistic data She has participated in many group and solo exhibitions in Europe and North America. Her works include modern decorative art as well as icons and decorated Easter eggs. Her icon painting techniques employ the traditional use of oils on wood or canvas as well as the more modern use of acrylics on wood. Her themes include traditional Byzantine sacred portraiture, biblical scenes, and Romanian saints (for example, her "Three Romanian Saints: Visarion, Oprea & Sofronie" executed in the late 1980s). Her works are found in the Manitoba Museum of Man and Nature in Winnipeg, in several Romanian Orthodox Churches, and in individual collections in Romania, Canada and the United States.[16]

ALMĂŞAN, ELENA

Personal data An architectural technician by profession, Elena Almăşan came to Canada from Bucharest, Romania in 1983 . She began painting in Canada because she "wanted to have an icon" of her own. Presently she lives in Hull, Quebec.

Artistic data She paints icons in water colours on cardboard or paper, copying patterns after famous models found in art books and magazines. She painted her first icon in 1985. At the end of the 1980s, she participated in a group exhibition organized by the Quebec Ministry of Immigration, "Canada - mon nouveau pays", shown in Hull, Sherbrooke and Montreal. She has donated several of her icons to the Saint-Pierre Channel Roman Catholic church in Hull, Quebec.[17]

APAN, VALERIU

Personal data A musician and painter of icons on glass. Came to Canada in 1980. Moved to Los Angeles, California in 1990,

Artistic data His glass icons are executed in the traditional manner and he makes his own frames. His icons were initially intended for home rather than formal, church use, and some were acquired by the Alberta Provincial Museum and, in 1985, by the Canadian Museum of Civilization in Ottawa-Hull. When the artist left for the United States, the Saints Constantine and Helen Romanian Orthodox Church in Edmonton, Alberta acquired 30 of his icons, now on display in the church.[18]

BĂDOIU, VIOREL

Personal data Icon painter on wood. Established in Montreal, Quebec. In the last few years has ceased painting.

Artistic data Practised a canonical type of iconography. Several of his icons were acquired by Anglican and Roman Catholic churches, such as Christ Church Cathedral in both Montreal and Ottawa.[19]

BODNAR, C. G.

Personal data In 1915, one of his icons was donated to the first Romanian Orthodox church in Montreal. He may have been a Bukovinian painter who never came to Canada. His icon may have been a gift from one of the first parishioners of the church, who mostly came from Bucovina.

Artistic data The only known icon by this artist is an oil painting representing "Saint John the Baptist" found in the chapel of the Annunciation Romanian Ortho-dox Church in Montreal. It originated with the Holy Trinity Church, the initial structure erected in 1912.

BOTEZATU, PETRE (PETBOT)

Personal data Born in Romania, he studied fine arts at the Faculty of Fine Arts of Bucharest University and obtained a teacher's diploma in 1967. For the next ten years, he pursued his personal studies and explorations while teaching art. His first solo exhibition in 1971 was followed by others in Romania, Austria, Canada and the United States. In 1988, he emigrated to Canada, settling in Ottawa-Hull. Since 1994, he has worked in Birmingham, Alabama.

Artistic data Petre Botezatu signs his works "PETBOT" and is known for the diversity of his output, both secular and religious. He works in fresco, oil, tempera, acrylic, mosaic and in large mural reliefs. Innovation and personal interpretation mark his religious style. Having made Hull, Quebec, his home in 1988, he began displaying his icons in private galleries and later in the Hyperion gallery, owned and operated by the Botezatu family. In 1990, he painted the ceiling of Gospa House in

Merrickville, Ontario, with frescoes, and a valuable icon by him was acquired by the Canadian Museum of Civilization in 1991. In 1994 he won a major international competition to paint the dome of the Baptist church at the multi-denominational Divinity School in Birmingham, Alabama (a replica of an Italian Renaissance style basilica). Botezatu rejects the official approach which entails the schematic repetition of images according to canonic dictates. Instead, he tries to understand the essence of a specific dogma, to reflect this understanding in his religious imagery, and to revitalize religious history and dogma. He has decorated more than ten cathedrals/churches. He has exhibited widely and is represented in numerous national and private collections here ands abroad.[20]

CÎRSTEA-TAURAND, IOANA

Personal data Ioana Cîrstea-Taurand began painting icons during her student years in Romania. She now lives in Quebec City.

Artistic data The artist paints a traditional type of icon on wood. The themes of her icons are treated in an ornamental manner with great care for detail. She also likes to enhance the decorative value of borders. Her work was presented in the exhibition *ICÔNE - EIKONA* at the Maison Hamel-Bruneau in Montreal in 1995.[21]

DE SILAGHI SIRAG, HELEN

Personal data Artist and poet, Helen de Silaghi comes from an aristocratic Transylvanian family. She studied art and calligraphy in Bucharest and has had several solo exhibitions in Romania, France and Italy. Before emigrating to Canada, she participated in the restoration of two churches in Romania. She came to Canada in 1949, settled in Toronto, and began working and teaching in her own private gallery. Her paintings are found in many countries, and since coming to Canada she has participated in over fifty art exhibitions. She lives in Burlington, Ontario.

Artistic data An occasional painter of religious works in oil on canvas, her style is outside the traditional canonical style. For her, the painting of is a manifestation of religious fervour. It keeping with this spirit, she donated one of her icons ("Mary with Child"), painted after a grave illness, to the Romanian Orthodox Church in Hamilton, Ontario. Another aspect of her religious vision is a work reproduced in the album, *Helen de Silaghi Sirag*, published in Bucharest in 1975; it is called simply "Icon" and represents, in a figurative but schematic style, Jesus Christ and his followers. The technique is oil on canvas, painted mostly with clear colours.[22]

DRĂGUŢESCU, ALEXANDRA-ELENA

Personal data Born in Galaţi, Romania, the artist is a professional iconographer who graduated with a master's degree in monumental art from the Nicolae Grigorescu University Institute of Fine Arts in Bucharest in 1977. She continued studying towards an arts teacher certificate at the Université du Québec à Montréal (UQAM). For many years she was an art teacher in a prestigious art high school in Bucharest, Romania. She continued her career as a teacher at the Stewart Hall

Cultural Centre in Point Claire, Quebec, after immigrating to Canada in 1992. She is married to another well known professional painter and iconographer, Titu Drăguţescu (see below). She now lives and works in Montreal.

Artistic data After graduation as a professional painter specialized in monumental art, Alexandra Drăguţescu together with her husband, Titu Drăguţescu, worked on the murals in four Romanian Orthodox Churches. She also restored a great number of icons on wood in tempera or oil technique. Since 1978 the artist participated in numerous exhibitions in Romania, Austria, Belgium, Netherlands, France, England and Canada. She became a member of the Union of Plastic Artists in Romania in 1990. Her icons, on wood or glass are painted in accordance with traditional Byzantine canons in colours enriched by the contrasting colour of the border and her works are found in private collections in several countries. She now concentrates on *objets d'art* restoration and icon painting. [23]

DRĂGUŢESCU, TITU

Personal data Titu Drăguţescu was born in Vîlcele, Argeş, and after 17 years of studies graduated in 1973 with a master's degree in monumental art from the Nicolae Grigorescu University Institute of Fine Arts in Bucharest. Between 1974 and 1992 he was an art teacher in a prestigious art high school in Bucharest, Romania. After immigrating to Canada in 1992, he began teaching the wood icon painting technic to Montrealers interested in this form of art. He is married to Alexandra Drăguţescu, another professional fresco painter and iconographer. Presently they live and work in Montreal.

Artistic data After graduating as a professional painter specialized in monumental art, Titu Drăguţescu began painting murals in six Romanian Orthodox Churches between 1978 and 1990. In four of these commissions he worked together with his wife, Alexandra Drăguţescu. A great number of altar icons on wood or cardboard in tempera or oil technique were also restored by the artist. Since his first exhibition in 1978, the artist participated in numerous exhibitions in Romania, Germany, Belgium, Netherlands, France, Italy, England and Canada. He was a member and vice-president of the Union of Plastic Artists in Romania between 1990 and 1992. He practices a very traditional wood icon painting, with great respect for the themes' treatment, in accordance with the Byzantine canons. The richness of his colours is greatly enhanced by the bright, golden border. His works are found in Romanian museums and in private collections in many countries and several art publications include illustrations of his paintings. The artist's works are permanently on exhibit in two Montreal art galleries. He also works as an art restorer of paintings and ceramics.[24]

DUBNEAC, FELIX

Personal data The Archimandrite Felix Dubneac was born in Bessarabia, formerly a Romanian province. From 1944 to 1949, he studied at the Academy of Fine Arts and at the Faculty of Theology of Bucharest. He came to Canada in 1967 and has presently retired to the Dormition of the Mother of God Orthodox Monastery in Rives Junction, Michigan.

Artistic data Before emigrating to North America, he has painted and restored the iconography in many churches and monasteries in Romania. His main technique at that time was the fresco. In Canada, he was painted (in oils) the iconostasis of the Saint George Romanian Orthodox Cathedral in Windsor, Ontario as well as large fresco scenes on its altar walls. The Saints Constantine and Helen Romanian Orthodox Church in Edmonton, Alberta is also decorated with his works. In 1989, he painted the dome of the altar of the Holy Resurrection Romanian Orthodox Church in Hamilton, Ontario. He also decorated several churches in the United States. His style is vigorous, his colours are warm, and his portraiture, which rigorously respects the canons, has a great serenity of expression.[25]

FLOREA, CONSTANTIN

Personal data Born in a small Romanian village, he began studying religious painting and restoration at the Theological Institute of Bucharest. As a student he participated in several major church restorations. He emigrated to Canada at the beginning of the 1990s and presently lives in Brossard, Quebec.

Artistic data He has a preference for religious mural painting but is versatile and works in fresco, oil and mosaic (Murano technique). He paints icons on wood and glass, engraves the wood frames, and uses charcoal and pencil for his portraits. He has participated in several art exhibitions both in Romania and Canada. His works are in collections both here and abroad. Dedicated to the restoration of religious frescoes, he undertook several restoration projects in Quebec (at the Church of the Annunciation and the Church of the Archangels Michael and Gabriel in Montreal, at the Chapel of the *Sœurs adoratrices du précieux sang de Jesus* in St. Hyacinthe, at the Church St. Dominique Savio in Montreal, and at St. Mary's Church in Greenfield Park). A traditionalist icon painter, he is respectful of canons. For Saint Mary's Parish in Greenfield Park he painted an interesting icon of Kateri Tekakwitha which was presented to the Kahnawake community on April 18, 1995. His dearest wish is to create a tradition for the restoration of religious painting in Canada.[26]

GONTESCU, ELISABETA

Personal data An amateur iconographer living in North Vancouver, she began painting as a hobby while an office clerk in Bucharest. Maria Tuluca, her sister, is an iconographer as well (she is listed below).

Artistic data Paints icons on glass in traditional manner.[27]

IONESCU (DELTA), NICOLAE

Personal data I. Delta (also known as Nicolae Ionescu), now deceased, was a Toronto painter. The Romanian-Canadian philanthropist, Nicolae Pora, has recorded that Ionescu came to Canada from Romania after World War II, with the third wave of massive Romanian immigration. I was unable to determine whether he was an occasional artist, or painted professionally.

Artistic data The only painting of this artist I have seen is owned by Nicolae Pora, who bought it at the first important festival held by the Romanian Cultural Association of Hamilton, Ontario (in 1971?). It is an interesting example of oil on canvas painted with both a sacred and lay character. It portrays the unusual concept of an icon within an otherwise profane painting. Represented is a prayer corner decorated with a typical traditional Romanian earthenware vase filled with wild flowers, an accurately represented icon lamp, and on the wall, covering three quarters of the painting, a canonical representation of Saint Nicholas.[28]

LĂCĂTUŞU, ION

Personal data Born in Romania, he studied fine arts at Bucharest University where he obtained his diploma in 1987. He left Romania for Paris and became a member of the French Artists' House enjoying numerous contacts in the Paris intellectual milieux. In 1993, he immigrated to Canada, and today lives and works in Montreal, Quebec. In 1995, he became a member of the Conseil de la peinture du Québec.

Artistic data He enjoys working in fresco, oil, glass, mosaic, tempera and ceramic, in both modern and sacral style. His religious paintings follow the traditions of Dionysius of Phourna. Though a specific canon can be his starting and finishing point, the icon *per se* makes room for exploration, inspiration and feelings, without which the message would be lifeless. His work in restoration has lead him to the rediscovery of old techniques and styles common to Byzantine art, though some elements remain specific to certain geographic zones. Since his arrival in Canada, he has mostly painted icons. His works were displayed at the Uniconcept Gallery in Montreal in 1993 and at the Romanian Cultural Centre Constantin Brâncuşi in 1994 and 1995. One of his icons was donated to the New Annunciation Church of Montreal and several others were acquired by private collectors.[29]

LIBEROVSKI, PAUL

Personal data Painter of Ukrainian or Romanian-Ukrainian origin, painted in Montreal in the 1950s (?).

Artistic data The present writer has seen only one example of his religious art, namely the Imperial Doors he painted in 1957 for the new iconostasis of the 1918 Annunciation Church in Montreal; these are displayed in the "New" Annunciation Church basement chapel built in 1972.

MATEI, L. (?)

Personal data Romanian iconographer from Bucovina. His paintings in Canada
are dated 1917 and can be found in Montreal and Hamilton, Ontario (?).

Artistic data The iconostasis of the "old" church (probably the Annunciation
Church built in Montreal in 1918) was painted by a Romanian-Bukovinian iconographer who signed and dated his works MATEI, 1917. According to Father
Popescu, parish priest, the iconostasis was brought entirely painted to Canada from
Bucovina. The icons are conventional representations. Presently, several icons
taken from the old iconostasis, are displayed in the parochial house. An icon
representing "Saint Basil the Great" signed L. MATEI and dated 1917 is on display
in the "Holy Resurrection Romanian Orthodox Church" in Hamilton, Ontario. It is
similar in style to the icons in Montreal. Father Nicolae Ciurea of Hamilton
believes that Matei may have been an itinerant religious iconographer who worked
for a while in Canada.[30]

MANOLESCO, IONELA

Personal data Born in Romania, Ionela Manolesco studied at Bucharest University where specialized in decorative arts at the Faculty of Fine Arts and obtained her
master diploma in 1962. After coming to Canada, she completed doctoral studies at
McGill University in Montreal, specializing in Middle Age and Renaissance French
Literature. She has published several volumes of poetry including a highly ac-
claimed rendition of François Villon's poetic work in Romanian. She lives and
works in Montreal.

Artistic data Iconographer, jeweller, poet, medieval scholar, --Ionela Manolesco
has a multifaceted personality. She loves her art and an overwhelming spirituality
emanates from her icons. The materials she uses in the creation of her icons are in
strict accordance with traditional Byzantine ways. The artist uses rare woods that are
aged and oil treated. Her icons owe a "fourth dimension" quality to the secret
natural ingredients of her colours. She favours the Byzantine imperial colours,
purple red and gold, to enhance the spiritual strength of her icons. Her knowledge
of jewels and precious stones is reflected in some of her works. Since 1979, she has
mounted more than fifteen solo exhibition in Montreal and other Quebec cities.
Her work has been diffused via various media including an internet address. Her
works are found in many churches, public and private collections (for example, the
Nicolet Museum of Sacred Art in Quebec, the Museum of Folk Arts in Bucharest,
and the Art Collection of the Cultural Affairs Ministry in France). The Canadian
Museum of Civilization in Hull, Quebec, acquired from her an interesting miniature Byzantine-style icon showing a Catholic Saint (St. Valentine) along with the
Quebec fleur-de-lis as a prominent motif.[31]

MIHĂILESCU, FLORIN

Personal data Born in Sinaia, Romania, he is a graduate of the Academy of
Commercial Studies in Bucharest, Romania and has also studied law. Since 1981, he

lives in Montreal and is presently completing a master's degree in political science
at the Université de Montréal.

Artistic data Wishing to own an icon he enrolled in a course on icon painting
offered by the Bulgarian iconographer, Svetla Velikova, at the Ville St-Laurent
Community Centre. As an amateur iconographer, he respects the canons by
reproducing approved models. His innovative sense inclines towards new combinations of colours and the use of rare woods, such as mahogany. He favours the use
of gold leaf and ensures the luminosity of his icons with gold powder. Painting
icons is for him a spiritual necessity that keeps him in touch with his Orthodox
roots and traditions[32].

MERINUK, JEANNINE

Personal data A resident of Richmond, British Columbia, Jeannine Merinuk was
born at St-Boniface, Manitoba. Having married a Ukrainian-Romanian, she
embraced the Orthodox faith and is now a follower of the multi-ethno-national
Canadian Orthodox Church.

Artistic data When they lived in Manitoba members of the Merinuk family
frequented Saint George Romanian Orthodox Church. Before moving to B.C.
Jeannine painted an icon that she presented as a gift to Rev. Fr. Mirone Klysh and
his family. This was an oil on wood icon, the subject of which was a traditional
representation of the Virgin Mary.[33]

MOCIORNITZA, ROSETTE

Personal data Born in Cluj, Romania, she obtained a law degree and married a
prominent Romanian industrialist. She and her family were forced to flee the
Communist regime. In 1970, the Mociornitza family settled in Montreal and
presently lives in Brossard, Quebec. Their home contains a fabulous icon collection.

Artistic data The artist studied of icon painting for several years in a monastery
with an elderly monk. She added to her knowledge by studying documents found in
many Romanian monasteries. She has exhibited in Western Europe and at the
Montreal Museum of Fine Arts in 1969 shortly after her arrival in Canada. Subsequently she mounted over fifty exhibitions and, in 1975, created the first Byzantine
museum in North America at the Bois-de-Boulogne Community Centre in
Montreal. (The Museum was later dismantled, but visitors can still view parts of
the collection in the Mociornitzas private home). The iconographer uses traditionally treated wood with distinctive covers and carved borders. The colours are rich
and sometimes highlighted with semiprecious stones and metal work. Her icons,
respectful of Byzantine canons, are painted generally on pine wood, covered by
seven or eight layers of alabaster powder, each one highly polished by hand. The last
layer is covered by gold or silver leaf on which the vegetal colours are applied. For
added ornamentation she uses whatever she fancies: enamel, sculptures, flowers or
arabesques, in an infinite variety of combinations. She is aided in her work by her
husband, Ionel Mociornitza, who commented on his wife's body of work, during
my visit at her studio in Brossard. In his view, she practices a neo-Byzantine type of

sacred art where the proportions and the specificity of the Byzantine style are identical to the old practices while her vision alone remaining personal. He considers her enamel technique, precious stones settings, and aging process highly original.[34]

OPREA, PETRE

Personal data Born in Southern Romania, Petre Oprea is a retired accountant who emigrated to Canada in 1989.

Artistic data He liked to draw as a child, but rekindled his taste for drawing only in recent years, to keep himself busy after coming to Canada. He uses pencils on cardboard and copies religious images from reliable sources. A deeply spiritual man, he is supported in his artistic endeavours by his two daughters, Gabriela Condruţ and Mihaela Păcurar (see below).[35]

PĂCURAR, MIHAELA

Personal data Born in Sibiu, Romania, she came to Canada in 1992 and now lives and works in Ottawa together with her father, Petre Oprea (see above).

Artistic data She is an amateur iconographer driven to this sacred art from childhood. When she was just 14 years old, her grandmother brought her to a monastery where the local priest, told her to begin painting saints. She likes to sketch religious figures on paper; although not necessarily canonically represented, these respect many traditional elements. She reproduces the same drawing in black ink on a piece of glass, and uses acetate colours to fill in the forms. The artist paints only when she feels a calling to do so, using old Romanian icons as her source of inspiration.[36]

PERETZ, ERASTIA

Personal data Born in Iaşi, capital of Moldavia, she grew up in an artistic family. Her father was a prominent figure in the Romanian theatre, and she expressed herself as a poet, writer, musician and painter. In 1931, she was declared Miss Romania and she married a distinguished actor. She lives in Richelieu, Quebec, and has slowed her artistic activities.

Artistic data Erastia Peretz's iconographic beginnings, according to her husband, coincide with her arrival in Canada. The desire to decorate their home with meaningful and traditional objets d'art, made her turn to religious painting. She began painting on glass and wood. She also worked metals, making coverings for her icons in the repoussé technique. Her icons on glass, copied from consecrated models, are traditionally naive, but some personal influences are also apparent. She allows the wood to suggest the form of her icons, which may, for example, be a Christ in a triangle. The wood is traditionally treated by her husband with well polished stucco layers. On this surface, she applies gold leaf, prepares the drawing and applies colours. The painting is then finished with a special coat of varnish to convey a patina effect. She has exhibited several times in Montreal and several articles have been published concerning her artistic activities.[37]

PORA, AMELIA ECATERINA

Personal data Born in Brăila, Romania, Amelia Pora studied with a prominent Romanian painter, Alexandru Ciucurencu. She holds a master's degree in fine arts from the Nicolae Grigorescu University Institute of Fine Arts in Bucharest. In 1963, she was admitted as a full member of the Union of Plastic Artists, the professional body of Romanian artists. In 1988, she and her husband, Ioan Pora, a distinguished Romanian jurist , emigrated to Canada, and they now live in Mississauga, Ontario, where she also paints.

Artistic data As an artist, Amelia Pora was always fascinated by colours and simplified forms. This greatly influenced her artistic career. Her works were present in the exhibitions organized by the Union of Plastic Artists since 1961. Upon immigrating to Canada, the natural beauty of the country inspired her to resume painting icons on glass. She likes this type of icon because, in her vision, icons on glass form a branch of the Romanian folk art unique in the world, due mainly to the exuberance of the colours, the great expressivity and the adherence to rules and canons specific to higher forms of art[38] In Canada she participated in four exhibitions. Her icons on glass have been acquired by collectors here and abroad. Two of her icons were donated to Saint George Romanian Orthodox Church in Toronto. Recently, the artist also donated to the Canadian Museum of Civilization in Hull, Quebec an icon representing Saint Paraskeva.

RASHID, VARVARA

Personal data Varvara Rashid née Munteanu was born in Bucharest, a descendant of one of Eastern Europe's greatest icon makers, Radu Munteanu.[39] In 1978 she obtained her high-school diploma in Architecture and since then concentrated on the family tradition of icon painting. The artist is married to Aladin Rashid, an architect of Iraqi origin with a PhD in Balkan culture. They immigrated to Canada in 1992, after living in Italy for two years The artist now lives and works in Vancouver, British Colombia.

Artistic data An artist of great creative talent, especially in the art of the icon, Varvara Rashid has also established herself in the field of restoration. She paints on wood, because according to tradition as kept in her family, icons must be painted on wood on account of Christ being crucified on a wooden cross. She uses the egg-tempera technique, because the egg is a symbol for the cosmos, and every colour has a specific meaning. Many of her works are embellished by the fine silver sheet embossed work carried out by her husband, Aladin Rashid. Since 1977 she has exhibited her icons in Romania, Germany, Turkey, Bulgaria, Yugoslavia and Hungary. During her stay in Italy she had many exhibitions, and her icons adorn several important churches in that country. She also has taught icon-painting technique in Rome, Italy. Her works can be found in private collection and galleries in Sweden, Germany, Austria, Denmark, Hungary and Italy, as well as in the Canadian Museum of Civilization.

SABĂU, Mrs. GEORGE

Personal data Mrs. Sabău was married to George Sabău and was one of the first female iconographers in Los Angeles, California.

Artistic data The artist was invited in 1958 to paint the iconostasis of the new "Descent of the Holy Ghost" Romanian Orthodox Church in Assiniboia, Saskatchewan.[40]

SINIUK, GEORGE (?)

Personal data George Siniuk may have been an itinerant artist from Bucovina. He came to Hamilton early in 1917 (?).

Artistic data The old church in Hamilton contained a small iconostasis carved and painted in a very original fashion, both on the front and on the back. It is now conserved in front of the new iconostasis. Father Nicolae Ciurea discovered an inscription on one of the doors, "George Siniuk din Bucovina - Bucovăţ Febr. 1917" (George Siniuk from Bucovina - Bucovăţ February 1917). But is this the name of the donor or the carver-painter?[41]

ŞTEFĂNESCU, ELENA

Personal data A construction engineer by profession, Elena Ştefănescu emigrated to Canada in 1958, worked for several years for the Montreal City Hall civil service department, and then retired to Ottawa, where she now resides.

Artistic data A gift received in the early 1980s, -- the monumental album, *La peinture paysanne sur verre de Roumanie* by Juliana and Dumitru Danco, -- inspired her to learn painting on glass, and she began copying the best Romanian glass icons. She strives for simplicity of form and takes few liberties with the original, except in the use of colours. She is known to have reproduced all the plates in the album, cited above, several times to meet the demand for her icons. He paints icons for enjoyment and gives all of her works to charities. Her icons were on display in 1984 at the Reginald J.P.Johnson Library in Montreal, at the Ottawa Public Library in 1985, and at the Civic Hospital (to which she donated her works). She donated one of her icons to the Canadian Museum of Civilization.[42]

TIMOFTE, VICTOR

Personal data Icon painter on wood (?). Established in Montreal.

Artistic data The artist practised a canonical type of iconography with a taste for geometric forms in his composition. A "Virgin Glycophiloussa" was acquired by the New Annunciation Church in Montreal.[43]

TOTH, ONDREY

Personal data Of Hungarian origin, he is married to a Romanian, and they frequent the Holy Resurrection Romanian Orthodox Church in Hamilton, Ontario, where he lives and works.

Artistic data An amateur painter, he has donated several oil on canvas icons, favouring the western tradition, to the church. The colours are rich, and the themes come from the New Testament: "Jesus and Children", "Sermon on the Mountain", "Good Friday", "Saint Trinity" and "The Miraculous Fishing."[44]

TULUCA, IRINA MARIA

Personal data Born in Romania, Maria Tuluca emigrated to Canada in 1976 and to live in Montreal. The loss of her valuable collection of ancient icons moved her to begin painting icons on glass as a hobby. She also practices the art of pottery. She and her sister, Elena Gontescu, also an icon painter (see above), now live and work in North Vancouver, B.C.

Artistic data She learned the art of icon painting on glass from several prominent Transylvanian artists. Her interest in this form of art allowed her to develop several original techniques, which she keeps a secret. She would like to dedicate all her time to the revival and teaching of this form of art. Several exhibitions in Montreal and on the West coast have contributed to her fame. She is well known by art amateurs, and her works are found in private collections around the world. Several articles and TV programs were dedicated to this painter who transformed her "hobby" into an art.[45]

ȚINCOCA, DANA

Personal data Born in Râmnicu-Vâlcea, Romania, she first studied at the Nicolae Tonitza College of Art in Bucharest. She holds a master's degree with a specialization in museology from the Nicolae Grigorescu Institute of Fine Arts of the University of Bucharest, graduating in 1989. Since 1991, she has lived and painted in Montreal.

Artistic data She paints in tempera and oil on glass and wood. Her subjects are varied: landscape and still lives. Her icons are inspired by old masterpieces.[46]

UNGUREANU, ILEANA

Personal data Ileana Ungureanu was born in Romania and immigrated to Canada in 1982. She began painting icons as geology student during her University years, being inspired by the study of form and colour of minerals. She is also an author. She now lives in Montreal.

Artistic data The preferred medium of the artist is copper worked in repoussé, but she also paints icons on wood and glass. She likes to give attention to details and uses vivid blues and red wine colours. Her favourite themes are the Virgin with Child and Christ Pantocrator. She exhibits her icons in Montreal's crafts shows.[47]

URSĂŢEANU, ION

Personal data He was born in Romania and immigrated to Canada in 1987. He now lives and creates in Winnipeg.

Artistic data The artist took up painting on glass from a Romanian roommate in an immigrant camp in Austria. He has painted over sixty icons, using oil on different surfaces such as glass, canvas and wool.[48]

VELESCU, VIORICA

Personal data Born in Brăila, Romania, she graduated in 1957 from the Nicolae Grigorescu Institute of Plastic Arts in Bucharest. She studied with prominent Romanian artists and left Romania in 1977 to settle in Geneva, then in Montreal. There she became a member of the Crimson Group and is now President of the Brâncuşi Exhibition Centre. She lives in Sainte Rose, Laval.

Artistic data Both as a painter and a sculptor, the artist experimented for several decades with various forms of contemporary art. Her interest in iconography was aroused while frequenting the New Annunciation Church in Montreal. The wish to contribute to the decoration of the new church made her paint an unconventional series of ten triangular panels representing the Passion of Christ. The colours are sombre but with an interior light, and her representation of sacred figures follows her own inspiration. For the Roman Catholic church of *Sainte Cunégonde* in Montreal she painted the "Martyrdom of *Sainte Cunégonde*". She continues to paint icons occasionally.[49]

VIZANTE, SONIA

Personal data A violinist by profession, she finished her musical studies in 1979 at the Ciprian Porumbescu Conservatory in Bucharest. She emigrated to Canada in 1981 and is presently associate concert master with the philharmonic orchestra in Hamilton, Ontario, where she lives.

Artistic data An amateur painter, Sonia Vizante was introduced to icons on glass by her former husband, Nicholas Tuluca, who is related to the artist, Maria Tuluca, of North Vancouver (see above). She paints in the naive style and finds challenging the reverse painting technique used on glass. Her first icon dates from 1982, and she has exhibited at City Hall in Toronto. She considers her painting a hobby with strong spiritual overtones and works only when she feels inspired.[50]

CONCLUDING REMARKS

1. Up to the Second World War, the painting of icons in Canada was an isolated phenomenon insofar as the Romanian community was concerned. The parishioners were generally content with photomechanical reproductions unless they had brought with them to Canada the authentic icons from Romania. A possible exception to this tendency is recorded in one of the first registers of the newly founded Romanian Orthodox parish in Hamilton: an entry for January 1918 seems to indicate that the church imported icons from

Bucovina for sale to its parishioners. Nevertheless, these could have been merely printed reproductions.

2. The strongest contingent of Romanian iconographers arrived in Canada from the late 1960s to the early 1990s -- the fourth wave of immigration that had left Romania primarily to escape the Communist regime.

    2.1. Many of them were professional painters who turned to painting icons as a living. They painted mostly on wood, and generally respected the canon.

    2.2. Amateur painters worked mostly as a result of a spiritual calling, the desire to own an icon, or as a hobby. With few exceptions, they preferred the simplest types of icons done on glass.

3. In Canada the bearers of the Romanian tradition of religious iconography came into contact with a broader ecumenical movement: Byzantine-style icons were prized by churches of various and different denominations: Roman Catholic, Anglican, Protestant, etc.: the art of Byzantine-style religious iconography transcended the respective religions of artist and the denominational borders of churches. This is best exemplified by the work of Petre Botezatu for the Baptist Divinity School in Birmingham, Alabama.

4. The expertise of Romanian artists in fresco painting and restoration has begun to be recognized specially in Quebec, where several artists were commissioned to restore murals, mostly in Roman Catholic churches.

5. New subjects departing from the established canon appear occasionally in some religious works: an Indian saint, several Catholic saints, and visual motifs with distinctly Canadian connotations (for example, maple leaves in a "Canadian Madonna" by Petre Botezatu and an icon of Saint Valentine with fleur-de-lis by Ionela Manolesco).

6. Romanian religious iconography in Canada is closely linked to the requirements of supranational religious bodies that cover the entire continent. Consequently, many iconographers are able to disseminate their art in churches and private collections in various parts of the United States as well as Canada.

7. Finally it seems that there is a new acquired taste for icons in Canada, a phenomenon which is slightly more pronounced in Quebec. However, not a single descendant from the first wave of Romanian immigrants in Canada is known to paint icons: for Romanians in Canada, this art appears to be lost in the second generation.

NOTES

1. There are many monographs and articles dedicated to this subject. For icons on wood see the classical study by I. Ştefănescu, *L'évolution de la peinture réligieuse en Bucovine et en Moldavie* (Paris, 1928). For icons on glass see C. Irimie and M. Focşa, *Romanian Icons Painted on Glass* (Bucharest, 1968) or J. Dancu and D. Dancu, *Folk Glass-Painting in Romania* (Bucharest, 1982).

2. I am indebted to Father Nicolae Ciurea, priest of the Holy Resurrection Romanian Orthodox Church in Hamilton, for his explanation and illustration of iconostasis registers. A detailed description of the iconostasis in Romanian Orthodox Churches is given by Corina Nicolescu in *Icônes roumaines* (Bucarest, 1971), p. 14.

3. Many thanks are due to the Rev. Father George Săndulescu who provided information and illustrations of the frescoes and new altar of the Windsor Cathedral.

4. In the booklet, *75th Anniversary 1916-1991 "Holly Resurrection" Romanian Orthodox Church* (Hamilton, 1991) , p. 33, there is an illustration of one of Father Dubneac frescoes.

5. Information kindly provided by the Rev. Father Mircea Panciuk of Boian, Alberta in a telephone interview in September 1995.

6. I am greatly indebted to Alexandru Nemoianu, resident historian of the Valerian D. Trifa Romanian-American Heritage Center in Jackson, Michigan and his wife Larissa, for providing me with several publications essential to the completion of this survey. This information comes from the *Historical Anniversary Album 1929-1979, (Jackson, Michigan, 1979), p. 86.*

7. Many thanks to the Rev. Fr. Petre Popescu and his wife who provided this information and showed me examples of Matei's work.

8. Information kindly provided by the V. Rev. Fr. Nicolae Ciurea and by *in situ* research done by the author.

9. The carver of the iconostasis in the New Annunciation Church in Montreal is Maestro Zambrano of Pasto, Colombia.

10. Information kindly provided over the phone by the V. Rev. Fr. Nicolai Zelea of London, Ontario, former priest of the Saint George Church in Toronto, by the V. Rev. Fr. Gheorghe Chişcă of Montreal and the V. Rev. Fr. Victor Malanca of Winnipeg.

11. Information kindly provided by the Rev. Fr. Constantin Iuga of Montreal, former priest of the Holy Resurrection Romanian Orthodox Church in Hamilton and by the Rev. Fr. John Jifcu of Timmins, Ontario.

12. Historical Anniversary Album...op. cit., p. 32 and 34.

13. Information provided by the artist and by the Rev. Fr. George Săndulescu of Windsor, the V. Rev. Fr. Nicolae Ciurea of Hamilton and the Rev. Fr. George Bâzgan of Edmonton in a series of telephone interviews in the fall of 1995.

14.   Joyce L. Collins, "Romanian Iconostasis", *Western Emerging Arts*, (Calgary, Alberta, vol. 5, March-April 1980), p. 22-24.

15.   Information kindly provided by the V. Rev. Fr. Gheorghe Chişcă of Montreal, Quebec in a telephone interview in October, 1995.

16.   The author is indebted to the Rev. Fr. George Săndulescu of Windsor and to Mr. George Alexe, the artist's husband, who in letters and extensive phone interviews offered essential information concerning the iconographer and her religious works.

17.   Interview with the artist on November 29, 1995.

18.   Information contained in a report by Dr. Robert Klymasz dated May 8, 1985 and in a December 8, 1995 phone interview with the Rev. Fr. Gheorghe Bâzgan, priest of Saints Constantine and Helen Romanian Orthodox Church in Edmonton, Alberta.

19.   Phone interview with the artist in September 1995.

20.   My warmest thanks to Mrs. Cora Botezatu, who provided me with an impressive bibliography and a live interview on September 1, 1995. As an art critic Mrs. Botezatu gave me an overview of the artist's creative process.

21.   Unfortunately I was unable to contact personally the artist.Some information was provided by Mrs. Ileana Ungureanu of Montreal. Comments on the characteristics of her icons comes from a manuscript by Claire Labrecque, *L'art de l'icône: Reflexions sur le concept d'exposition ICÔNE - ΣIKONA*, (Montréal, 1995) p. 5. I take this opportunity to thank Dr. Klymasz for signalling it to me.

22.   Information collated from an interview with the artist on October 23, 1995, several scrapbooks and articles and the album, *Helen de Silaghi Sirag* (Bucharest, 1975).

23.   Many thanks to the artist who provided me on June 1996 with this information and an illustration of one of her icons.

24.   The artist kindly provided me with this information and illustrations of his work.

25.   Many thanks are extended to the Archimandrite Felix Dubneac, who promptly answered my questionnaire and to Mother Gabriela, Superior of the Dormition of the Mother of God Orthodox Monastery, Father Nicolae Ciurea of Hamilton, Father George Săndulescu of Windsor and Father Mircea Panciuk of Boian, Alberta who all kindly provided information on the artist's life and activity in Canada and the United States.

26.   The artist and his wife were extremely cooperative in providing the author with all pertinent information. Several articles and illustrations followed to complete the live interview. Useful information was taken from Dana Ţincoca's article, "Tradiţie şi modernitate : Constantin Florea" in *Luceafărul Românesc* (Montreal, Quebec), An 1, N° 4-5, March-April 1991, p.1.

27.   Phone interview with the artist in November 27, 1995.

28.   All the information regarding this painter came from Mr. and Mrs. Nicolae Pora, who kindly allowed an interview and invited me to see their icon collection on September 4, 1995 in their Metcalfe, Ontario house.

29.   The artist expressed his views in an interview on August 21, 1995. He kindly gave me a guided tour of his studio and provided me with several bibliographic references.

30.   The religious paintings of Matei (?) were made known to me by Father Petre Popescu of Montreal and Father Ciurea of Hamilton. A typologic study could possibly provide the answer to the question of the artist's identity in both cases.

31.   The artist was extremely helpful in providing abundant illustrative material and pertinent information for the completion of this report. During several phone interviews and by filling questionnaires, she outlined her interests and aspirations and I am greatly indebted to her for her cooperation. A great deal of information came from Angela Comnène, *Recherches d'art néo-byzantin au Canada* (Ottawa, 198-) and from the INTERNET presentation, *Ionela Manolesco Medieval Art: Paradoxical Icons*, at *artists"tharsissia.com*

32.   Illustrations and information kindly provided by the artist in a written questionnaire and a phone interview on December 3, 1995.

33.   From a phone interview with the artist on December 3, 1995.

34.   Information collated from an interview granted by Rosette and Ionel Mociornitza on September 6, 1995, from a booklet, several scrapbooks, letters and articles dedicated to her art and career.

35.   Interview given by the artist and his daughter, Mihaela Păcurar, on November 21, 1995.

36.   Interview given by the artist and her father, Petre Oprea, on November 21, 1995.The artist demonstrated her pleasure in drawing religious figures by sketching several religious representations for my own documentary file.

37.   The present writer did not have the opportunity to admire Mrs Peretz's works, but her husband, in a phone interview on November 26, 1995, kindly provided all the information included in this note. I am indebted to the Rev. Fr. Dr. Cezar Vasiliu of Montreal and to his wife, Zoe, for giving me several useful tips for my present research. They offered me a copy of the *Calea de lumină Parish Bulletin* of the Saint Nicholas Romanian Orthodox Mission in Montreal, An II, N° 17, September 1995; the article, "Aniversarea bisericii", on page 12 includes a photograph of an icon on glass by Erastia Peretz, donated by the artist to the Saint Nicholas church.

38.   All information was kindly provided to the author in a manuscript letter, résumé and questionnaire received from the artist. Extremely graciously, the Pora family invited me to see their private icon collection and provided me with pertinent illustrations.

39.   I am greatly indebted to Dr. R. Klymasz, who kindly gave me all the information and pertinent illustration regarding the life and work of Varvara Rashid. Most of the biographic data and artistic comments come from an article by Michael Scott, "Putting

faith in old traditions and a new life" in: *The Vancouver Sun,* Saturday Apr. 18, 1992, p. D 4-5 and from the exhibition catalogue: *Icone di Varvara e Aladin Rashid, Personale, dal 18 dicembre 1991 al 7 gennaio 1992, Piazza del Popolo - Roma.*

40.   Information gathered from the *Historical Anniversary Album...,* *op. cit.,* p. 51-52. It seems also that the 1912 church "Saints Peter and Paul" in Flintoft, near Assiniboia has "perhaps the finest iconostasis of any Romanian church in Canada...made in the Romanian monastery at Mt. Athos in Greece, or...built in Jerusalem".

41.   The author once again thanks Father Ciurea for providing this information. In an interview on October 26, 1995, Father Ciurea supplied many essential details on the past of the Romanian Orthodox Church in Canada.

42.   The artist provided ample illustrations and information to the author during an interview on November 26, 1995. I thank her for her generosity in donating one of her icons to the Canadian Museum of Civilization.

43.   The only information available was provided by Father Popescu from the New Annunciation Church in Montreal.

44.   Information provided by Father Nicolae Ciurea on October 26, 1995.

45.   Due to the distance between our cities, I was unable to see personally the painter's work. I am indebted to my Vancouver friend, Stela Dumitrescu, and to the artist's son, Mihai Dumitrescu, for providing all the information included in this note.

46.   The artist supplied ample illustrations and information in a letter dated October 7, 1995.

47.   Information supplied by the artist in a telephone interview in June 1996.

48.   Thanks are extended to Father Victor Malanca of Saint Demetrius Romanian Orthodox Church in Winnipeg from whom I learned of the artistic activity of Mr. Ursăţeanu, who, when approached, kindly completed and returned a questionnaire and illustrations of his work.

49.   The main source of information for the artistic profile of Viorica Velescu is the anthology by Ionel Jianou et al., *Romanian Artists in the West* (Los Angeles, Ca.,198?), p. 182. In an interview on September 10,1995, the artist outlined her approach to icon painting and its spiritual implications.

50.   Phone interview given by the artist October 26, 1995.

ABOUT ICONS
ABOUT MYSELF
ABOUT CANADA[*]

by
Vladimir Blagonadejdin

My name is Vladimir Aleksandrovich Blagonadejdin. I come from Russia, from the town of Volgograd (formerly Stalingrad) on the banks of the Volga River. I am thirty-nine years old and I have a degree in architecture. At the age of thirty I was accepted as a member of the USSR Union of Architects, and in 1988, having passed my certification in Moscow, I was given the right to have my own artist's studio.

All of my creative life I have been painting icons. I began immediately after finishing the High School of Physics and Mathematics. Through all my student years and all the years I have been employed as an architect, I have been working at improving my skills in iconography, travelling in search of old craftsmen, who are still rare, but who can be found in the central areas of Russia. I have shown them my work and have questioned them about many interesting and necessary things needed for my work. Everything to do with icon-painting, icons and frescos was destroyed after the Revolution.

I began collecting and saving the old icons in ruined churches from destruction. I studied them, restored them and painted my own icons. As the years passed I added to my knowledge and skills, but I never stopped and never will stop being excited by, admiring and studying the old craftsmen, so that I may, if only in a modest way, attain the high level of their creative art. The dream of my life has always been and still remains to become a first-class professional. This is both an aspiration and an obligation to all the wonderful people, teachers, craftsmen, who have taught me my ABC's, my culture and about architecture, painting and life, who believe in me.

There are many interesting schools of icon-painting, many interesting artists, but my favourite is the Moscow school, and my favourite artist is Andrei Rublev. For this reason my favourite film is also A. Tarkovskii's film, "Andrei Rublev". While improving my icon-painting skills, I tried to master the various schools which appealed to me. And by now I am able to paint in the style of various schools of icon-painters. While reinforcing my skills, I painted in various situations, under all sorts of circumstances. I painted when I didn't feel well, when I was cold, when I was too hot, when I was depressed, when I was happy; I painted when it was dark, when it was light, at night, during the day, when things went badly with my paints

---

[*]   Translated from Russian

and under all kinds of other extreme circumstances. Sometimes I deliberately made crude mistakes in technique in order to investigate the consequences and I conducted a lot of experiments.

Of course it is better to paint icons in a good studio, without being pressed for time, with good paints, brushes, gold and varnishes. The old-time icon-painters produced icons of exceptional beauty as regards colour, composition and execution probably because they were in no hurry to achieve results. I particularly like to paint large, complex, but interesting, well-executed icons, with the lives of the Saints and holy figures - to paint a lot, over a long period of time, patiently and persistently. But, the results justify all the creative difficulties. Overcoming these difficulties is a wonderful experience.

I like the thrill which comes over me when, in anticipation of the final result, I start my work. I don't like to paint cheap, souvenir-type icons, which do not follow the doctrines laid down by the church nor the techniques established by tradition. This is cheap handicraft, not craftsmanship. I am convinced that an icon should be executed skilfully, should be valuable, that it should be a family treasure in a home, to be conscientiously looked after, honoured and carefully handed down from generation to generation, to be an heirloom. I love large-scale works done mural-fashion on iconstases and fresco wall-paintings. I like the difficult process of searching, conceptualizing and of finding solutions to problems, all of which is at times terribly taxing. However, I know that I am sure to find the very best approach and therefore I am always confident of my abilities when I start to work.

Of course, everything that is beautiful is expensive and it is difficult to sell expensive icons. But, all the same, I love to paint large, difficult icons. And when the customer has the means to go along with my proposals and my execution, that is wonderful.

In my work I zealously adhere to the doctrines of the church and respect them profoundly and I always remember that in compositions and in subject-matter these canons have been selected over the centuries and that we do not have the right to ignore them, nor, in fact, does the church allow us to. In any case, in this area there is a lot of room left for creativity. Here we are talking about the use of colour and form, as well as improvements in how we approach the other elements in the composition and the question of raising the level of sophistication in terms of the actual technique of painting, the degree of subtlety and the thoroughness and the overall skill involved. I like to depict the saints on icons as good, sorrowful and beautiful.

Of course, one has to be very familiar with the Bible and other writings, in order to portray all those depicted on an icon and all that activity and the whole history of the subject. How pleasantly and confidently a subject can be painted when you know all about it. However, I do not hesitate to ask questions and to learn, and I react calmly to criticism, particularly to justifiable and informed remarks and to the wishes of specialists. I always enjoy talking with specialists who know their business. Whenever I meet someone like that it always puts me in a good mood, as if I were encountering a member of my family. And I always approach a colleague in icon-painting or architecture with the idea of seeing how I can help him and only later do I start to consider what kind of person he is. I am not afraid of competitors, because I have confidence in myself. I even find competition interesting.

Naturally most of my work has been done in Russia. It's true the conditions weren't very good: there was no paint, no brushes, no gold and a lot of interference. But, on the other hand, there was Russia, the faith, the people, all of that was inspiring. The museums have a great many masterpieces of old Russian painting. Of course I visited all the best museums many times. I love the Russian museum in St. Petersburg, the Tret'yakovskaya Gallery and the Andrei Rublev Museum in Moscow. I loved to spend hours studying the museum icons which made the custodians of the museums somewhat nervous. I spent many long hours carefully examining the icons. I loved to visit the churches of Moscow, Kiev, St. Petersburg and the little Russian towns of Yaroslavl, Suzdal, Vladimir, Ivanov, Palekha, Mstery and many others. Most of the churches in the villages have been destroyed and they are still standing in ruins. But the churches and cathedrals with their beautiful architecture and wall-paintings stand mournfully silent, their rusty metal onion-domes moaning in the wind.

This moaning echoes constantly in my heart. Two years ago, in the winter I visited the Ivanovskaya Oblast, going from village to village. And there, amid the driving snow and frost, in the village of Verkhnyi Landekh, I stood before two ruined cathedrals. They had been destroyed and their bells removed, but although their bells no longer rang, they remained proud, beautiful and unbowed, accompanied by the wailing of the half-loose metal roof plates of their domes and their smashed gates and railings - astounding examples of the iron-and bronze-mongers' art.

Not everyone can stand this awful spectacle. But in many people the very sight arouses the need to do something. I swore to myself then and there that for the rest of my life I would do everything within my power to preserve and develop our genuine Russian art. I am convinced our children have to be brought up with such spectacles. Let them see for themselves the terrible mistakes committed by uneducated, illiterate people and let them feel that they have a duty to correct such mistakes.

I have not overwhelmed my own son with passionate speeches, but I have made every effort to show him my work, my interests, what I read and what I write, what I plan to do, what moves me, what problems I have, what is really important in my life and what is of secondary importance. And I think he has understood me. My son is now seventeen years old and he helps to paint icons, knows all the technical side of my work, the whole process and he likes it. He is now preparing to enter the Architectural Institute in order to learn to become my assistant, my supporter and my successor. God grant him success! Among the icons brought to Canada, there are three done by my son. People do not see the differences; and I say nothing and feel very proud.

When I have asked some icon-painters whether they can paint icons outside of Russia, away from home, they have told me that they cannot. They don't feel the right mood, the inspiration, the conditions are wrong, the whole atmosphere. However, once they return home, everything comes back and they are once again able to work. But I can paint anywhere and under any circumstances. During the 1990-1991 season, I spent four months painting icons in Jerusalem (Israel). Of course there they paint icons with an entirely different mood. The whole environment recalls Jesus Christ, one feels His presence all around. It is as if all the biblical writings were taking place during one's lifetime, in one's presence. And it becomes one's duty to capture this as perfectly as possible and as extensively as possible. A visit to the temple of the Holy Sepulchre on Mount Golgotha creates a powerful impression. I saw the place where Christ was crucified, the prison where he languished, awaiting sentence, a part of the Holy Cross, I kneeled in front of the Holy Sepulchre. Such impressions are a great joy for an icon-painter and are a source of great creative inspiration. You feel that you are participating in all the events depicted on an icon, that you are becoming part of the image. It is all splendid, pleasing and fascinating. From these feelings and these impressions, from working in such an environment, I feel myself to be a happy man and I am grateful to the Fates for the privilege. All of this can be related to the realm of poetry. But the prose of life consists of the fact that the churches, and particularly the Russian churches, are urgently in need of restoration, of being inventoried and of attention. But all my professional proposals did not encounter the understanding they merited on the part of the representative organizations and religious missions. It was evident that they have created a quiet and staid life for themselves in Jerusalem [...].

After Jerusalem, I spent some time in Nikosia on the island of Cyprus. There I met Greek artists and icon-painters and worker monks and icon-painters from the island of Crete. Their works are not bad, but they are more of a souvenir type. There is none of the subtlety of painting such as is found in the works of the Russian icon-painting schools. This problem also exists in the modern icon-painting studios of the Moscow Patriarchate, where the main emphasis is also on quantity and not on quality. They base themselves not on the iconography of the fifteenth and sixteenth centuries (the "Golden Age" of icon-painting in Old Russia), but rather on the school of the eighteenth and nineteenth centuries, when iconography was riddled with a formalism and an excess of the relief gesso style.

Now I move from the general to the particular, that is to say, to my creative and life credo, the one I also follow in my icon-painting.

In working with icons a feeling of moderation is also important. It is very difficult to stop. One feels the need to redraw, to rework, to add or to increase the intricacy, seeking exactly the right nuance in quality and in splendour, and even sometimes in laconic beauty. Sometimes, one has to put the work aside for a certain time, giving oneself time simply to move around in front of it, to observe it from various points of view, under different lighting conditions, while remembering to note down one's observations. Sometimes, on the other hand, I come to the conclusion that I have over-loaded an icon, that there is too much that is superfluous. However, I do not despair and I do not try to rectify the situation, but rather I study the work, drawing conclusions, thus enriching my experience for later works.

Books on icon-painting, based on schools of painting and on techniques, are rare and are mainly devoted to describing what has already been done. I enjoy looking at them, reading them and comparing the opinions and judgements of the authors and theorists. Sometimes I will find a good deal of useful advice in these books. But there are books which are interesting, but which have terrible consequences for me. For example, the book by my favourite Russian writer Vladimir Soloukhin, "Black Boards and Letters from a Russian Museum" [English translation, *Searching for Icons in Russia*, New York, 1971 - editor]. The author writes extremely well and interestingly about icons, about their value and their significance in world culture and this started the present "boom" with all its criminal consequences. Icons began to be stolen, bought up and churches to be robbed. So that it's hard to tell whether this book caused more harm or good. Harm, most likely.

Soloukhin himself only published the book after he himself had amassed one of the most valuable collections of icons in the country. Collecting icons is a very expensive and very serious pleasure. Every icon may be regarded as unique, since each icon is hand-painted, hand-done. In possessing an icon (a genuine one), a man should understand that his icon is unique in the whole world. There is no other such icon in any museum anywhere in the world, nor in any collection, even in the collections of the most wealthy people. There are similar ones, better ones, worse ones, but no one else has an icon exactly like that unique one.

Sometimes it seems that an icon is alive, that every element is made of natural, living materials (wood, polished stones, chalk, egg, tissue). An icon should not be mechanically processed, just as the gold in it should not shine brightly with a polished surface. The gold should gleam, and the icon should breathe.

Being very familiar with the techniques involved in preparing the boards and the gesso (the base) for the painting of an icon, one can either make the surface with craquelures or without them, in the "old" style and ideally smooth, fresh - however the client wishes it. And the thickness of the paint emulsion may also be controlled depending on the effect one wishes to achieve and the gold may be applied in various ways. In earlier times in the icon-painting studios there were specialists for preparing the wood, after which the board was passed to another craftsman for the gluing of the *pavoloka*, [*pavoloka*: expensive imported silk (or linen) materials - translator] and then to another for the gesso, then to the gilder and finally to the artist-icon-painter. And even here there were specialists. Some painted "hillocks", others trees, still others the clothing and finally there were those who painted countenances.

Painting countenances (faces), fingers (hands), legs and the uncovered parts of the body was the most difficult of all. The technique of painting countenances involves six even and fine layers of egg-tempera emulsion. Regardless of the dimensions of the portrayal, there are six coats. Initially the icon is not painted, but is coated, that is, a thin, transparent and even layer of egg-tempera emulsion is applied with a brush. The impression given is as if six fine plates of glass of different colours were being stacked one upon the other. Sometimes even through all these payers of paint one can see the pencilling under the first layer. Then, after the coating is applied, the icon is ready for painting, using a fine brush. The whole is finished with white intensifying tints. Of course the work is both difficult and laborious, but the results justify all the difficulties. I usually spend the summer preparing the boards and the gesso, in the autumn I do the drawing and through the long winter evenings I paint the icon. I paint several icons at the same time, as it is more convenient for me to work in this way and makes better use of time and materials. When working on large orders I station my assistants, each in his place, according to his abilities so that they will feel good about their work. I give the complex and demanding work to those who are best...

In the summer of 1991 my friend and his Canadian wife visited me. When she saw my work she said that she had never seen such work in Canada and that Canadians would be interested in getting to know my work. Three months later, I received an invitation from the Canadian "Peace Train Foundation". Without much hesitation I collected up my finished icons, prepared clean boards, brushes, paints and everything else necessary for my work and set off for Canada with an enormous amount of luggage. I was welcomed with a great deal of good will and was introduced to interesting people in whose company I visited churches and museums in the cities of Toronto, Ottawa, Montreal and Kingston.

And how I was amazed, overcome and depressed when I saw the empty walls in churches and iconostases made up of photographs and reproductions [...]. The most awful thing is that the people, particularly the young people have become used to this and say that they don't need icons, that they are expensive and that they have become used to photographs. In Russia, too, there used to be a similar attitude, when all the icons and the churches had been destroyed and ruined and when many of the master-icon-painters were killed off, when archives were burnt down. Only now have they begun to understand that they almost destroyed the most important things in life. Now there is no tsar, no God, no faith, nothing and nobody. Instead of icons they have either a hastily drawn caricature or a photograph, while instead of faith, they have trendy sham. Offerings have disappeared, patronage has disappeared, beauty has disappeared, craftsmen and icon-painting schools have disappeared. And again here in Canada, nobody seems to have time for icons. I haven't been lucky enough to encounter any patrons, nor serious collectors nor even connoisseurs of this type of art. Maybe there are some in Canada, but I have never met any at my exhibitions.

However, it was pleasant to see how some Canadians brought carefully wrapped 18th and 19th century icons to my exhibitions. With great interest, satisfaction and gratitude I told them everything I could on the subject, my own kind of modest expert opinion. I told them about the style of painting, about the boards, about which school was probably involved and when their work had been painted and of course everyone wanted to hear about the value of his icon. It was very pleasant, when one woman brought along her icons made of stitched material to show me. Beautiful works executed with great skill and with taste. I saw the skilful works of a woman icon-painter from Russia (an immigrant), who after clashing with a local priest doesn't want to work or see anyone. I also met a Mr. Schlieper who studied with the Russian school of Novgorod icon-painting and who has been painting icons in Canada for seventeen years now. At the moment he is decorating the Ukrainian church in Edmonton. Several other local artists also sent me photographs of their icons. But these could scarcely even be called caricatures of icons. I would very much have liked to visit the United States for which I had already acquired a visa, but my exhibition in Montreal took up a lot of time so I wasn't able to go and my visa expired. However, some of my icons travelled to the United States (taken by a friend). They were exhibited in Holy Trinity Monastery where people said that finally they had been able to see real icons. The icon-painters in the monastery do not paint such complex and expensive icons, but rather they paint simple, inexpensive works on plywood, with the *pavoloka*. All in all, everything has been planned in order to produce quick, simple and inexpensive work. There is no question of complexity, of a school of painting or of craftsmanship.

Is it possible, I wondered, that no one wants these skills or is interested here in Canada? [...]. I decided not to talk about icons, but to paint them in such a way that Canadians could see and understand what a real icon was and understand that no photograph, no matter how beautiful, can compare with a genuine, living icon painting in beautiful bright colours on wood, on white gesso, on gold. So I began to work, to work the way I like to work. Drawing on all my resources and potential and, having deployed my skills and bearing in mind my resources, I set up a strict regimen. Every day I worked, worked, worked, nineteen hours out of the twenty-four. Sometimes it was very difficult, sometimes it was unbearably difficult. But complaining is not part of my game-plan. And at the same time I also believed in myself. I would be able to do it or I wouldn't. I was able!

Letters from home helped. From my beloved son Denis, my wife Nina (a beautiful woman with refined taste), my mother, my grandmother, from all my relatives and friends. In Russia we have extensive and very close families. All of them have received a higher education, apartments, cars, country houses, all have interesting specialities. We often get together, we look after one another. We are an old church family and have a church surname. My great-grandfather was a priest (an archpriest) before the revolution. My grandmother's father was also a priest (he was shot during the last war). My grandmother's brother was also an archpriest in Novosibirsk (he is now a pensioner and may God grant him good health). So my roots are ecclesiastical, but no one was an icon-painter, only my great-grandfather was interested in icon-painting. Then again painting icons was dangerous in those days. Even when I began to paint in the 1970's there was an Article in the Criminal Code under the terms of which I could have been jailed for four years and had my property confiscated for criminal activity, i.e., the painting of icons. So one had to be very careful when studying and painting icons.

Now I have a small exhibition in order to demonstrate to Canadians what icons are. I myself am satisfied with what I have done and feel that I have worked hard and well. However, again I tell myself that one could and should paint better and more, for the wild barbarians have destroyed so much of the Russian spirit, of the Russian soul, of the Russian icons. Every icon-painter should contribute as much as he can to replenish our culture. And time, once again, will become the judge and the expert, discovering, noting, forgetting and glorifying. It is a pity that man's life is so short and that we have only one life to lead. Therefore we should make haste to leave more good things behind us.

Having seen my work, all the clergy wanted to have such icons in their churches. There were a great many compliments and much delight. Some people prayed to my icons, some wept as they prayed [...].

An icon-painting school must be organized in Canada. It won't take a lot, just the place and the desire. But all the same, I decided to start by carrying out an experiment and, with the help of my Canadian friend the Doukhobor Kuz'ma Tarasov, who has helped me not with words but with actions, to organize two-day icon-painting workshops in his home. The first time there were six participants, all interesting people of varied backgrounds, but with a great desire to learn to paint icons. The workshops were structured so that over a mere two-day period each student had the opportunity to try preparing a board with the *pavoloka*, with the gesso, to make glue, prepare the paints, to work with real gold, to find out what it means to soak an icon; and the whole of the second day was devoted to the complex techniques involved in painting images. Of course church music was played as a background throughout the whole workshop and Russian borsch was served for the meal. During the breaks there were books on icon-painting to browse through. Of course the capabilities of each participant were immediately apparent to me. But the wonderful thing is that in Canada there are people who want to learn how to paint icons. A month after the first workshop, we staged another one and it went beautifully. Now people want it to become a regular thing [...]. I am not concerned with the organizational side of things and as far as the language problem is concerned, for the moment I am being helped by an interpreter. The main thing is the question of finding accommodation.

This is precisely what I proposed to the clergy in the churches of Canada. They have many beautiful buildings and they need wall paintings, but of course they have no money to pay for them I told them that we could organize an icon-painting school attached to a church, that is, an atelier where icons would be painted and sold for the benefit of the church. So things are moving along little by little and [at least] are not standing still. No, they don't want extra worries, work and bother. This is really bad, very bad. And it is why so few people attend church and why there are no offerings. The community-housing facilities affiliated with churches are full of all sorts of people, only there are no icon-painters, no craftsmen and no ateliers. However, people can learn how to embroider with gold and beads, to paint icons, to gild and to transform the shamefully bare walls of churches into genuine temples. The most important thing is that no one is concerned about this [...]. Everything is devoted to paying off the churches themselves, which either don't want to or cannot become involved with this question. It would seem that in this country there is money and resources for these problems. That means that some need to be helped, some encouraged, while some may need to be coerced. There is no need to pressure the client, but based on his resources the work should get under way and proceed stage by stage. Money has appeared for the church. Things got done and more money appeared. More was done. It takes money to make money. But every year every church should pay some attention and devote some of its resources to this question. Then, after a certain time the church will have trained its own icon-painters in its school - to make proposals for new art-projects and these proposals may be used to appeal for [more] funds. So these are the problems and issues that concern me.

I continue to paint icons and am finishing very complex triptychs and six very complex, but interesting icons. I still have several blank boards, but I already know what will be painted on them. I am often asked how long it takes to paint an icon. I reply that this depends on both my inspiration and on the size of the icon, on its complexity and on the client. Sometimes it takes me a week, sometimes a month and sometimes even three months. However, it is best if I paint several icons at the same time. I am also asked how long it takes to learn to paint such icons. Some icon-painters say the equivalent of a minimum of fifteen years. I, however, say that this depends on the capabilities, the talent and the desire [of the artist]. But I am convinced of one thing and that is that one goes on learning for one's whole life. There is no limit to man's potential, but one has to work at the outer limits of this potential.

It often happens that on seeing my work, but not seeing me, people think that they will meet an old man, a monk or an ascetic. They ask what rituals and what prayers I practise before I paint an icon and if I fast [...]. Of course, I am a man, a believer and superstitious, but I am chronically short of time for learning all these fasts and rituals and for taking part in holy days and church services. When I work, I listen to modern music, sometimes classical music and sometimes spiritual music and I very much like the operas of the Russian composers Borodin, Glinka and Rimskii-Korsakov. I love Tchaikovskii, Musorgskii and I love the great singers, Chalyapin, Mikhalov, Lisitsian. I love to watch all kinds of films, historical, musical, comic, detective and adventure films. I love to drive in my car to my country house, to go fishing, to spend time with my family and friends. I am very fond of travelling through the little towns and villages of Russia and in other countries. I have visited Mongolia, Japan, Israel and Cyprus. I am interested in places where there is a lot going on, a lot of activity [...]. I prize the craftsmen who work for me in Russia. I value their talent and their capacity for work very highly. I call them my gold reserves. There aren't very many talented young people, but I have them working for me. I waited all my life for them and the wait has paid off. They also love working with me, they have faith in me and they respect me, but above all, both for myself and for them it is a question of less talk and more action! [...].

In Russia, my impression of Canada was of course totally different than it is now. Everyone in Russia who has not visited Canada has the same impression as they have of America as a whole and Canada is seen in the image of a centre of an American Manhattan, with skyscrapers, glass and concrete, super-machines, super-

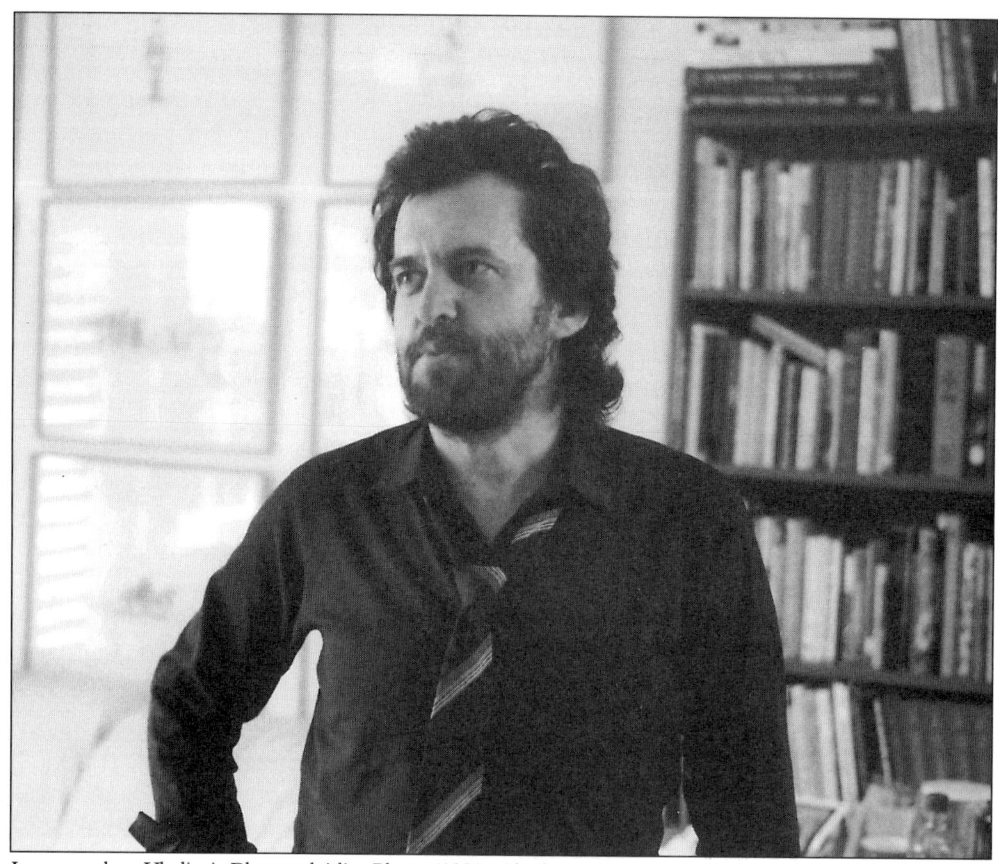

Iconographer, Vladimir Blagonadejdin. Photo (1992): Shirley Klymasz.

rich people, luxury and an all-encompassing high-level culture, with freedom and justice. This is how people in Russia see Canada. I, knowing practically nothing about Canada, simply loved this country. It seemed to me that Canada was very like Russia. And although I have seen Canada and the Canadians in a somewhat different light, I was not wrong overall and I remain faithful to my feelings for this unbelievably beautiful land of a thousand lakes.

When I visit homes where people speak Russian, I forget that I am in another country, a long way from Russia. Everything is so Russian, like back home, even the scenery I see out of the windows, with birch trees, grass and a blue sky. I visited some famous Canadian lakes with the Canadian friend I am staying with in Kingston. Once we climbed a high mountain from which there was the most beautiful view of lakes and islands and my friend, Bob Fisher, said, "Look Volodya, this is the real Canada!" And for a long time I looked, loving Canada and remembering Russia.

Kingston, Ontario
May, 1992

"ICONS FOR CHILDREN"

[NOTE: The commercial viability of religious iconography in the 1990s is reflected in the following letter dated April 29, 1995, written by Christina Senkiw of Etobicoke, Ontario and addressed to R.B. Klymasz, Curator, Canadian Museum of Civilization.]

I was very pleased to hear that you read about my work ... Here are a few notes in point form about my series of drawings "Icons for Children":

- the series was designed in 1983 to fulfil a demand for icons for children up to age 12
- the style was designed to appeal to children of that age, and the price was kept low for the parents
- the icons serve as gifts for special Ukrainian occasions ie. Christening, First Communion, Birthdays, Namesdays, Blessing of Icons in Church
- the originals are done in colour pencil or watercolour crayon on art board
- the originals are reproduced in limited editions of 40, 75, 100, or 200 - depending on the theme
- the reproductions are handmade photographs done on Cibachrome paper and dry mounted on cardboard
- customers purchase their own mats and frames
- 8" X 10" reproductions sell for $30, 11" X 14" for $60 (an affordable price for young families)
- the original drawings sell for $600-$800
- most popular titles are: "Guardian Angel with Boy" (3 versions), "Guardian Angel With Girl" (3 versions) and "Madonna" (4 versions)
- other popular sold out titles: "St. George with Dragon", "Girl with Easter Basket", "Boy with Easter Basket", "St. Nicholas with Angel and Devil", "St. Nicholas with Girl"
- over the years I've done around 30 original drawings which were reproduced in editions
- in total I've sold about 2500 reproductions in the Toronto area
- the series sold well in Montreal, Winnipeg, Edmonton and in major Ukrainian U.S. centres
- these "icons" have never been advertised or promoted anywhere, they sell themselves by word of mouth
- customers are parents, grandparents, aunts and uncles, and teachers (women predominate)
- customers are generally children of immigrants who have been educated in Ukrainian schools and youth organizations and understand Ukrainian cultural and church traditions
- the favourite subject is the "Madonna and Child" especially if the Madonna is wearing a Ukrainian costume
- the parents always like to see the children pictured in embroidered outfits

I don't know if you wanted this much information but I had fun putting it all together. It strikes me that this "Icon Series" presents an interesting profile of popular taste - which cultural ideas are treasured and passed on to the children and which are left behind.

"WITH GOD'S HELP..."[*]

by
Tatiana N. Vartanova

I, Tatiana Vartanova, was born in the city of Kaliningrad in the environs of
Moscow on the 2nd of February, 1950. My father was a pilot at the time and my
mother - a housewife. I do not remember a great deal about my early childhood,
except that we did not even have our own separate flat but rather lived in a single
room in a communal apartment. And the families who lived in the other two rooms
were complete strangers to us as well. There was a communal kitchen with a large
coal stove in it, and each family also had its own oil stove which was fuelled by
kerosene. This was the way people prepared their meals. We did not have a bathtub
either, and so we used to go to the steam bath. I did not like going to the steam bath
very much at all, because there were lots of people there and it was noisy and
stifling. And after we were finished, particularly in the wintertime, Mama would
wrap me up very, very snugly when we went out into the street so that I wouldn't
catch a cold. This irritated me to no end, since it prevented me from breathing
freely. And in this manner we would march home on foot with our basins and our
washing. Four of us lived in our room - papa, mama, me and my older brother. Yet
there seemed to be enough space for everybody. We slept there, and ate there, and
did our homework there. I even studied music for nine whole years and finished the
music high school. I did not have any particularly great talent, however it was
considered to be in good taste for children to study music, and so I was given
lessons. Even later on, when I became older and didn't particularly want to study
music, I was obligated to do it. After I became an adult I came to appreciate the load
of activities that I had during my childhood. It taught me how to work consistently.

My interest in the applied arts came to the fore after I had grown up a little. I
really liked plays, especially historical plays, and I began to draw sketches for scenery
for the performances and built models of my favourite scenes. And generally
speaking I fell in love with painting. I collected postcards and reproductions of the
classics of world painting and set up exhibits of them in my room. By that time I
was already 14 years old and we had been given a separate apartment. It had only
two rooms. My parents lived in one of the rooms and I lived in the other.

By that time I had already tried to make my first icon. Why, I don't know. I
cannot explain it. Whatever the case, I was drawn intuitively to the secrets of the
icon, though I had not been given any kind of religious upbringing. I took a drafting
board, drove nails into it and stretched wire around them. I applied wall putty over
the wire and then tried to paint over it. This was all very clumsy, of course. Only
much later on did I find out how properly to prepare the groundwork for painting

---

[*]   Translated from Russian

icons. And then somehow one summer my mother and I were in a summer home in the environs of Moscow. There we became acquainted with a family, unfortunately I do not remember their names, who suggested that my mother show my drawings and sketches to an artist friend of theirs. He became my first teacher of painting and drawing. Yuri Efremovich Efremov was the head of the Graphics Studio, the only one in Moscow. He loved his work and was a good artist, but above all he knew how to teach and loved his students. It gave us a great deal of pleasure to draw, paint and cut out etchings on linoleum according to our drawings. We had presses for printing etchings, and later on Yuri Efremovich was able to acquire an offset press and we became acquainted with the art of the lithograph. My studies were so interesting, and I liked them so much, that I did not miss a single class in one and a half years. And I had to travel far - an hour and 40 minutes one way and an equal amount on the return trip. At the same time I was in the process of completing my general education, and so I was busy from morning till night.

When I finished school in 1967 I decided to become an artist. Mama didn't want me to do this for she had dreamed that I would become a doctor, however this idea was really not to my liking at all. And once again Yuri Efremovich came to my rescue. He was able to persuade Mama otherwise, and then he suggested that I become a student in the theatre department of the very well known Art School named after the Commemoration of 1905. He also helped me to prepare for my entrance exams.

The examinations were very long. The ones for painting, drawing and composition lasted three days each. And every day they were followed by exams for the academic subjects, with each one of these lasting four hours. After it was over I would go into the studio where Yuri Efremovich was waiting for me. We set up a similar arrangement in the studio and I drew or painted until the evening, with him showing me my mistakes. And when I returned to continue my examinations in the morning I already had some experience and was better able to cope with my assignments. In this manner I did very well, passed my exams and began my studies. Only 75 students a year were accepted, and of these only 15 were in the theatre department.

I liked my studies very much. They were unusually interesting and the teachers themselves were outstanding people. For example Tatyana Ilinichna Selvinskaya, the daughter of the famous poet Ilya Selvinskii, taught us composition, while Tatyana Borisovna Serebryakova, the daughter of the well-known Russian artist Zinaida Serebryakova taught us how to paint theatre scenery. Her experience was extraordinarily unique. Our teacher for history of the arts was the wife of the composer Rodion Shchedrin. We studied a great deal, from 8 to 10 hours a day. We had classes in painting and drawing every day, and in addition we had composition, scenic painting for the theatre, history of the arts, theatre and costume, philosophy and other subjects as well. We went to school 6 days a week and on Sundays we usually drew sketches and painted studies. Twice a year, in the winter and in the summer, we had examinations at which he had to present as many of our works as possible.

Once a week our theatre group was supposed to go to the theatre as a practice. We went to the MKHAT [Moscow Art Academic Theatre - translator] and to the Bolshoi Theatre, where T.B. Serebryakova worked. This was a fantasy kingdom, where under the tutelage of highly qualified professionals we learned to make pearls out of peas, mother-of-pearl out of rice, crimped velvet out of cheap flannel and many other magical things. We also learned how to decorate back drops and wings. In February of each year we underwent practical training in the various theatres of Moscow. I particularly loved to go to the Taganka Theatre, for which T.I. Selvinskaya did the sketches for the scenery for the production of P. Weiss' "Makinpot". I really enjoyed the rehearsals of Shakespeare's "Hamlet" with V. Visotsky in the role of Hamlet.

In the summer of 1970 an incredible event happened to me. The head of our group was Alexander Moskalionov ["Sasha"]. He was quite a bit older than us and already had his own family. Both of his brothers were priests, and this interested me more than anything else about him. He had some unusual literature about God, about the church, and about spirituality. This was completely incomprehensible, but terribly tempting. He and his family lived with one of his brothers and I liked visiting them very much. Everything there was unusual: the furniture, the books, the icons and even the smell.

And then the spring of 1970 arrived. Sasha all of a sudden asked me to go to the Pskov Region with him to paint murals in a church. His suggestion simply took my breath away and I said: "Yes, of course, however I don't know how to do that. Why did you choose me?" He replied: "I know how and will tell you what to do. I chose you because you like to work and you will keep quiet." And it was necessary to keep quiet, because at the time it was a dangerous thing to work in churches. If the authorities were to find out that we students were involved in painting murals in churches we would have been deprived forever of our right to study. Of course I agreed.

We began to get ready. Sasha did the sketches, we bought the paints and other necessary materials, and as soon as the holiday season commenced we travelled to the village of Palkino in the Pskov Region. We were billeted in a house for pilgrims which stood next to the priest's house. We each had a very small room where we slept for only a few hours, since we spent all of our time in the church. Services were conducted in the summer section of the church while we worked quietly in the winter section, and no-one was the wiser.

I did everything that Sasha told me to. He did the main work while I did the support work - transferring the drawings onto the wall and doing the decorative patterns. I was particularly good at painting the sky. I made use of the knowledge that I had gained in my classes in scenic painting for the theatre. Before we arrived the interior of the church had been painted with dark green colour and reminded one more of a bomb shelter than a temple. Now all the ceilings and cupolas had been turned into a bright, clear sky. The church even began to seem higher. We worked from morning till late evening and only during special holidays, when the

Christians were not at work, did we rest. During these periods I loved to read books on spiritual themes.

But nevertheless one man, an old deaf and dumb communist, noticed that we were there. He monitored our activities for more than two months. He could not understand what we were doing there, since we did not communicate with anyone and went into the church using the side entrance which faced the cemetery in order that no one would see us. In the end he reported us to the police.

And so one day in August, at 6 o'clock in the morning, our little house was surrounded, we were awakened, ordered to get into cars (each of us into a different car so that we could not talk between ourselves), and then driven to the office of the chief of the regional police.

Sasha was taken into the chief's office to be questioned and I was told to sit in the corridor. And as for me, I sat there wondering what I should do. You see, he would be saying something in there, but then what would I say in turn? And suddenly I saw a door that looked like it led to a storage room. I opened it quietly and went in. It did indeed turn out to be a storage room and it was located right in the office of the commander, except that the entrance to it was from the corridor. I sat down there very cautiously and was able to listen to everything that was being said. Don't tell me that this wasn't help from God! Sasha made up a whole story for the investigator and that one didn't even realize that we were artists. He thought that we were actors, since our student cards said that we were students of the theatre department. Sasha made up a story for him along the lines that we were simply on holidays and were observing the types of people residing in the area for use in our future acting roles.

When the chief asked him to read the statement over and sign it, I realized that the interrogation was over, and so I quietly went out of the storage room and sat down again on my chair in the corridor. Sasha came out of the office and looked at me with a terrible fright in his eyes: what would I say? However I knew that I would say the very same things as he and walked in calmly. And when the chief asked me as well to read and sign my statement I even had the nerve, in reply to his question "Is everything correct?", to answer "No, not entirely". "Then what have I written down incorrectly?", the startled chief asked. I replied: "Look, you haven't even put the punctuation marks in properly. But don't worry. It's nothing. I'll fix it." He nearly burned up out of embarrassment and apologized profusely. We returned home on foot and laughed a great deal about how well everything had turned out.

However that wasn't the end of it. They began to summon us to the police station every day and ask us the same things over and over again. It already began to play on our nerves. And after a week had passed they drummed up a "case". They claimed that we had been seen going around everywhere propagating religion and that we had hung little crosses around the necks of children at the lake by force. This was a stupid lie, since we had not gone anywhere and didn't even know that there was a lake there. But you can't argue with the authorities. They said that it was so, and that was that. And they even ordered us to get out of the village immediately. What were we to do? We had another three weeks of work left.

The next morning we had to march demonstrably to the bus station with our things so that the entire village could see us. We left. But we only went as far as Pskov. There we placed our things in a locker and went off to see the city. We hoped to return secretly to the village at night by taxi. However the driver drove us there so quickly that we arrived before dark. And at this time all the villagers were standing by the side of the road waiting for their cows to come back from the fields. And that same deaf and dumb communist was standing right in front of all of them. When I saw that I cried out: "Sasha, on the floor!" We threw ourselves down and an empty taxi sped by the inquisitive crowd. The taxi driver was terribly astonished, however he did as we asked and took us to an unfinished cow shed in a field and then drove away very quickly.

After it had grown dark we went to the Father's house by way of the back gardens. The priest's wife fell into a panic: "Oh, what will happen if you are seen here?" Ah, nothing will happen, no one will find out. The Father immediately gave us some old blankets that he had in the house and we went to the church. We completely covered up all the windows with the blankets so that the light inside could not be seen from the street. After we had finished doing this and had checked to see that everything was indeed dark, we were then able to work in light both day and night. A few days passed in this manner before we were able to complete everything, though this time in an abbreviated version. We only left the church in darkest night through the cemetery to go to the priest's house to sleep there for a couple of hours. During the day the Father came to the church by the same path to bring us some bread and milk to eat. Through a crack I saw the old deaf and dumb communist peeking through the windows of the church, suspecting something, however he never was able to find out anything. After we had finished the work, we took down the heavy scaffolding planks with the help of the Father and left the village of Palkino, also by night.

By 1971 it was time to complete my studies. In my youth I adored Spain. I was interested in her art, her architecture, her history, and even the inquisition. That is why I tried to choose plays with Spanish themes. Before my diploma I had done sketches for scenery to Verdi's opera "Don Carlos", and now for my diploma work I chose V. Hugo's play "Torquemada". The secrets of the Spanish middle ages were the inspiration for my work on the sketches. My diploma work was very well received and my sketches were taken for an exhibit. Unfortunately, however, they were never returned. And this was how my student years ended.

In February of 1971 I met my future husband for the first time, and in August I married him. His name was Ilya Vartanov and he was a student of the Institute of Foreign Relations.

After completing my studies I decided that I would not go to work in the theatre. I did not like the theatre atmosphere. It had been interesting to study there, but to work there - not at all. It was much too Bohemian, while I favour more of a chamber atmosphere. After I had defended my diploma I was assigned to some theatre or other in Saratov as principal artist. I refused to go and was left without a job. However I knew what to do. I loved graphics and decided to become involved in commercial graphics. Yuri Spiridonov, the husband of a classmate of mine, worked as a leading artist in an advertising group and took it upon himself to teach me. I had to work many long hours - drawing and discarding, drawing and doing everything over again. I learned how to design labels for wines and cognacs and packaging for cigarettes, candy, chocolates and perfumery. I had to learn commercial type, the rules governing the design of these commodities, as well as other nuances. My studies were quite successful and soon I was given a job in the Commercial-Artistic Industrial Group "Prodoformlenie" [Product Design - translator], where I worked until 1974.

By then I had withdrawn from the church completely, since my husband was studying in a political institute and was a member of the CPSU [Communist Party of the Soviet Union].

The artists in this industrial group were given wonderful Dutch paints to work with. All of us worked at home for the most part and brought our originals to the Artistic Council once a week, on Fridays. Our sketches were accepted or rejected by the Council. If they were accepted, the artist was required to present them to the Greater Municipal Artistic Council, which met once a month. If the work was affirmed there as well and the client also approved it, then the work was sent to production, i.e. to be printed. But if somebody didn't like the sketches, then the work was rejected and the artist received nothing. And so one had to work very hard and run around with the finished work as well. As I have already said, my work was going along quite successfully. I was fortunate enough to be with a group of leading artists and was therefore able to design many wine, cognac and vodka labels. I was even given a studio at the Industrial Group.

I had to work a great deal at the "Mezhrespublikanskie Vina" [Inter-Republican Wines - translator] Distillery, and especially at the distillery's experimental institute "Magarach". There I designed a well-known series of labels for fruit and berry wines. I also thought up a very famous label - "Streletskaya Gorkaya Nastoika" [a Russian brandy-type of bitters - translator], which became so popular that it was called "The Fellow with the Axe" by the people after the archer with the pole-axe that was portrayed on it. The work was not easy. We did not have any computers or any other kind of technology. Everything had to be done manually. And to draw by hand a type that has to be printed - this is the work of a jeweller.

In May of 1973 my daughter Ksenia was born. Things became even more difficult. However I was able to keep on working. With the help of my parents I managed to work and even be with my little one as well.

In 1973 my husband completed his final year at the institute. He was supposed to undergo his practical training abroad from the fall until the New Year. However he decided not to go but rather to work in Moscow in the editorial offices of TASS [Telegraph Agency of the Soviet Union], where he had held a half position during all the years he was studying. His work there was going well, and so he decided to upgrade his skills during his practical training and then go to work as a full-fledged journalist at TASS after graduating from the institute. And that's exactly how it turned out. He completed his practical work very successfully. However in the spring of 1974, when it became necessary for him to fill out the state application forms for a full-time job at TASS and for permission to go abroad, the unexpected happened. He mentioned in the application forms that his father had been sent to Siberia in 1947 and then subsequently rehabilitated in 1956.

One night in 1947, when his parents were living in the Caucasus, their entire Assyrian settlement was surrounded and the inhabitants were driven out of their homes, pushed into trucks and taken off somewhere. As it turned out, it was to Siberia. Therefore when Ilya was about to write about his father in the application forms I said: "Don't write that. You see nobody arrested your father or interrogated him personally. Without any investigation absolutely everyone was simply taken away to Siberia." He answered that he had nothing to hide, that the Party had looked into the matter and was aware of everything and that everything would be all right. However the Party decided otherwise and he was denied employment both at TASS and abroad. Even marvellous references from the Institute, where he was their best student and an active communist, and the fact that he enjoyed the reputation of being an excellent journalist with the Arab editorial staff at TASS failed to help. As a result he remained without work. After receiving such a shock Ilya began to question the "fairness of the CPSU".

His fellow classmates suggested that he go to the State Committee for Economic Ties and offer them his services as an interpreter, but fill in the application forms in a different way. The new application forms were accepted and he was offered a job as an Arab interpreter in Egypt.

In November of 1974 I, my husband and our one and a half year old daughter Ksenia flew to Cairo. At first I stayed at home with our daughter, but eventually I began to think about what I could do. And I came up with something. With the help of magazines I began to model and sew women's dresses. And I earned quite a bit of money doing that.

[Editor's note: T. Vartanova continues with a lengthy description of her experiences as a political refugee before arriving in Canada in 1990. This section is deleted.]

After our return home [Moscow], we suffered from the human vacuum around us. Therefore we made an effort to try to find new acquaintances within the dissident circles. We began to go to the library and look through the newspapers to find articles that were critical of the dissidents. When we found one we would copy down their names and then go to the Central Moscow Address Bureau with this information to get the address of one person or another. We even went to that address to make their acquaintance. However it turned out to be not that simple. Not one of the political dissidents wanted to enter into a relationship with us. They were frightened already, and they suspected everyone and everything. They were afraid of us as well. And so we shuffled on from door to door without any results. And then one day Lev Regelson, a religious dissident, agreed to meet with us. At the time Lev was one of the leaders of the Committee for the Defence of the Rights of the Believers, to which the well-known priest Gleb Yakunin belonged. A few days later we met with Lev. We had a good talk and he sent us to two dissident priests who were already well-known by then - Father Alexander Menyu and Father Dmitri Dudko.

It was very shortly after that Ilya and I went to see A. Menyu. He greeted us warmly and compassionately. From that time on my church life was revived. My husband also attended mass. Now the Party could not prevent him from doing so since they had kicked him out, of course.

A little while later we became acquainted with D. Dudko as well. His parish was situated closer to our home and we went there more often. Father Dmitri also conducted a marriage ceremony for my husband and I. After the service Father Dmitri would often invite friends to dinner in the church house. I liked to go there very much to listen to the discussions initiated by the priest. His guests all held similar views. Thanks to these two priests we began to broaden our contacts with people and we acquired friends within the circle of those in the intelligentsia who were believers.

Alexander Manishin, a psalm reader at the Patriarch's cathedral, used to visit Father Dmitri's temple. Father Dudko knew that I was an artist and that I wanted to learn how to paint icons, so he introduced me to him and asked him to take me on as a helper in the cathedral. And so in the spring of 1977 I went to the cathedral for the first time. At the time a strange, but very good woman named Irina worked in the cathedral as a restorer. She used me to help her restore a huge painted icon that was approximately 2.5 x 5 metres in size. It was a depiction of the "Ascension of Christ" for behind the altar. In the cathedral I was taught how to remove oil paints, to glue and strengthen damaged areas, to apply a grounding of "levkas" [a mixture of alabaster or chalk with glue which is used as a grounding layer on wood - translator] where it had been lost and to tone. Priest Gerasim, who was also an artist, took part in the work. I spent all my free time away from the industrial group in the cathedral. After this huge restoration work was over I continued to act as an assistant for all the work done in the cathedral.

I began to take up icon painting in the cathedral. At first I learned the techniques of preparing the icons and tried to apply them. Then I learned how to apply gold and to paint with molten metal. I also practised my icon painting under Ksenia Pokrovskaya, a parishioner in Father A. Menyu's church who painted icons in the style of the 14th and 15th centuries.

A little later, after I had already become quite familiar with the principles of working on an icon quite well, I met the priest Anatoli Volgin. He was a great master and painted marvellous icons. He had even compiled a textbook on learning how to paint icons in which he included wonderful tables and illustrations. It is thanks to him that I have the ability to paint icons. He taught me strictly, demand-ingly, and he made me repaint images many times over, correcting my mistakes. Together we tried to make slaked gold and studied the iconographic canons. Father Anatoli permitted me to use his ecclesiastical library which included many books from France and America, even though this was not particularly safe during those years. His wife, Mother Nina, taught me how to restore woven fabrics and embroider new icons using a very old Russian stitch. I travelled to the Troitse-Sergieva Lavra [an important monastery - editor] for consultations about icons.

In Canada I was once asked: "How is it that you, a woman, are painting icons?" Yes, possibly in the middle ages it was like that, however now these are totally different times. You see in Russia, instead of creating and strengthening the Church as the Apostles had called upon others to do, the Bolshevik men destroyed and ruthlessly looted Her - yet it was weak women who stood to the death for every temple. And I believe that when we are given a Benediction, we must implement It with honour. And besides, icon painting is not a spiritual calling but a profession.

At the end of 1978 I realized that not everything was satisfactory in the relations between me and my husband. However I do not want to dwell on this. I shall simply say that we parted in November of 1979 when my second daughter Maria was born. And in 1981 we officially divorced. Father Dmitri Dudko thought that I was right in doing so.

In the spring of 1979 I finally lost the patience and strength to fight with the KGB and the Industrial Group and so I quit my job of my own accord. Someone helped me to get a job in the commercial firm "Detski Mir" ["Children's World" department store - translator], but as what! - a fireman. This work, as a fire safety inspector, suited me very well at the time. I was already expecting my second child and had to spend more time at home. My work consisted of being in the department store for a period of 24 hours to make sure that the employees followed the fire safety regulations, after which I could stay at home for three days. I continued to work in the cathedral on a contractual basis. I took restoration work home or else I created some new work or other. In this way I was able to be with my children, continue to work in the cathedral and have a small, but regular salary from "Detski Mir".

In the fall of 1981 our fire brigade was abolished and they let the civilians go and hired on military personnel. I did not want to transfer over into the military and was therefore let go. However I remained in "Detski Mir" in charge of the guard dogs. At the time the department store was guarded at night with the help of a pack of huge German shepherds. It was my job to look after them, feed them, and put them in position at night to guard the store. Although I still worked for a 24-hour period, I found that I had more time for the cathedral. You see, once I had done everything necessary for the dogs in the morning I was allowed to leave until the evening. Of course I went to the cathedral for the whole day. During that period restoration work was being carried out in the cathedral on two huge icons from Afon which had been painted with oils - "the Martyr Panteleimon" and an image of the Virgin "Skoroposlushnitsa". They were intended for the grand altar.

Once in a while I also restored woven materials in addition to icons and paintings. In 1980-1981 I restored a large Shroud with the image of the Saviour on it. It was completely threadbare and eaten through by worms. I had to transfer the Shroud onto new velvet piece by piece. As well I had to carry out the restoration of the image of Christ himself, which was painted in oils, in the same manner. In addition to this I also restored a number of embroidered icons. I liked to embroider new Icons in my spare time and I have three of them with me here in Canada.

In 1981 a young artist by the name of Nikolai Tarasenko came to the cathedral. Later on he developed into a wonderful master, working exclusively with oils. He and I worked together in various temples for almost ten years. He did not work permanently in the cathedral but was my unfailing assistant for all the large and rush jobs. For example he helped me every evening while I was working in the church in the village of Nikolo-Arkhangelsk in the environs of Moscow to restore the main iconostasis of that cathedral, which we restored for the celebrations of the 1000th anniversary of the Christening of Rus.

The elder of the cathedral, N.S. Kapchuk, had asked me a long time ago to work full time in the cathedral. This meant that I would have had to spend eight hours each day there. However I was able to accept his offer in the spring of 1983, when my mother went on pension and agreed to sit with the children. In April of 1983 I became the principal artist in the cathedral. It was my job to keep all of the icons in good shape both inside the cathedral building itself as well as in the vestry. There were a few thousand of them in all, both large and small.

Once in a while I had to do some graphic design work. My earlier experience in the industrial group helped me in this regard. For example it was impossible to gain entrance to the Temple at Easter without a special invitation. I did the designs for the invitations not only for Easter, but also for other events and international conferences that took place in the cathedral.

We lived in the cathedral as one family, helping out in all the needs of the cathedral when necessary, such as preparing for the holidays and for large patriarchal receptions. We even counted the money.

At the beginning of the 80's the ownership of two small state houses which were located on the territory of the cathedral was transferred over to us. We decided to build a christening altar with a baptistry in one of them. We also erected a new two-tiered iconostasis for which I painted the top tier of icons.

In the second house we organized a hotel and a large hall for receptions that could hold two hundred people. The mural for the huge ceiling was painted by an entire team of artists. I restored two large icons for that hall - Sergei Radonezhski and an icon of the Holy Mother the Redeemer.

In the second half of 1986 we began to restore the main iconostasis of the cathedral. A whole team of gold gilders was invited to gild the body of the iconostasis with gold. I was given all the icons to do. There were ninety of them, both large and small. I invited a number of people to assist me. They did the easy technical work while Nikolai Tarasenko came every evening to help me tone the icons. I removed the old surface varnish and subsequent layers of images from almost all of the icons myself. Sometimes the icons were in pretty good condition and I only had to remove the old varnish which had darkened. However some of them were in terrible condition, with three or four layers of images laid on with a whitewash paste. I had to expend a lot of energy to clean off this ugliness. An old Russian organic method helped me to clean it neatly right down to the original layer of the icon. Such layers were painted with oils by fine masters using the method of thin layers of scumbling and with beautiful gold decorative patterns on the clothing. I have a number of photographs of these icons with me in Canada. Sometimes after the cleaning it turned out that the damage amounted to almost 60%. In these instances it was very difficult to finish repainting the icon in the original manner in which it had been painted in the 19th century. We worked every day from morning until night. Often I even slept in my studio in the cathedral. With God's help the work was finished on time. It was a great satisfaction to me to realize that we had managed to complete this colossal task and that the cathedral would look so beautiful with a younger looking iconostasis for the celebration.

In the second half of the 80's Metropolitan Vladimir Rostovski was the Exarch of Western Europe and had a residence in Paris. Two books and, later on, a number more were published in Paris in celebration of a thousand years of Christianity in Russia. The Metropolitan commissioned me to do the designs for the covers of these books. I painted the backdrop for the stage when the cathedral choir went to sing in Paris. I often painted icons for various celebrations or anniversaries. Once I painted a miniature landscape on an Easter egg. Later on this turned into yet another form of my creative activity. Every Easter I painted ten wooden eggs. Each year I liked to choose a new theme, and I remember some of them: Russian monasteries, folk tales in the Palekh style [Palekh is a settlement in the Ivanovskii Region of Russia which is famous for its intricate paintings on lacquered wooden articles such as little boxes, etc. - translator], Russian costumes, Russian temples and decorative patterns. I received, in addition to my work in the cathedral, private commissions to restore icons and paintings, paint new ones, and decorate wooden eggs with views of old Russia. And so in this way my work is now in Germany, Austria, France, and the USA, as well as in other countries to which some of my works from the cathedral were presented as gifts.

I also did some work in other cities. At the beginning of the 1980's I restored and painted a number of icons in the town of Kadnikov in the Vologda Gubernia [Gubernia is the old Russian term for province - translator]. The team of gold gilders that gilded the iconostasis in our cathedral with gold was often invited to work in the most diverse locations. Whenever the work involved icons they always requested that I go along with them. I accompanied them whenever it was convenient for me to do so and when it was not to the detriment of the cathedral. That's how we worked in the Pochaevskaya Lavra in Western Ukraine, in the Remote Caves in the Pecherskaya Lavra in Kiev, in the Optina Pustin [a monastery - translator] in the environs of Kozelsk, where there are two large icons which I restored (Pokrov [the highest of the saints - translator] and Ilya the Prophet), in the village of Bratovshchina in the Moscow Region where we restored a section of the iconostasis, in the Lithuanian city of Druskinikae where I fixed up a number of icons, and in the village of Nikolo-Arkhangelsk in the environs of Moscow where I worked for a while restoring the murals on the walls. In Russia at the time it was not customary to compile a professional portfolio. We simply worked and were well known in many circles. This was enough to ensure our popularity and for us to

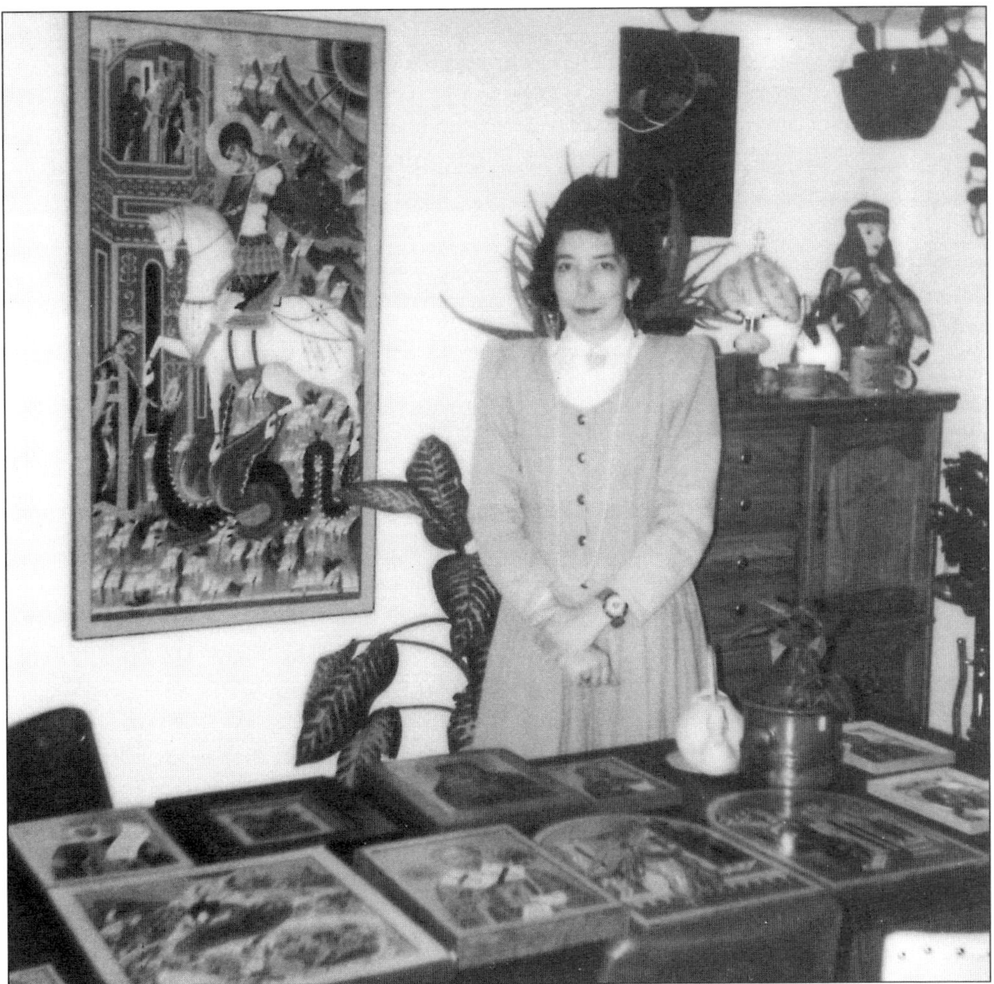

Tatiana Vartanova with some of her icons. Photo (1994): Shirley Klymasz.

receive commissions. And now it is only here, in Canada, that I am working on my portfolio.

In 1989 I was invited to Canada to paint murals for a new church. I declined the offer at the time because my mother was seriously ill. When I was invited a second time, in 1990, my mother had already recovered and I agreed. I arrived in Ottawa with my two children in August of 1990. The Russian church there has ten icons that I painted for it as part of a celebration series.

Delayed in Ottawa, we decided to remain in Canada for good. Mike Bell, a lawyer and a very good friend of mine helped me a great deal in this matter. The only way to remain in Canada was to prove to the government that my work would make a significant contribution to the culture of the country. And in addition, I had to prove that I could support myself and my school age children on the income I made from painting icons. In February of 1993 we were given the status of landed immigrants in Canada. I remember with gratitude the assistance of the Russian families Eletskii, Mokievskii, Shklyarevskii and Grindal.

I have painted almost fifty icons over the four years that I have been living here. They were painted for Orthodox and Catholic churches, for private individuals and for exhibits. My first minor exhibit took place in the Church of Saint Brigitte in 1992. By April of 1993 I already had a major exhibit in a gallery in downtown Ottawa. The third took place in the small town of Merrickville. In the fall of 1993 I was able to travel to Germany and Switzerland to show my icons to private individuals and at a minor exhibit.

I became friends with the Newland family. She was my English language teacher. Her husband Peter restored articles made out of wood and was a wonderful master at this. I taught him how to prepare boards with dowels for the icons and icon cases according to all the rules, which he now does for me.

In addition to painting icons I restore icons and paintings. I have restored around twenty-five of them. For the most part I have done this for private individuals, though it is true that I worked for three months in the Catholic church of Saint Brigitte where I restored two columns. By using the old Russian method of removing the surface images I was able to preserve the original painting on the columns as distinct from the two neighbouring ones, on which the original had been completely washed off and repainted.

Now all the icons have been sold and I am working on new ones. No endeavour fascinates me more than painting icons. I put a tremendous amount of energy into this. However I derive a great deal of pleasure and satisfaction out of it.

Ottawa, Ontario
November, 1994

SOME GUIDELINES FROM THE
CANADIAN CONSERVATION INSTITUTE

[NOTE: The following is excerpted from a letter dated April 9, 1992, written by Dr. Leslie Carlyle of the Canadian Conservation Institute in Ottawa, an agency of the Government of Canada, and addressed to John Kohler, Assistant Conservator with the Canadian Museum of Civilization.]

... with regard to your inquiry on the use of Masonite as an artists' support, and the plans to use egg tempera, acrylic paint and 24 carat gold leaf for a contemporary Ukrainian icon executed in a traditional style.

In our seminars on Modern Artists' Materials, we have been recommending that artists use Masonite as a support for painting - but include various provisos:

It is most important that the Masonite surface be adequately prepared to receive the preparation layer. This involves sanding with a fairly coarse sandpaper to achieve a roughened surface. The surface is then dusted off and degreased with alcohol (rubbing alcohol). To be on the safe side, it is best to choose untempered Masonite, since the tempered version may not offer as good a bond to the preparation layer.

Since the edges of Masonite panels are prone to chipping, they should be sanded until they are quite round and the corners should be rounded slightly for the same reason.

Masonite will change in dimension somewhat according to changes in relative humidity, therefore it is important to observe the following precautions:

- coat both sides of the board with the same preparation layer in the same thickness.

- ensure that when the board is framed there is adequate allowance for dimensional changes in the frame rebate, and a cushioning material (synthetic felt or velvet ribbon) is attached to the inside rebate edge. The board should also be backed - that is sealed in the frame with a smooth even support directly behind the board but not attached to it. Ideally, the frame could be deep enough to take the painting, followed by a thick sheet of Styrofoam (a rigid lightweight, stable foam - another choice might be Ethafoam). The Styrofoam or Ethafoam should be a minimum of 1/4 inch thick, and exactly the same overall dimensions as the Masonite. The frame could be sealed and the Styrofoam held in place by a third board which fits over the back and is attached to the back of the frame ...

Large boards (over 2 to 3 feet square) have a tendency to warp significantly if they are not properly supported. Most contemporary artists' manuals recommend that a wooden frame (like a strainer with cross bars) be glued (not nailed) to the back of the Masonite board. While this is usually adequate, there can be long-term problems with this method, especially if the work is exposed to high enough relative humidities to cause significant dimensional changes in both the wood and the

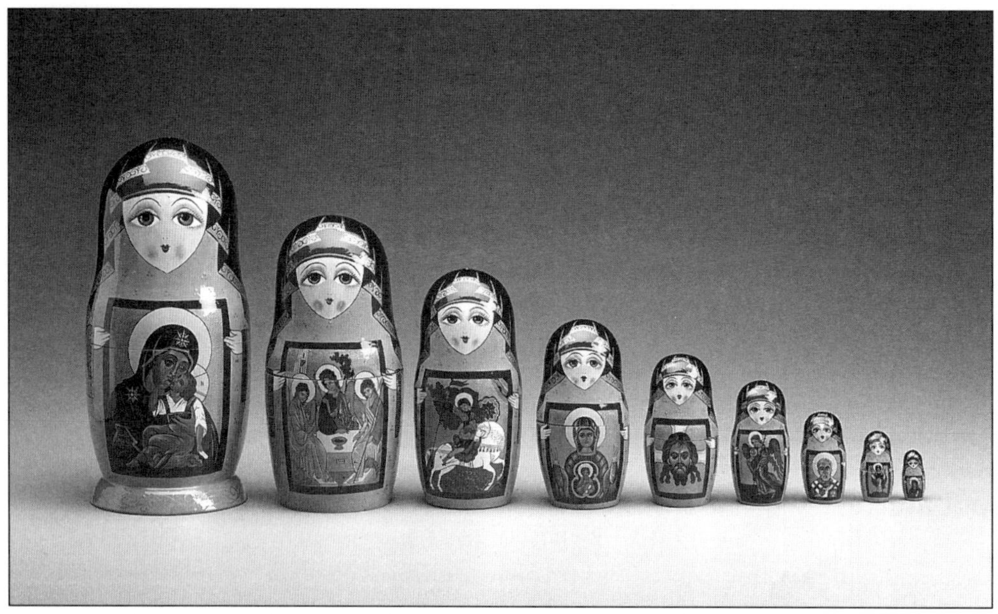

Set of wooden nesting dolls from Russia — a procession of nine nuns, each bearing a different icon. (cat. no. 94-807.1/9.) Photo: Harry Foster.

Masonite. The Masonite can dish where it is not supported by the wood - so the wood frame's outline can be seen in the undulations on the surface of the board. Treatment of warped or distorted Masonite panels is difficult and not always successful. Therefore, it is best to provide the Masonite board with an even support on the back. The framing method suggested above for smaller pieces may offer the best solution for a larger piece as well.

Regarding the paint materials:

If the artist would like to use egg tempera, it will be necessary to ensure that the preparation layer is made with a traditional chalk/glue gesso - not an acrylic ground. There could be problems with bonding between egg tempera and an acrylic ground. If the artist has not had experience with preparing a traditional chalk gesso ground, they would be best off to purchase one of the good quality ready-mixed powders intended for this, since the correct proportion of chalk and glue will have been worked out.

If the egg tempera is used as an underlayer to the acrylic paint, there should not be a problem - however, the two media should not be mixed, nor should the egg be applied over the acrylic at any time in the execution of the painting.

The use of the 24 carat gold leaf should not pose any problems since it is an inert material. However, it will be important to ensure that it is genuine by purchasing it from a reputable dealer.

I am enclosing a diagram of the framing of the Masonite board, and a handout on framing.

Of course, the best, most stable support of all, is an aluminium honeycomb panel ... but Masonite, prepared according to the above, should be quite adequate.

A CALL FOR PROPOSALS FROM
A PARISH IN MISSISSAUGA, ONTARIO

[NOTE: The following specifications originate with a "request for proposal" issued in the first half of 1995 by the steering committee for an entire church iconography project at the Dormition of the Mother of God Ukrainian Catholic Church in Mississauga, Ontario.]

This is a two step process to award an entire church iconography project, to be completed in the traditional Ukrainian manner, to a capable artist with a proven track record. Work is to commence in the fall of 1995.

Background

Location:
: The Ukrainian Catholic Church of the Dormition of the Mother of God (St. Mary's) is located in Mississauga, Ontario.

Parish information:
: The Parish, which celebrates according to the Julian calendar, serves approximately 800 hundred families. The community includes a wide range of members, ranging from newly arrived immigrants from Europe (Ukraine, Poland, etc.), to members whose ancestors have resided in Canada several generations. Many families remain close to their Ukrainian traditions, while many others, including a large portion comprised of mixed marriage families, are less tied to their Ukrainian roots. The Parish is served by a taxpayer supported school, which fosters an understanding of Ukrainian religious and cultural traditions among its students.

History of building:
: The building is about 25 years old. The building is steel frame construction, with exterior marble brick finish and interior plaster walls. The structure follows a traditional Ukrainian form, with one central cupola, framed by four cupolas in each corner of the structure. The interior design is geometric, with sharp, angular lines, rising in a slight inward inclination, and features a largely unobstructed nave.

Paintable area:
: The sanctuary measures approximately 33 feet wide (10 metres) by 16 feet deep (5 metres) [at the base], and is about 36 feet (11 metres) high. The nave measures approximately 70 feet (20 metres) square, and rises to 115 in the central cupola.

Existing decoration: The only permanent decoration is a one-tier marble iconostasis, approximately 8 feet high (2 metres) with icons by Father
Juvenalij Mokrytsky, in the Byzantine/Ukrainian style.

Step One:

In phase one of this process, applicants are invited to provide the following information:

- √ curriculum vitae, including a demonstration of significant experience in traditional Byzantine/Ukrainian iconography and polychromy
- √ photographs, slides or video
- √ pricing approach (cost plus, fixed price)
- √ artistic flexibility
- √ an understanding of the theological significance of iconography,and its contribution to advancing the faithful in their experience of God
- √ spirituality consistent with providing direction for such a significant theological work
- √ an understanding and application of contemporary construction and painting materials, sufficient to provide recommendations and guidance to the steering committee responsible for this project
- √ artistic qualification and experience in a projet of this magnitude
- √ insight and understanding necessary to develop and execute a plan consistent with the existing edifice, and the style adopted to date, as portrayed in the iconostasis
- √ personal availability, together with adequate supporting resources/personnel, to assure completion of this project, which will likely continue for a period of ten years.

Step Two:

Based on the initial submissions, selected applicants will be invited to provide more detailed information for the second phase. In the second step of the selection process, applicants will be asked to provide:

- ☞ a detailed composition and workplan for the sanctuary
- ☞ an outline indicating the major themes and approaches to be used in the nave (including the cupola), side aisles and choir
- ☞ a full sized figure (90x60 cm. approximately) indicative of a style proposed and painted using the proposed materials
- ☞ a detailed specification of materials to be used, with appropriate justification, based on the existing substrate, indicating considerations of adhesion, durability of finish and colour, ease of work, cost and any relevant factors to be considered; a listing of preparatory work to be completed, if any; a listing

of required tools or equipment (such as scaffolding which will be repaired); and

☞ a detailed costing for completing work in the sanctuary, for materials, artist and assistants, as well as other costs to be borne by the Parish community:

   ☞ artist's fees

   ☞ fees for assistant(s)

   ☞ projection of casual labour required

   ☞ travel and living arrangements required

   ☞ paint materials proposed, as suitable to the structure

   ☞ brushes and other applicators, cleaners, scaffolding, canvas, glue, and other materials (as specified above).

General Notes

Architectural drawings and a video will be made available to those who are invited to participate in the second phase of the selection process.

The finalist will be required to demonstrate adequate insurance coverage (liability, worker's compensation) as well as proof of required work permits.

The selected individuals or group will be required to obtain the documents necessary to work in Canada. The Parish will confirm the offer of work and may provide other assistance, if necessary, to assist in this process.

EAST CHRISTIAN ICONOGRAPHY IN CANADA: AN ANNOTATED BIBLIOGRAPHY

by
Robert B. Klymasz

INTRODUCTORY NOTE

This listing reflects various aspects of icons and iconography with emphasis on print materials produced in Canada from 1915 to 1995, inclusive. (Monographs originating with foreign publishers are generally excluded.) The following classificatory scheme is used to tag individual entries by alphabetic letter(s) (these appear to the left of each entry):

A.	*General (overviews, surveys, outlines)*
B.	*Icons and iconography in/from the Old World*
C.	*Exhibitions (reviews, catalogs, lists)*
D.	*Individuals (iconographers, collectors: about/by them)*
E.	*Devotional aspects, customs*
F.	*Icons in imaginative literature, fiction*
G.	*The iconostasis*
H.	*Other.*

Materials in languages other than French or English are noted accordingly. Cyrillic has been transliterated in keeping with a modified version of the international scholarly system. In most cases copies/originals for unpublished or obscure materials listed below are housed by the CMC's research archives unit where they are available for consultation by appointment.

Banting, Larissa. "In the Image of God...Marianna Savaryn", *ACUA Vitae* (Edmonton), 3:3 (December 1993): 5-6 (with b/w
D   foto-ill). About Edmonton iconographer, Marianna Savaryn.

Barbeau, Marius. "Slavic Cultural Influences on the North Pacific Coast." Unpublished typescript [1956], 100 pages. CMC archives, Barbeau
H   collection. (Shorter version also available ["Slavic Cultural Influence on the Art of the North Pacific Coast"], 16 typescript pp.) Critiqued as overly speculative, Barbeau's diffusionist work included comments on the halo as an intrusive, Slavic element in indigenous art ("For Russian icons had introduced among the natives at large this symbol of sacredness and divinity", p. 2). See especially pages 1, 2, 4, 8 and 9 in document first cited above.

Bilash, Radomir B. "Peter Lipinski, Prairie Church Artist," *SSAC* [=Society for the Study of Architecture in Canada] *Bulletin*
D   (Edmonton?), vol. 13, no. 1 (1987): 8-14. Reprinted in *Alberta Past*, vol. 4, no. 2 (1988): 1-3. With notes and 5 b/w foto-illustrations.

Blagonadejdin, Vladimir. "Russkie ikony v Kanade. Ob ikonax, o sebe, o
Kanade", Ottawa, May 1992. i+17 pp. Unpublished contract-report
D   in Russian. CMC archival/accession finding no. 92-29. With English
translation: "Russian Icons in Canada: about Icons, about Myself, about
Canada", i+13 pp.

The *Byzantine Ukrainian Rite.* Ottawa: Canadian Catholic Conference,
A,G   1975. See "Iconostasis" and "Icons": 101-105

Canada Post Corporation, Philatetic Service, Ottawa. *Commemorative
Stamp Bulletin* for "Christmas 1988-Icons / Noël 1988 - Les icônes",
H   issue date 27 October 1988. Pull-out leaflet, 5 page-sections, bilingual, 5 col.
foto-illus. "Designed by Ernst Roch and Tom Yakobina of Montreal, each of the four
Christmas stamps depicts an icon from a different tradition of the Eastern Church"
(from news release dated October 12, 1988).

Carlyle, Leslie. Ottawa: Department of Communications, Canadian
Conservation Institute. [Conservator's recommendations regarding "a
H   contemporary Ukranian (sic) icon executed in a traditional manner".] Letter
dated April 9, 1992, addressed to J. Kohler, CMC. [2 pp. (letter) and 6
pp./attachments with diags. and illus.]

"Cerkovne mystectvo /Church Art", in *Vadym Dobrolizh: Al'bom.*
Edmonton: Wadym Dobrolige Memorial Fund & Slavuta Publishers,
D   1985: 59-84 [=foto-illustrations, b/w, col.]. In Ukrainian.

CHavaha, Kost'. "Prylbyc'komu ikonostasu misce u xrami, a ne v pidsobci
kramariv" [=The iconostasis from Prylbytsk belongs in a church not
B   in a backroom of hucksters] , *Nasha meta* [Our aim], Toronto, vol. 46, no. 30
(Sept. 10, 1994): 2, 4. (Reprinted from *Ratusha*, L'viv, Ukraine.) In
Ukrainian.

Chirovsky, Andriy
SEE under CHyrovs'kyj, Andrij

CHyrovs'kyj, Andrij. "Preliminarna propozycija pro rozmishchennja ikon v
Sobori Sv. Ivana Xrestytelja v Ottavi" [=Preliminary proposal for the
H   placement of icons in the Shrine of Saint John the Baptist, Ottawa], Ottawa,
December 7, 1991, 9 pp. Diagrams and notations, mostly in Ukrainian.

___________. [review of:] Stéphane Bigham's *Les chrétiens et les images.*
Les attitudes envers l'art dans l'Eglise (Montréal-Paris, 1992) in
A   *Logos* [Lohos]: *A Journal of Eastern Christian Studies* (Ottawa),
H   vol. 35, nos. 1/4, 1994: 598-9.

__________. instructor. [Materials re course no. THO 2196 on "Theology
and Spirituality of Icons".] Ottawa: Saint Paul University,
H   Metropolitan Andrey Sheptytsky Institute of Eastern Christian Studies, 1995.
"Goals and Methodology" with "statement of purpose" and "methodology of
the course", 3pp; course outline, 4pp; "Bibliography", 4 pp.

Cinq-Mars, Marcelle. "La Vierge Marie dans l'imaginaire des croyants:
analyse des prières déposées à l'icône de Marie, Mère de Dieu, Porte
E   du Ciel." *Culture & Tradition* (Québec/St. John's), v.13 (1989): 42-53 (with
1 b/w foto-illus. and 4 tables).

Collins, Catherine (Winnipeg Art Gallery). "Condition Reports: Icons of
Taras Snihurowycz", Winnipeg, 1994. 77 pp. +covering letter dated
D   July 11, 1994, from C. Collins to David Theobald, Head, Art Conservator,
Conservation and Technical Services Division, CMC. This document
describes the condition of 30 icons by T. Snihurowycz offered to the CMC as a
donation. Of these, 17 were subsequently acquired by CMC for its collections. "As
you will observe his methods and materials are quite unique and very much in the spirit
of traditional icon painters who were 'naive' painters that relied on local materials"
(from the letter cited above).

Collins, Joyce L. "Romanian Iconostas", *Arts West* (Calgary, Alberta),
vol. 5, Mar.-Apr. 1980: 22-4, foto-illus. On the work of M. and G.
D,G   Morochan in St. Demetrius Romanian Orthodox Church, Winnipeg.

Comnène, Angela. *Présence de l'art néo-byzantin au Canada.*
Sherbrooke. Québec: Editions Naaman, 1982. 101 pp., maps, illus.
A   A brief, regional survey from Labrador to B.C.

Crosby, Louise. "Reviving an Art Form that Dates Back 2,000 Years",
The Citizen (Ottawa), December 2, 1982: 27. About iconographer,
D   Heiko Schieper. See also entry under his name.

Croteau, Denis. "L'icône de Marie, Mère de Dieu, Porte du Ciel: Esquisse
d'un cheminement spirituel." *Culture & Tradition* (Québec/St.
E   John's), v. 13 (1989): 34-40.

Darevych, Darija. *Myron Levyc'kyj.* Toronto: Ukrajins'ka spilka
obrazotvorchyx mystciv, 1985. List of Ukrainian Catholic churches
D   painted ("Cerkovna polixromija"), p. 120.

Dawes, David. "Glimpses into Heaven - Iconography is Alive and Well in
B.C.", *Christian Info News* (Vancouver, B.C.), Nov. 1995. On the
D   activities of three iconographers (V. Blagonadejdin, E. Hartley, and S. Mattila) with 3
foto-illus.

Dribnenky, Bernard. "The Icon as the Liturgical Visual Aid - Proclaiming
the Presence of the Risen Lord", *Beacon Ukrainian Rite Bimonthly*
E   (Ottawa/Toronto), vol. 29, no.1 (January/February) 1995: 24-25.

Dwirnyk, Joseph. *Rôle de l'iconostase dans le culte divin.* Montréal:
Faculté de théologie, 1960 (="*Theologica Montis Regii*", 13).
G   128 pp. (with bibliography, p. 9). Part 1: from its origins to the present; part 2:
theological considerations. Separate Ukrainian version also published: *Rolja ikonostasu v
bozhestvennomu kul'ti* (Montreal/Yorkton), 147 pp., errata slip at end.

Early Russian Icons / Icônes russes primitives (travelling exhibition).
Listing of 32 icon-items with introductory note. Ottawa: National
C   Gallery of Canada [c. 1967], 4 pp., bilingual. The travelling reproductions were
taken from, *USSR: Early Russian Icons*, preface by Igor Grabar, New York/Paris:
Graphic Society/UNESCO, 1958.

The Father Alexander Schemenn Bookstore, Montreal. Price list for
summer 1993, 13 pp. Section for "Icons", pages 5-6, lists works by J.
A, H   Baggley & R. Temple, M. Quenot, E. Sendler, A. Ugolnik, A. Tregubov, L. Ouspensky
& V. Lossky, L. Ouspensky (tr. A. Gythiel).

Fineman, Mark. "Cyrpus Icon Crusade Pays Off: Church, government
scour world to recover stolen Byzantine treasures", *Ottawa Citizen,*
B,   *July 3, 1993, p. C7 ("Religion" section").* Author is identified as an
H   associate of *The Los Angeles Times.*

Galavaris, George. "'Christ with Saints Alexandra and Agatha': A Russian
Icon in the National Gallery", *National Gallery of Canada Bulletin,*
B   vol. 26, 1975: 24-38 (with 17 illustrations [Fr./Eng. captions], notes, Fr.
résumé at end).

Goa, David J. "Icon and the Presence of the Kingdom / The Making and
the Meaning of Holy Image" in his draft (version 2, dated July 6,
C   1995) for a 5-part "Video Companion to 'St. Onuphrious Church' Exhibit",
CMC. Edmonton, July 1955: [22-27].

__________. "The Symbolism of Vestment / Le Symbolisme du vêtement
liturgique", pp. 39-40 (with 1 foto, col.), and "Sacred Objects /
A   Objets sacrés", pp. 41-44 (with 7 fotos, b/w), in David J. Goa, ed., *Seasons of
Celebration: Ritual in Eastern Christian Culture / Temps de célébration; Les Rites
dans la culture chrétienne d'Orient.* Edmonton: Alberta Culture, Provincial
Museum of Alberta, 1986.

__________. "Three Urban Parishes: A Study of Sacred Space", in

Material History Bulletin no. 29. Ottawa/Hull: Canadian Museum of

H Civilization and National Museum of Science and Technology, 1989: 13-23.
  See especially "Image and Likeness: The Icon", pp. 13-23.

__________. [Exhibition review:] "Spirit of Ukraine: 500 Years of
  Painting", *Muse* (Ottawa), vol. 10, no. 1 (spring 1992): 70-71. With

C, B cover showing reproduction of 15th century icon, "Miracle of St. George."

__________ and Anna E. Altmann. *Eastern Christian Ritual: A*
  Bibliography of English Language Sources. Edmonton: Provincial

A Museum of Alberta, 1988 (=Human History Occasional Paper No. 5),
  vi+121 pp. See "Subject Index" at end, pp. 68-73.

Granger, Lesya. "Icons and Folk Art in Canada: A Changing Context" (27
  pp. + 9 figs.), and "Thesis Proposal" [to "examine the transference

A,H of the icon painting tradition from Ukraine to Canada and its further devel-
  opment in the Canadian context"], various versions, 2, 3, 4 pp.
  Written in fulfillment of master's level graduate studies in fine arts,
  Carleton University, Ottawa, 1995.

Greenhill, Pauline. "A Study of Outdoor Household Shrines in Toronto."
  Unpublished contract report, circa 1981, v+50 typescript pages, col.

E, slides and photos available separately. CMC archival

H finding/accession no. GRP-A-4. See especially chapters four ("AZULEJOS"
  [=Portuguese ceramic tile images depicting Christian saints and other
  religious entities]) and five ("Devotion to Saints"), pp. 25-36.

Hartley, Edward. "Saint Herman of Alaska Chapel". Surrey, B.C.: [c.
  1985]. 14 pp. + cover pages. Typescript-brochure describing "ikons" and

A, E other features in chapel built in 1976.
G, H

Harvey, Bob. "Icons Are Beautiful Symbols of Faith", *Ottawa Citizen*,
  January 29, 1994, p. C4 ("Religion" section). Features brief

D interview with iconographer-monk, Rev. Gregory Abu Assaly from Colorado, about
  his work in Ottawa's St. Elias Church. With a b/w foto-illus. See also entry under St.
  Elias.

__________. "Religious Art a Challenge: Brush Powerful Weapon, Says
  Romanian Painter Now Living in Ottawa", *Ottawa Citizen*, November

D 23, 1991, p. G10 ("Religion" section). About artist, Petru Botezatu.

(Hodowansky), Sister Angelica, "Icons: Theology in Colour", in *Material*
  History Bulletin no. 29. Ottawa/Hull: Canadian Museum of

E Civilization and National Museum of Science and Technology, 1989: 113-
  114. Includes a b/w foto-illus. showing icon ("Our Lady of Victory") by Fr. J.
  Mokrycky, p. 114.

Holowaychuk, Anthony. *Catholic Faith Guide: Presenting the Catholic
  Faith in the Context of the Byzantine Ukrainian Rite.* Toronto:
A, E, G Basilian Press, 1990. See "ICON" and "ICONOSTASIS" in index at end.

Hordynsky, S [vjatoslav]. "Byzantine Art". *Encyclopedia of Ukraine,*
  University of Toronto Press, 1984 (vol. 1): 336-338, with biblio.
A at end, and 8 col. illustrations (single leaf, non-paginated insert).

_________. "Icon". *Encyclopedia of Ukraine,* University of Toronto
  Press, 1988 (vol. 2): 294-297. Section headings: "History", and "Research".
A, With biblio. at end, and 20 b/w illus., and 10 col. illus. (as non-paginated insert). See
G also adjacent entries (pp. 297-9): "Iconography" and "Iconostasis" by S. Hordynsky and
  I. Korovytsky with biblio. at end and 9 b/w illus.

_________. "Painting". *Ukraine: A Concise Encyclopaedia,* vol. 2,
  University of Toronto Press, 1971: 557-569. With biblio. at end; note also
A non-paginated insert (2 leaves) between pp. 558 and 559, showing icons, mosaics,
  frescoes, and miniature paintings.

_________. "Pro nashe suchasne relihijne mystectvo" [=About Our
  Contemporary Religious Art], in *Lohos* (Waterford, Ont./Yorkton,
A Sask.) vol. 1, no. 2 (Apr.-June) 1950: 95-100, 4 b/w foto-illus. In Ukrainian.

_________. "The Ukrainian Icon" in *Dux Ukrajiny /Spirit of Ukraine:
  500 Years of Painting. Selections from the State Museum of
A, Ukrainian Art, Kiev.* Winnipeg Art Gallery, 1991. Exhibition
C catalogue. Same article in Ukrainian ("Ukrajins'ka ikona", pp. 87-89). A
  French version of this article ("L'icône ukrainienne") published in separate French
  addendum *(L'Âme de l'Ukraine: 500 Ans de Peinture),* pp. 25-27.

_________. "Vystavka relihijnoho mystectva v KUMF" [=An exhibition
  of religious art at the Ukrainian Canadian Art Foundation, Toronto],
C *Novyj shljax/New Pathway* (Toronto), vol. 59, 35 (August 27, 1988): 9. In
  Ukrainian. A review of an exhibition featuring 170 works. See entry below under
  Ukrainian Canadian Art Foundation, Toronto.

Ibbotson, Anthony. "Heiko Schlieper: Iconographer", *Canada Crafts*
  (Toronto), vol. 4, Nov.-Dec. 1979: 22-26. With 8 foto-illus.
D

"Icon Exhibition at St. Michael's Long term Care Centre", *Ukrainian
News/Ukrajins'ki visti* (Edmonton), October 1994, p. 17. An
announcement of an exhibition to feature over 100 icons by T. Snihurowycz of
Winnipeg. C.H. Schlieper to give a short presentation on icons prior to the exhibition
opening.

C,
D

Icône-Eikona. Exposition à la maison Hamel-Bruneau, Ville de Sainte-Foy,
Québec, du 14 avril au 11 juin 1995. "Liste des oeuvres", 4 pp. The
exhibition featured anonymous works from the 16th to 19th centuries (Romania,
Russia, Greece...) and works by iconographers mostly residents of Québec: Marthe
Bélanger, Céline Boucher, Ionna Cirstea-Taurand, Mercourios Dimopoulos, Titu
Dragutescu, Nicolas Majdalani, Rosette Mociornitza, Lise Ouellet, Oleg Pankine, Frère
Sylvain, Denise Rioux, Jeanne Vanasse, Svetla Velikova, Paul I. Voevodine.

C

"Icons to Iconoclasts", *Border Crossings,* Winnipeg, spring 1992: 54-
63. Features three articles inspired by exhibition, *Spirit of Ukraine*: (1) "The Walls
of Remembrance" by Myrna Kostash, pp. 55-59; (2) "Moving to the Clear" by Bill
Pura, pp. 60-61; and (3) " The Chronology of History" by Sharah M. McKinnon, pp.
62-63. (With illustrations.)

C,
F

"The Ikon Room", The Vatikan [sic] Restaurant, Toronto. A full-page col.
advertisement in *Eye* (Toronto), Aug. 18, 1994, p. 13. "Lunch and
Dinner Monday to Saturday Served in THE IKON ROOM, Dancing Wednesday to
Saturday".

H

*Ikonohrafija Svjato-Mykolajivs'koji Cerkvy / The Iconography of St.
Nicholas' Church.* Toronto: St. Nicholas Ukrainian Catholic Parish,
1977, 174 pp. Bilingual (Ukr./Eng.) throughout. Includes the following
chapters: "Iconography and Its Meaning" by M.N. Barida; "The Decoration of the
Church of St. Nicholas" by I. Syrotynsky; "Iconography of the Chappel [sic] of the
Divine Wisdom" by M.N. Barida. With notes, bibliography, foto-illustrations (b/w,
col.).

A

Ikonostas [=Iconostasis]. Toronto, 1970, 12 pages. In Ukrainian. A list of
donors with amounts gifted to fund iconostasis in "Ukrainian Catholic Church Sw.
Pokrowy" in Toronto. Copy held by UNF Library, Toronto.

G

"Ikonostas: joho znachennja j pobudova" [=The iconostasis: its meaning
and construction], *Ukrajins'ki visti* [Ukrainian News], Edmonton,
May 20, 1971 (issue no. 20): 3. In Ukrainian.

G

"Ikonostas - mystec'ka ozdoba ta liturhijna potreba nashoji cerkvy" [=The
iconostasis - artistic embellishment and liturgical requirement of our
church], *Visnyk Cerkvy sv. O. Mykolaja* [=St. Nicholas Church Bulletin],
Toronto, April 15, 1976: 6-8.

G

"Ikony / Holy Icons". Bilingual (Ukr./ Eng.) entry in *The Ukrainian Wedding Church Service*. Winnipeg: Oseredok/The Ukrainian

E Cultural and Educational Centre, n.d. (c. 1980. "Prepared by Rev. N. Rauliuk, Hamilton, Ont." 6 leaves.

Ikony: Tvory Tarasa JUrija Snihurovycha /Works by Taras Yuri Snihurowycz. Winnipeg: Ukrainian Cultural and Educational Centre,

D, C 1993. No pagination [8 pp.]. Exhibition catalog in English and Ukrainian with 93 items listed, 3 introductory statements and col. illus.

Ilarion, Mytropolyt. *Fortecja pravoslavija na Volyni: Svjata Pochajivs'ka Lavra. Cerkovno-istorychna monohrafija*. Added t.p. in Eng.:

B "Fortress of Orthodoxy in Volyn. Holy Pochaiv Lavra. An historical monography [sic]." Winnipeg, 1961. 398 pp., footnotes, b/w illustrations, bibliographical survey (pp. 374-383). In Ukrainian. Especially following sections: "CHudotvornyj obraz na Pochajivs'kij Hori" (28-30), "Koronacija Pochajivs'koji ikony Bozhoji Materi" (140-149), "Sproba vykrasty CHudotvornu Pochajivs'ku Ikonu" (208-209), "Rozmaljuvannja Soboru" (219-222), "CHudotvorna ikona Bozhoji Materi" (260-266), "Ikonostas" (276-280).

__________. *Ikonoborstvo. Istorychno-dohmatychna monohrafija* [=Iconoclasm. A historical-dogmatic monograph]. Winnipeg:

A, vydannja Ukrajins'koji hreko-pravoslavnoji cerkvy v Kanadi, 1954.

B, 239 pp. In Ukrainian.

E

Interpol Ottawa. "Art Theft Notice, File No. 90IP0884. The following [ten] icons have been stolen from a church in Hines Creek, Alberta,

H Canada between June 17 and June 24, 1990." Ottawa: National Central Bureau, Interpol Ottawa, Cultural Property Unit, October 1990. Descriptions for each missing icon include a b/w foto-illustration. See subsequent recovery notice dated March 3, 1992 (Interpol Ottawa file no. 90IP04884) for six of these icons recovered in Vancouver, B.C., January 23, 1992; and following publication.

__________, The International Criminal Police Organization. *Theft of Cultural Property in Canada, 1993/Vol de biens culturels au Canada,*

H *1993*. Ottawa: Royal Canadian Mounted Police Public Affairs Directorate for Interpol Ottawa. PAD.268/ copyright Minister of Supply and Services Canada (1993). "Compiled by the Cultural Property Unit from Information received during 1992." vi+86 pp. Bilingual throughout, b/w illus. See especially p. 4 ("Six icons recovered"), p. 19 (icon by T. Snihurowycz), and pp. 81-84 (6 icons from Hines Creek, Alberta, recovered), and iconostasis (recovered) from Hines Creek, Alberta.

"Interview with Nazar Polataiko" [iconographer], *Anchor / JAkir* (monthly
   youth journal of the Ukrainian Orthodox Church of Canada,
D   Winnipeg), October 1994: 3. With 1 b/w photo.

Isajevych, JAroslav. "'Ikona': novyj chasopys v Ukrajini",
   Bat'kivshchyna/Batkivschyna (Toronto), vol. 53, no. 5/6 (May-June
H   1992): 8. In Ukrainian. About plans for a new periodical, "Ikona", to be published
   in L'viv, Ukraine.

Izyk, Semen. "Souvenir Icons", in his *Smiling through Tears: Memoirs
   from Second World War*. Winnipeg: the author, 1994, p. 140, with
E,   b/w reproduction of icon-card marking the occasion of the author's
F   (author=priest) first liturgy upon release from a concentration camp.

Jones, Michael Owen. "Ukrainian Byzantine Icon Painters and Paintings in
   Canada: A Preliminary Report on Researching a Tradition."
A   Unpublished contract-report, Los Angeles, October 1994, 16 typescript
   pages, with list of "selected works on icons and folk art", pp. 14-16. CMC
   archival finding/accession no. 95-13.

__________. "Folk and Academic Traditions among Byzantine Icon
   Painters in Western Canada." Unpublished contract-report, Los
A,D   Angeles, October 1995, 75 typescript pages, with "selected references", pp.
   74-5. CMC archival finding/accession no. 95-F0034. "This preliminary
   investigation of Canadian icon painters and paintings, focusing especially on self-taught
   artists and the folk tradition, involved travel to the provinces of Manitoba in June and
   British Columbia in August 1995, to meet with iconographers and to examine
   iconographically decorated churches in order to prepare a report that will: provide
   information about the state of religious iconography in Canada; address several issues
   related to the museum's icon project in progress; [and] recommend future research
   directions and priorities, particularly in research on icon painters from a behavioral
   perspective in folkloristics." The report has five parts: "Introduction", "Selected
   Iconographers in Manitoba" [R. Desilets, T. Snihurowycz, G. Robertson], "Selected
   Icon Painters in British Columbia" [A. von Kuegelsen, S. Protic, V. & A. Rashid, E.
   Hartley], "Academic Versus Folk Art and Artists", and "Recommendations for Future
   Research."

Kazymyra, Bohdan. "Chudotvorna ikona Bohomateri peremohy" [=The
   miracle-working icon of Our Lady of Victory], in *Kalendar Holosu*
B,D   *spasytelja na 1987 rik* [=Redeemer's Voice Press Almanac for 1987] (Yorkton,
   Sask.): 33-44. Traces the history of this particular icon including the installation of a
   copy by JUvenalij Mokryc'kyj in Regina, Sask. In Ukrainian.

Keddy, Bathany. "Icons of a New Era", *Shared Vision* (Vancouver), no. 81
(May 1995): 8-9. Col. cover and two fotos. About iconographer,
D   Vladimir Blagonadejdin.

Keleher, Serge. "Ukrainian Church Iconography in Canada: Models and
Their Spiritual Significance", in David J. Goa, ed., *The Ukrainian*
A   *Religious Experience: Tradition and the Canadian Cultural Context*. Edmonton:
Canadian Institute of Ukrainian Studies, University of Alberta, 1989: 47-55
(with 11 col. foto-illustrations).

Klymasz, Robert B. "The Holy Icon", in his *Folk Narrative among*
Ukrainian-Canadians in Western Canada, Ottawa:
F   CCFCS/NMM/NMC, 1975: 59-60. Same in his doctoral dissertation, "Ukrainian
Folklore in Canada: an Immigrant Complex in Transition" (Folklore Institute, Indiana
University, Bloomington, Indiana, 1970: 170-171, and in facsimile publication,
Ukrainian Folklore in Canada (New York: Arno Press, 1980). This is a humorous
folktale from the Old Country recorded in Manitoba.

__________. "Searching for Icons in Canada: A Brief Report", Ottawa:
A   CMC, August 29, 1994. Unpublished, 4 typescript pp. Subsequently published
inaccurately in *Sacred Art Journal* (Torrance, California), vol. 17, no. 1 (Pascha issue),
1996:40-43 (with editor's critical comments at end).

Kohut, Kathy. "Churches Display Saskatoon Artist's Skills", *Star-Phoenix*
["Religion and Life" section], (Saskatoon), Sat. November 1, 1975:6.
D   With 1 b/w foto-illus. Interview with iconographer, Theodore Baran [1911-1995].

Kol'esarov, JUlijan D.M. [=iconographer, Julian Kolesar]. *Russki ikony na*
Horn'ici i Panoniji [=Russian icons of the Hornitsa and Panonia
A,B   districts of Carpatho-Russia], Montreal, 1983. A self-published typescript in
three parts: 90+179+254 pp. Many b/w illus. In Carpatho-Russian. Part 3
includes a bibliography, pp. 250-1. Copy of complete work in National Archives of
Canada (the Julian Kolesar Papers [MG 55/31, No.38]).

Koljankivs'kyj, M. "Oxtryrs'ka Bozha Maty" [=The Ostrikh Mother of
God Icon], *My i svit* [We and the World] (Toronto), no. 143 (vol.
A   19), March-April, 1968: 5-7. In Ukrainian. About author's recently acquired
icon.

Komar, Mykola. "Borusivs'ka ikona Presvjatoji Bohorodyci" [=The icon
of the most glorious Mother of God from the village of Borusiv,
B,   eastern Galicia, western Ukraine], *Svitlo/The Light* (Toronto), vol. 57,
E   no. 9, (859), September 1994: 314-316. In Ukrainian. Historical
F   legends from as early as the 17th century and other materials concerning this revered
icon noted by the author who visited the village of Borusiv in 1992.

Korchahin, Klym. "Istorija Pochajivs'koji Ikony" [=A history of the icon
of Pochaiv], *Nasha meta / Our Aim* (Toronto) vol. 45, no. 25 (June
B   20, 1992): 2-3. In Ukrainian.

Koval', Roman. "Ukrajins'ke cerkovne mystetstvo v Kanadi" [=Ukrainian
church art in Canada] in Oleksander Baran and O.V. Gerus, eds.,
A   *Zbirnyk tysiacholittja xrystyjanstva v Ukrajini 988-1988* (added title in English,
The Millennium Collection - Christianity in Ukraine 988-1988), Winnipeg,
Ukrajins'ka akademija nauk v Kanadi, 1991, pp. 249-267. A critical survey in
Ukrainian by an artist-iconographer, with 4 b/w fotos, and sub-sections on "Vitrazhi"
[=windows, stained glass], pp. 262-264; "Mozajika" [=mosaics], pp. 264-266; and
"Suchasne i majbutnje" [=The contemporary and the future], pp. 266-267.

Kozak, Pat. "Builder's Dream Becomes Reality", *Progress/Postup*
(Winnipeg), vol. 33, no. 39 (November 8, 1992: 4. With one foto-
D   illustration. Activities of iconographer, Gary Robertson, Elma/Janow, Manitoba.

Krat, Pavlo (1881-1952). *Posljidne xozhdenije Boha po zemli, abo Boh na
revoljuciji* [=God's final wandering on earth, or God at the
F   revolution], [?Winnipeg, 1915]. In Ukrainian. Copy at Ottawa Univ.
Library. v+148 pp., and errata [2 pp.] at end. A collection of short stories
constituting humorous, anti-clerical narratives written in an imaginative folkloric style
with links to apocryphal literature. The first two stories include imaginative descriptions of icons in context: "Car na molytvi" [=The tsar at prayer], pp. 1-2 and "V
kanceljariji s'vjatoho Mykoly" [=In the office of St. Mykola], pp. 3-5. In the first story
cited above, the Tsar of Russia, in his hour of need, turns for help to an icon of St.
Mykola and offers to bribe the Saint.

Krawchuk, Andrii. "Icons and Iconography", in his *Finding Aid No. 2 to
the Special and Rare Books Collection of the Ukrainian Catholic
A   Seminary Library in Ottawa,* Ottawa: UCS Press, 1990: 32.

Kushnir, Myxajlo. "Svitohljadovi osnovy ukrajins'koji ikony" (with added
title in English: "Basic Conceptions of Ukrainian Icon"), in *Lohos*
A   (Yorkton, Sask.), vol. 32 (1981), no. 3: 165-173. In Ukrainian.

Labrecque, Claire. "Concept d'exposition..." Unpublished, 3-page
typescript, dated April 11, 1995. Separate English translation also
C   available Outlines an approach for an exhibition on icons curated by the writer.
For more information, see separate entry above under *Icône-Eikona*.

Labrecque, Nathalie. "André Rublev et l'icône de la Trinité", *Relations*
B,D   (Montreal), juillet-août 1978: 212-216. (With 17 footnotes.)

__________. "L'imitation du Christ selon Rublev," *Relations* (Montréal), v.
D   38, no. 443 (décembre 1978): 337-341. (With 17 footnotes.)

Labrecque-Pervouchine, Nathalie. *L'iconostase: une évolution historique
      en Russie.* Montréal: Éditions Bellarmin, 1982. 292 pp. With
G   glossary, pp. 265-281; biblio. pp. 287-292, and 33 illustrations. (=Author's doctoral
      dissertation in medieval studies, University of Montréal, 1978).

Lacroix, Marie-Josée. "Rosette Mociornitza: peintre d'icônes", *Le bel âge*
      (Montréal), vol. 4, no. 7 (mai 1991): 104. With photo of R. Mociornitza.
D

Lazar, Bishop of Vancouver. *The Ikon as Scripture: A Scriptural and
      Spiritual Understanding of Orthodox Christian Ikonography.*
E   Dewdney, B.C.: Synaxis Press 1970, 54 pp., 49 b/w plates-illus. Serialized as
      follows in various issues of *Canadian Orthodox Missionary* (Dewdney, B.C.), 17: 2 (no.
      155), March/April 1993: 12-14; 17:3 (no. 156), May/June 1993: 8-13, and other issues.

Liam, Laurence. "The Basilica Face-lift: Edmonton Catholics Fear
      Iconoclastic Renovations", *Alberta Report* (Edmonton), vol. 18, no.
E, H   44 (Nov. 25, 1991): 50-51.

Loewen, Brad. "A Ukrainian Church Exhibition at the Canadian Museum
      of Civilization", *Material History Bulletin 29* (spring 1989): 81-88.
D   Especially section on "Early Church Painting in Saskatchewan" with tables for churches
      decorated by Stephen Meush and Paul Zabolotny, pp. 83-87.

Lozynsky, T., ed. *He Dwells in Our Midst: Relfections on Eastern
      Christianity.* St. Catharines, Ont.: St. Sophia Religious Association,
E   1988. 87 pp. With many col. illustrations. See especially, "The meaning of
      icons", pp. 30-31; "The iconostasis", pp. 34-35; and "At the icon corner"", p. 75.

Mack, Lloyd. "Blending Tradition and an Artistic Flare", *Lloyminster
      Meridian Booster*, October 17, 1993, p. A14. With 3 foto-
D   illustrations. Reprinted in *Ukrainian News/Ukrajins'ki visti* (Edmonton), 67:1
      (January 1994). About iconographer, André Prevost, and his iconographic work in
      process, at the Ukrainian Catholic Church in Lloydminster.

Makaryk, Irena R. "Iconography and Symbolism" in her study, *About the
      Harrowing of Hell (Slovo o zbureniu pekla): A Seventeenth-Century
F   Play in its European Context.* Ottawa: Dovehouse Editions, 1989: 87-96 (with
      notes).

Marko, Olya (Winnipeg). "Byzantine Style Icon Painters of Manitoba".
Unpublished contract-report, dated March 16, 1995, 13
A, D   typescript pages.

Marunchak, Myxajlo H. "Rozmaljuvannja cerkvy sv. Andreja" [=The
Painting of St. Andrew's Church], in his *Studiji do istoriji ukrajinciv
A,   Kanady, Tom I. (Studies in the History of Ukrainians in Canada,
D   Vol. I., The Selkirk Settlers and the Ukrainian Community in Point Douglas)*,
Winnipeg: Ukrainian Free Academy of Sciences, 1964/65: 187-189. In
Ukrainian. Written for Marunchak by the iconographer, S. Hordyns'kyj, this brief
essay describes the latter's iconographic representations in St. Andrew's Church,
Winnipeg, painted over the summer of 1964.

Masiuk, Shara. "Theology in Imagery and Icons for Education", *Ukrainian
News/Ukrajins'ki visti* (Edmonton), November 1994, p. 14. About
D   local iconographer Marianna Savaryn and greeting cards showing her icons.

Mazuryk, O. "Znachennia ikony u vizantijs'kij cerkvi" [=The icon's
significance in the Byzantine church], *Nasha meta (Our Aim)*,
A, D   Toronto, June 4, 1988. In Ukrainian.

McDougall, Anne. "André Roublev: peintre d'icônes / Andrei Roublev:
icon painter", *Vie des arts* (Montréal), 32 (128) autumn 1987: 42-
B   7, 75. Parallel bilingual text. 6 col. foto-illus. "Back from a
C,   cultural trip in the Soviet Union, our contributor describes her visit in
D   an old Russian monastery converted in 1960 into a museum dedicated to icons."

Ménard, Pauline. *Les icônes pour aider à mieux prier*. Montréal:
E   Compagnons de Jésus et de Marie, [198?], 44 pp., col. illus.

Mociornitza, Rosette. *Icônes: la douce obsession du passé*. Montréal:
A, D, E   Humanitas Nouvelle optique, 1988. 62 pp., col. illus.

Montas, Lise. "Le Musée d'art byzantin de Montréal: Les icônes de
Rosette Mociornitza", *Le Médecin du Québec* (Montréal), 15: 7
D   (juillet 1980): 121, 123-125. Rosette Mociornitza as collector and iconographer.

Moreault, Éric. "L'icône, une forme d'art encore très vivace", *L'appel*
(Sainte-Foy, Québec), April 23, 1995. A review of exhibition, *Icône-
C   Eikona* (see entry above).

"Mother of God of Canada" [=icon by Vera Senchuk, Winnipeg,
commissioned by the Ukrainian Orthodox Church of Canada on its

D,H   75th anniversary (1993)], in program booklet published to honour the
      Metropolitan Wasyly Fedak in Oakville, Ontario, June 17, 1995, pp. 6-8. In

      Ukrainian and English, with col. reproduction/card, insert [p. 6]. An explana-
      tory statement that includes a section entitled "Canadian Symbolism".

Mushynka, Mykola. "CHyji ce ikony: slovac'ki, karpats'ki, kostel'ni chy
      ukrajins'ki?" [Whose icons are these: Slovak, Carpathian... or
B,   Ukrainian?], *Journal of Ukrainian Studies* (Edmonton), 6:1 (spring
H   1981): 79-89. In Ukrainian. See also under T. Vynnnytsky, below.

[Obituary:] "Baran", *Star-Phoenix* (Saskatoon), Thurs. January 5, 1995: C1.
      With 1 b/w foto-illus. About the life and work of icoinographer,
D   Theodore Baran (1911-1995).

Osakiwsky, Ihor. "Muralist Beautifies St. Michael's Church", The
      Ukrainian (Montreal), vol.1, no. 2 (July 1974): 3. About
D   iconographer,Wladimir Denysenko.

O'Toole, Lawrence. "No Short Cuts for Belsky on Those Giant Murals",
      The Globe and Mail (Toronto), May 18, 1971: 33. About the work of
D   Ivan Belsky, "the Canadian artist who painted the murals in St. Josaphat's and St.
      Mary's, both Ukrainian Catholic churches in Toronto." With 2 b/w fotos.

*Ottavs'ka Matir Bozha Neustannoji Pomochi/The Icon of the Mother of God
      of Perpetual Help of Ottawa* [Ottawa, 1991?]. Bilingual (Ukr./Eng.)
E   foldout leaflet with col. foto-illus. At end of Eng. version: "Father Vladimir
      Shewchuk...". "On June 2, 1991, a copy of a very ancient icon, the Mother of God of
      Perpetual Help was installed in the Ukrainian Catholic Shrine in Ottawa. The purpose
      of this brochure is to provide a brief story concerning the icon." Sub-headings: "Origin
      and History", "The Icon", "Miraculous Power", "The Mother of God of Perpetual
      Help", "East and West", "Copies", "In Ukraine", "In Canada", "The Shrine", "Travels to
      Ottawa", "Pilgrim Place", "The Great Moment", "Indulgences", "Invitation to Pilgrim-
      age". See also entry under V. Shevchuk.

Ouellette, Fernand. "Les icônes", *Liberte* (Montréal), octobre 1994: 122-
      129. With 11 bibliographical footnotes. A review of Kurt Weitzmann et al, *Les
H   Icônes*, Paris, 1982.

Peers, Glenn Alan. "The Iconography of the Archangel Michael on
      Byzantine Icons." Master's thesis for the Department of Art History,
B   McGill University, Montreal, Quebec, 1986. x+87 pp. With bibliography, 8
      figs./illus., and abstracts in French and English.

Pervouchine-Labrecque, Nathalie. "L'icône de la Vierge de Vladimir",
    Ecrits du Canada français (Montréal), vol. 21, no. 3 (hiver 1988-
B   1989): 55-67, with notes at end.

Pidhirnyj, M. "Ikonopysna majsternja pry Duxovnij seminariji" [=The icon-
    writing atelier at the Holy Spirit Seminary (Ottawa)], *Novyj*
D,   *shljax/The New Pathway* (Toronto), vol. 64, no. 32/33 (August 7-14,
H   1993): 16. In Ukrainian.

__________. "Vidrodyty u novomu stare" [=Reviving the old in the new],
    in *Novyj shljax/The New Pathway* (Toronto), vol. 64, no. 24 (June
D   12, 1993): 10. In Ukrainian. With 1 b/w foto-illustration, describes the activity of
    Ihor Andrijiv's "Icon Art Studio" in Ottawa. English transation available.

Plokhy, Serhii. "The Symbol of Little Russia: The Pokrova Icon and Early
    Modern Ukrainian Political Ideology," *Journal of Ukrainian Studies,*
B   vol. 17, no. 1/2 (summer 1992): 171-188. With b/w illus.

Pochajivs'ka Bohorodycja / The Pilgrim Icon. Winnipeg: Central Jubilee
    Committee of the Ukrainian Catholic Church, 1982. 48 pp. B/w
E   illus. Bilingual (Ukr./Eng.) throughout. "This booklet is intended to serve as a
    kind of manual for this new devotion. It contains a short history of the Icon [of
    Pochaiv] as well as prayers and songs...", p. 5.

Polishchuk, Viktor. "Vystavka ikon dlja vidznachennja tysjacholittja"
    =An icon exhibition marks the Millennium], *Nasha meta (Our Aim),*
C   Toronto, May 28, 1988: 2. See also entry below under "Ukrainian Canadian Art
    Foundation." In Ukrainian.

Polatajko, Nazar. "Ikona stritennja Hospodn'oho" [=The icon of the Lord's
    Presentation in the Temple of Jerusalem], *Anchor / JAkir* (monthly
A, B   youth journal of the Ukrainian Orthodox Church of Canada, Winnipeg),
    February, 1995: 2. In Ukrainian.

Popov, Il'ja A. "Otvet Vasilij Bokov o tom otkuda vzjalis' ikony"
    [=Vasilij Bokov's reply concerning the origin of icons], in his
B,   *Rasskazy iz istorii Duxoborcev: izlozhennye dlja prepodovanija v*
F,   *vosskresnyx sobranijax dlja detej i na vechernix sobranijax Sojuza*
H   *molodezhi* [=Stories from the history of the Doukhobors: intended for
    teaching at Sunday gatherings for children and at evening gatherings of the
    Union of youth]. Grand Forks, B.C: Izdanie Soveta Sojuza Molodezhi,
    Sojuza Duxovnyx Obshchin Xrista, 1956: 5. (Mimeograph format). In
    Russian. a For English version, see his *Stories from Doukhobor History* (Grand Forks,
    B.C.: U.S.C.C., 1992), pp. 13-15 ("Vasiliy and the Ikons"). See also udio-recording of

Vasili Bokov and the Ikons, a Doukhobor play in Russian about a Doukhobor martyr, V. Bokov, as recorded by K. Peacock in Grand Forks, B.C., 1963 (on deposit with CMC sound archives).

Poulin, Anne-Marie. "Iconographie actuelle du Sacré." *Culture &*
    Tradition (Québec/St. John's), v. 13 (1989):9-32 (with 3 b/w foto
A   -illus.)

__________. "L'iconographie actuelle du sacré au Québec: le cas de
    l'icône miraculeuse de Montréal." Master's thesis (Arts), Québec:
A   Université Laval, 1992. xvi+134 pp. (with 54 col. illus.)

__________. "Tendances de l'iconographie actuelle du sacré au Québec."
    Contract-report, [ii]+31+[i] typescript pages, dated March 7, 1995.
A   CMC archival finding/accession no. 95-12. (English translation also available: "Report
    on Tendencies in Contemporary Religious Iconography in Quebec", March 7, 1995, 33
    typescript pages.)

Povroznyk , Ljubov. "CHudotvorna ikona Materi Bozhoji z Korchmyna v
    Krakovi" [=The miraculous icon of the Mother of God from
B   Korchmyn in Cracow]. *Nasha meta* [Our Aim], Toronto, January 29, 1994
    (vol. 46, no. 4): 3. Legendary information. In Ukrainian.

Préclaire, Madeleine. "L'ange et l'icône: pour une approche du
    symbolisme religieux", *Critère* (Montréal), v. 30, no. 30 (printemps
A, H   1981): 169-185. With 26 footnotes.

Pro obrazy i molennjesja do svjatyx [=About images and praying to saints].
    Rossburn, Manitoba: Ukrainian Evangelical Literary Society, circa
E   1928: 28 pp. Iconoclastic pamphlet.

"Pro zarvanyc'ku chudotvornu ikonu Bozhoji Materi" [About the
    miraculous icon of the Mother of God from Zarvanycja], *Nasha
H   doroha* (Edmonton), vol. 26(1995), no. 1: 5-6. In Ukrainian.

"Proekty: vidnovlennja ikonostasu kolehijal'noji kaplyci" [=Projects: the
    renovation of the iconostasis in the college chapel], *Bohoslov / The
G   Theologian* (published by the Theology Students association of St. Andrew's
    College, Winnipeg), no. 3 (fall 1994): 11. In Ukrainian, with 2 b/w photos. The
    project is headed by iconographer, Nazar Polatajko (see separate entries above under his
    surname and under "Interview with..."[etc.]).

Prokopchuk, Ivan. *The Black Icon. A Story...* Aurora[?], Ont.: Island
Grove Press, 1992. An imaginative narrative, set in Ukraine. The icon appears
F   in chapter ten (pp. 41-46).

Puhalo, Bishop Lazar
SEE UNDER Lazar, Bishop of Vancouver.

Raymond, M. "Les icônes de la Galerie Temple" [à Londres], *Vie des
arts,* 49 (hiver 1967-1968): 67. English summary at end, p. iii.

*A Reformation Debate: Karlstadt, and Eck on Sacred Images. Three
Treatises in Translation.* Translated by B.D. Mangrum and G.
B, H   Scavizzi. Ottawa: Dovehouse Editions, and the Centre for Reformation
and Renaissance Studies, Victoria University, Toronto, 1991. xi+115 pp.

Rondeau, Yolande. "Des images cousues d'or", *Châtelaine* (Montréal),
vol. 20, no. 12 (décembre 1979): 20-21, 24. Icons viewed on a tour
A, C   of five of Montreal's thirteen Orthodox churches and the private museum of
D, G   iconographer R. Mciornitza.

Rotoff, Basil, Roman Yereniuk, Stella Hryniuk. *Monuments to Faith:
Ukrainian Churches in Manitoba.* University of Manitoba Press,
D   1990. See especially "Major Manitoba Ukrainian Artists", pp. 115-136, "Works of the...
Artists", pp. 171-176 and "Other Artists", p. 182. "Artists" highlighted with some detail
are Theodore Baran, Dmytro Bartoshuk, Sviatoslav Hordynsky, Roman Kowal, Jacob
Maydanyk, Leo Mol, Olga Moroz (nee Evanchyn), Vera Senchuk (nee Lazarovich), and
Hnat Sych. Others listed on p. 182 are B. Kostur, R. Patchkowsky, I. Suhacev, and J.
Wolaniuk.

Roy, Lucien. *Une icône de la Mère de Dieu: Notre-Dame de la Porte.*
Sillery, Québec: Éditions Inter Renouveau, 1985. 67 pp. Written by a
E   Roman Catholic priest in defense of the "miraculous icon of Montreal"/Notre-Dame de
la Porte, this testimonial traces its history (from 1981) and includes an appendix listing
some of the favours received by adherents. The first chapter provides background
notes on icons and iconography.

Roy, Gabrielle. "The Well of Dunrea", short story in her *Street of riches,*
tr. Henry Binsse. Toronto: McClelland & Stewart, 1957: 73-86 (in
F   1991 reprint edition). Original French titles: "Les puits de Dunrea", *Rue
Deschambault,* Montréal: Beauchemin, 1955: 123-143. "Abruptly Jan rushed
toward the chapel and emerged from it holding an icon of the Virgin. His icon in front
of him like a shield, he walked toward the burning house...the eyes of the image shone
as though they were alive." (p. 82)

Sahas, Daniel J. *Icon and Logos: Sources in Eighth-Century Iconoclasm.*
An annotated translation of the Sixth Session of the Seventh
B, H   *Ecumenical Council (Nicea, 787), containing the Definition of the*
E   *Council of Constantinople (754) and its refutation, and the Definition of the Seventh*
Ecumenical Council. Toronto: University of Toronto Press, 1986. xvi+215
pp. plates, biblio., appendices, index. See especially the introduction, pp. 1-44, and
the b/w reproductions of two icons (1983) painted by Father Theodore Koufas of
Toronto.

Sangwine, Jean. "Flickering Candles, Stylized icons and Bustling Humanity
Make a Russian Cathedral a Place for Journeying beyond Time and
B, E   Place", *The United Church Observer* (Toronto), vol. 53, no. 10 (April 1990): 2.
A report on visits to Russian Orthodox Cathedrals in Helsinki, Finland, and Leningrad,
Russia.

Sbornik" izobrazhenij javlennyx" i chudotvornyx" ikon" Presvjatyia
Bogorodicy, v" pravoslavnoj cerkvi proslavjaemyx" [=Collection of
E   image-apparitions and miracle-working icons of the Most Saintly Mother of
God, as venerated in the Orthodox church], Montreal, 1980. 63+iii pp.,
with 179 illustrations. The 179 icons are arranged according to the church calen-
dar/feast days honouring the Mother of God and other holy days. This is a photocopy
of first edition published in Moscow, 1866.

Scheffel, David. *In the Shadow of Antichrist: the Old Believers of Alberta.*
Peterborough, Ont.: Broadview Press, 1991. Especially section on
E   "Sacramentals", pp. 141-151; and pp. 164-165, 169, 183, and passim elsewhere.

Schlieper, Heiko C. "Icons and Art: An Icon Painter's View / Les Icônes
et l'Art: Le point de vue d'un peintre d'icônes", in David J. Goa,
D   ed., *Seasons of Celebration: Ritual in Eastern Christian Culture /Temps de célébra-*
tion: Les Rites dans la culture chrétienne d'Orient. Edmonton: Alberta Culture,
Provincial Museum of Alberta, 1986: 45-48 (with 1 col. foto-illus.).

Scott, Michael. "Putting Faith in Old Traditions and a New Life",
Vancouver Sun (Saturday Review), April 18, 1992: D4-5. With 6
D   foto-illus. plus section cover. About iconographer, Varvara Rashid, and husband
Aldin.

Shepertycky, Martha R. "Taras Yuri Snihurowycz and His Icons", in
Renate Pillinger - Erich Renhart, eds., *The Divine Life, Light, and*
D   *Love, Euntes in mundum universum: Festschrift in Honour of Petro B. T. Bilanuk.*
Graz, Austria: Andreas Schnider Verlags-Atelier, 1992: 323-330 (with 4 col.
illus.).

Shevchenko, I. Section on "Art" in entry for "Byzantine Elements" in,
    Ukraine: A Concise Encyclopaedia, vol. 1, University of Toronto
A   Press, 1963: 937.

Shevchuk, V. "Ottavs'ka ikona Materi Bozhoji Neustannoji Pomochi"
    [=The icon of the Mother of God of Perpetual Help of Ottawa],
E   *Postup [Progress]* (Winnipeg), vol. 33, no. 34 (September 8, 1991): 5. In
    Ukrainian. A report on the Icon's installation, June 2, 1991. See also entry under
    "Ottavs'ka Matir Bozha...[etc.]."

Shewchuk Marie and Patricia Lacey. *Journey of Faith: Ukrainian
    Millennium.* Toronto: Servants of Mary Immaculate, 1987. "... a
E   project of studies to assist the Parish and school community prepare for and celebrate
    the Millennium of the Baptism of Ukraine." ..."designed as a teachers' guidebook". See
    Unit 2, Theme 5: "The Icon: Presence of the Holy", pp. 65-67. Separate Ukrainian
    edition published *(Shljaxom viry: ukrajins'ke tysjachorichchja)* with section on the icon, pp.
    62-64.

Shurrow, Mary. "Icon Workshop at St. Basil's", *Postup/Progress*
    (Winnipeg), vol. 33, no. 16 (May 3, 1992): 2 (with two b/w photo-
E   illustrations).

Smindak, Helen. "Today's Weddings: Blending Ethnic and Modern", in
    The Ukrainian Weekly (Jersey City, N.J., U.S.A.), Sun. Sept. 25,
E   1994 [vol. 62, no. 39]: 11, 16, and 17 (with 3 b/w fotos). The article includes
    references to icons. Of special interest here is the Perozak-Pedenko wedding, Hamil-
    ton, Ontario, Wed. June 12, 1994. Captions for two of the fotos are from this wedding:
    (1) "Ivanna Perozak and Victor Pendenko carry icons as they leave St. Vladimir's
    Cathedral. The icons were held during the ceremony [in Hamilton] by their starosty
    (match-makers)... [etc.]"; (2) Icons, wreaths and candles from the church ceremony
    are displayed along with two korovai wedding breads at the Perozak-Pedenko wedding."

St. Elias Antiochian Orthodox Church, Ottawa. ["*Brochure*"], 1994?, 32
    pp., illus., diagrams. "This brochure is a guide to the icons that will beautify St.
H   Elias Church. The plans were made by Fr. Gregory [Abu Assaly] and myself. This
    brochure illustrates the names of the icons as well as their location. It gives a brief
    explanation of their liturgical purpose and spiritual meaning. At the completion of this
    beautification process, St. Elias church will be the best example of Byzantine Iconogra-
    phy in Canada and the States" [p. 1]. The brochure includes cost-estimates in dollars
    (U.S./Cdn.).

St. Mary's Ukrainian Catholic Church, Mississauga, Ont. "Request for
    Proposal" [1995]. 3pp. Specifications for "an entire church iconography
H   project to be completed in the traditional Ukrainian manner...Work is to commence in
    ... 1995." Separate English and Ukrainian versions. See also entry below under
    Zakydalsky.

Stepovyk, Dmytro V. "The Ukrainian Icon in Canada" in *Art and Ethnicity:*
the Ukrainian Tradition in Canada. Hull, Quebec: Canadian

A   Museum of Civilization, 1991: 39-45. Also separate French version ("L'icône
ukrainienne au Canada") in *Art et ethnicité: la tradition ukrainienne au Canada*,
pp. 39-45. Original version (handwritten) in Ukrainian, dated Montreal, May 31,
1989, "Ukrajins'ka ikona v Kanadi", 12 pp., CMC archival finding/accession no. 95-16
(photocopy with author's notations).

Struck, Doug. "Israel's Icons: Immigration Brings a Flood of Russian
Art", *The Gazette* (Montreal), July 17, 1993, p. i5 ("Art" section).

H   Author is identified as associated with *Baltimore Sun*.

Svientsitsky, I. "Iconography of Galician Ukraine in the Fifteenth and
Sixteenth Centuries. Lviv 1928. vi + 190 typescript pp., 160 figs.

A,B,C   An English translation by Dennis Sowtis (Toronto) commissioned/received in 1988 by
the CMC at the request of the curator for the Museum's East European Programme
and provided by the Multilingual Translation Directorate, Secretary of State, Government of Canada. Original bibliographical data in Ukrainian: *Ikonohrafija halyc'koji*
Ukrajiny XV-XVI vikiv (L'viv 1928), xii + 98 pp., by I[larion S.] Svjencickyj [1876-
1956]. At top of title-page: *"Zbirky Nacional'noho Muzeju u L'vovi"* [=The Collections of
the National Museum in Lviv]. The English translation is preceded by two pages of
"remarks from the translator."

Tataryn, Myroslaw. *Praying with Icons: An Introduction for Children*.
Ottawa: Novalis, St. Paul University, 1988. 32 pp. (with "icon

E   packet" attached inside back cover, featuring 12 col. reproductions, each
about 9 x 5 cm., showing icons by JUvenalij Mokryc'kyj). Separate French
edition, *Prier avec les icônes : une présentation pour les enfants*.

"Theodore Baran - Church Artist, *Where It's At*, Saskatoon Gallery and

D   Conservatory Corp., April 1973 [2 pp., with 2 b/w foto-illus.].

"Theodore Baran: Obituary", *Progress/Postup* (Winnipeg), vol. 36, no. 7
(February 12, 1995): 7. (Reprinted from *Star Phoenix* [Saskatoon],

D   Thurs. January 5, 1995, p. C1.)

Ukrainian Canadian Art Foundation, Toronto. "Icon and Religious Painting
Exhibit (June 5-August 31, 1988)". List of 173 works, citing

C   artist/collector, title, and price. [6 pp.]. For review of exhibition, see above under
S. Hordynsky ("Vystavka..."[etc.]), and under V. Polishchuk.

Ukrainian Churches of Manitoba: a Building Inventory. Winnipeg:
Manitoba Culture, Heritage and Recreation, Historic Resources, 1987.

D   See especially "Appendix V: Artists", pp. 378-380.

University of Toronto, Robarts Library. Print-out for all holdings under
A   subject area, "Icon", as of Aug. 1, 1995 [82 pp.].

Vachon, Paula. "A Report on Romanian Religious Iconography and
         Iconographers in Canada (A Contemporary Overview with References
A   to the Past)." Unpublished typescript dated December 1995, 52 pages, with
         12 col. illus. CMC archival finding/accession no. 96-F0001. Includes "Over-
         view of Romanian Immigration to Canada", "Artists' Profile", and "List of Romanian
         parishes in Canada."

Varenycja, Iryna. "Seminar ikonohrafiji LUKZhK Edmontons'koji
         Eparxiji" [=An iconography seminar, Ukrainian Catholic Women's
E   League, Edmonton Eparchy], *Ukrainian News (Ukrajins'ki visti)*, Edmonton,
         June 29, 1988: 10. In Ukrainian.

Vartanova, Tat'jana. "Biografija" [=Biography]. Contract-report in
         Russian, [Ottawa] dated November 27, 1994, 26 typescript pp.
D   English translation available (CMC archival finding/accession no. 95-10), 52
         typescript pp.

Volyns'kyj, JEvtymij. "Plashchanycja Uspennja Presvjatoji Bohorodyci:
         cikava istorija plashchanyci z Ukrajiny, jaka chudom opynylasja u
B,   Vudstoku, Kanada" [=A Good Friday shroud of the Assumption of
H   the Most Holy Mother of God: an interesting history of a Good Friday
         shroud from Ukraine that miraculously ended up in Woodstock, Canada],
         Nasha doroha (Winnipeg), vol. 23, no. 3 (August-September 1992): 5-6. In
         Ukrainian.

[von Kuegelgen, Anna Petrovna, iconographer.] Unpublished transcript of
         interview conducted May, 1986, with iconographer's daughter,
D   Martha von Rosen-Olds, about latter's mother (deceased at time of inter-
         view) and her 68 icons donated to the University of British Columbia's
         Museum of Anthropology in Vancouver. [24pp.]

Vynnytsky, Taras. [Letter to Editor:] "Falsification of Culture in
         Slovakia," in Canadian Association of Slavists, *Newsletter*, vol. 28,
B   no. 71 (winter 1988): 15-17 (with notes). A polemical comment on a recent
         publication ("Slovak Icons of the Sixteenth to Nineteenth Centuries" by S. Tkach). See
         also under M. Myshynka, above.

Weatherbe, Stephen. "Icons and the Word Made Flesh", *Alberta Report*
         (Edmonton), vol. 10, April 18, 1983: 46-47.
A

Zakydalsky, Oksana. "Mississauga church to decorate interior", *Ukrainian Weekly* (Jersey City, N.J.), Sun. Apr. 9, 1995: 16. "A proposal for
H   the iconographic decoration of the Ukrainian Catholic Church of the Dormition of the Mother of God (St. Mary's) has been issued."

Zel'ska, Ivanna. "Ukrajins'ki ikony v pol's'kyx muzejax" [=Ukrainian icons in Polish museums], in *Lohos* (Yorkton, Sask.), vol. 28, no. 1
C   (Jan.-Mar.), 1977: 15-22. In Ukrainian. A favourable review of an exhibition catalog published in Poland in 1968.

FALLING INTO THE EYES OF AN ICON:
A THEOLOGICAL POSTSCRIPT

by
Andriy Chirovsky

Icons from the Point of View of the Church's Tradition

While folklorists, ethnographers, and art historians all have their reasons for studying icons, the point of view that needs to anchor any such discussion is one that is rooted in the icon's *raison d'être*. It was the early twentieth century cleaning of a fifteenth century icon by Andrei Rublev that spurred modern interest in the ancient ways that were, up to that point often considered primitive or backward in comparison with the achievements of the Western Renaissance and following centuries. When students of art got a closer look at the subtlety of Rublev's famous icon of the Trinity (depicted as the three angelic visitors received by Abraham at the Oak of Mamre in Genesis 18) , they were forced to begin to accept the icon on its own terms. Byzantine icons of Greek or Slavic or other origins were static, and flat and did not follow linear perspective, but they were by no means primitive or underdeveloped or naive. There were masters at work in this realm, expressing through a very strict vocabulary of line and color not only their talent, but also a highly sophisticated aesthetic which was almost entirely subordinated to the Rule of Faith. From early on and especially after the iconoclastic controversies of the eighth and ninth centuries, icons were seen not just as art on a religious theme, but rather as bearers of the Church's official teaching, of the living reality of continuity with the full revelation of God in Christ which Eastern Christians call Holy Tradition.

The Theology of Icons

Whereas in the Western Church religious images were seen more as a visual aid for the illiterate and as decoration for the House of the Lord, Eastern Christians looked at icons through the prism of intense Christological debate. Eastern Christianity had divided after 451, when the Council of Chalcedon sought to express the paradox of Christ's Divine humanity by simultaneously stressing unity of subject or *hypostasis* and fullness of both the human and Divine natures or *physeis*.

For many reasons, including social tensions, terminological misunderstandings, and ecclesiastical as well as civil politics, the Church was divided between those who saw Chalcedon's expression of who Christ is as an authentic continuation of earlier teaching on the one hand, and those who looked upon the Council's statement of the faith as one that abstracted the human from the Divine in Christ by speaking of two natures or *physeis*. Thus, the opponents of Chalcedon were labeled Monophysites, because of their insistence on absolute fidelity to the letter of the teaching of St. Cyril of Alexandria and the Fathers of the Council of Ephesus in 431. When Cyril had used the phrase "one nature of the incarnate Word of God", he was emphasizing unity of subject in Christ and opposing the abstraction of Christ's humanity from his divinity.

By 451 further nuance had crept into the discourse and the triumphant party at Chalcedon had begun instead to use the word *hypostasis* to delineate the unity of subject, and spoke of two *physeis* or natures to safeguard the real and simultaneous humanity and Divinity of Christ. All of this may sound like a lot of theological nit-picking to the modern reader, but the issues were acute enough to rip apart the Church in the centuries that followed. Only recently have ecumenical dialogues allowed the two sides to see that their differences were more in the realm of terminology than substance of teaching, but it took over 1500 years for tempers to cool.

More importantly, for those who wish to understand why icons in the Eastern Churches have a theology underpinning them, while the Christian West sees these images as simply art on a religious theme, the rift over Chalcedon left Eastern Christianity haunted by the question: "How far is the humanity of Christ absorbed by His Divinity?" Many tried to find a compromise position between the adherents and the opponents of Chalcedon, creating new controversies over the question of whether there is one will and one activity in Christ, or two. All of this must be understood for the iconoclastic controversy and the finally triumphant theology of icons to make sense.

While there were doubtless political, economic, and cultural forces at play in the Iconoclast struggle, the vehemence of both sides must, in the end, be seen as a result of lingering doubts about the validity of depicting Christ, if Christ was understood to be God, and God was by definition uncircumscribable and undepictable. The "iconoclasts" or icon-breakers, either accused the "iconodules" or icon-venerators of idolatry (because they attempted to depict the Divine, who is undepictable) or they accused the iconodules of the heresy of Nestorianism, which abstracted Christ's humanity from His Divinity (because they were depicting solely the human Jesus.) Clearly, the iconodules were in a difficult situation. They needed to elaborate a theology that would justify their position and remain faithful to the Chalcedonian insight that Divinity and humanity in Christ must neither be separated nor allowed to fuse. Thus, the defenders of icons focus on the incarnation of God in Christ as legitimation of their depiction of one who is Divine yet human.

This is the very core of the theology of icons: they must always depict a reality that is simultaneously divine and human. In the case of icons of Christ, both his real human corporeality and his transcendence as the Son of God must be expressed. In the case of the Theotokos and the saints, the reality of the Divine action within the real flesh of the human being must be preserved. Thus, certain conventions become the usual vehicles of the expression of this paradox: static, hieratic frontality along with a careful manipulation of perspective and proportions. Restraint and ebullience coexist side-by side in a style of expression that is regulated by the Tradition of the Church in order to correctly present this very central dogma.

The Theology in Icons

Once the most central doctrinal issues surrounding an adequate depiction of the Incarnation of Christ and the action of the Holy Spirit in the saints are established, icons are seen as convenient vehicles for further teaching -- a veritable theology in colour, shape and line. Far from being some static *deposit* of non-written teaching, as some later Western theologians would define Tradition during the debates surrounding the Reformation, the Christian East has preferred to think of Tradition as a process, the process of the handing-on of a living faith from generation to generation. This emphasis on process allows one to understand how the iconographic canon can be sometimes rather rigid, and at other times quite flexible. The basic composition of most major iconographic themes has changed little over the centuries, and yet there is an astounding variety of emphases and approaches by particular iconographers, whether Masters or simple village artisans.

A case in point is the masterful treatment of the Trinity by Andrei Rublev. He abided by the rule (often broken, and often restated) of not depicting the Father, whom no one has seen. He therefore used the Genesis scene of Abraham's reception of three Divine messengers (the Greek for messenger is *angellos*), to whom Abraham spoke alternately in the singular and the plural. In this Rublev was completely true to earlier models, passed on by generations of believers. What he changed was the particular emphasis which he gave to the three figures and the relationship among them. By radically simplifying the composition (originally known as "The Hospitality of Abraham") to the point of excluding Abraham, Sarah, servants and nearly all extraneous elements, he rendered one of the most penetrating insights into the internal life of the Holy Triad: Father, Son, and Holy Spirit. "The Hospitality of Abraham," with all the additional compositional elements remains even today as a standard icon-type, but alongside it, since the fifteenth century, a myriad of simplified Rublev-type Trinity icons have multiplied, though rarely with anything near his simplicity and depth.

Central to the understanding of how the content of icons is monitored and preserved in fidelity to this ancient yet living Tradition, is the Orthodox notion of reception. Unlike the Roman Church, which has objective, external criteria by which one can recognize which gatherings of bishops carry the august designation and infallible authority of an ecumenical council, for the Orthodox things are never quite so clear. Considerable attention has been paid in recent years to this question. Most Orthodox theologians claim that a Council needs to be *received* by the whole Church in order to be recognized as Ecumenical. Something similar may be said with regard to icons. Variations on a theme develop, and entirely new icons are created, but whether they are received by the Church, by the whole people of God, is another matter, one that cannot be perceived except through hindsight.

Thus, certain icons carry potent messages that have been received, confirmed by centuries of undisputed use. A good example of this is the icon of the Nativity of Christ, where Mary is turned away from the infant Jesus. This is a striking demonstration of the ascendancy of theology, of doctrine, over sentimentality. Every human heart expects to see a tender love between Mother and Child in this scene. Instead, Mary turns her face from Jesus in order to make a Christological statement. One cannot behold God and live, according to Exodus 33:20. Thus, the infant is God! Thousands of iconographers have copied this composition without knowing the theology in this icon. Millions have no doubt venerated such icons without fully comprehending the full import of its teaching. But for those who do know in every generation, this one compositional element is a powerful bearer of the Revelation — the Word expressed beyond words.

There are many such theological moments in icons. Happily, there is a steadily growing body of literature that examines icons not only from an artistic, but from a theological and spiritual perspective.

The Spiritual Preparation of the Iconographer

Just as the icon's content is regulated by the living Tradition of the Church, so also the process of its creation is subject to the blessing of the

Church. There are many who think of themselves as iconographers because they copy icons, or use the eminently recognizable hieratic style of icons for their own compositions, but who are not in living, sacramental communion with the Church. Many Eastern Christians would be hesitant to call such artists iconographers, or to accept their work as icons. There is a definite spiritual and sacramental component to the preparation of the iconographer for the work upon which he or she is to embark.

The iconographer is expected to have the permission and blessing of his/her spiritual Father or Mother. The importance of this first step cannot be minimized, as it immediately sets forth the criterion of humility, which allows one's work to be a true bearer of Holy Tradition rather than simply a prideful activity of the individual will. The icon should not be signed, as a further indication of the humility of the iconographer, who allows for the power of God to act, rather than asserting one's own will. Frequently the materials to be used will be blessed as well. There is an ascetic discipline which accompanies each stage of the creation of an icon, from the preparation of the board, to the gilding and writing of the icon itself, and its final preservation. Prayer and fasting are seen as essential components of the iconographers interior attentiveness to the grace of God. This constant prayer and attendant fasting is achievable outside monastic settings, but it is made easier by a monastic environment. For this reason, over the centuries many iconographers have been monks or nuns. It is a commonplace of Orthodox spiritual thought that all Christians are called to the same life as is lived in the monasteries. Therefore even lay iconographers are expected to adhere to a discipline of prayer and fasting. That many have not is often visible from the lack of spiritual depth in many icons even though they may still have artistic merit. In the end, an icon's value in the Church is judged not according to its prettiness, but rather by virtue of its ability to help the faithful unite with God. With such a lofty purpose in mind, it is no wonder that much is required of the iconographer.

This, of course, is not to say that the images painted by the spiritually ill-prepared cannot be bearers of Divine presence, or that they are wholly without worth for the Church and the individual believer. Orthodox theology and spirituality are always maximalist in their orientation. The ideal is presented, so that we may aspire to the ideal. To set down minimum expectations would be to begin at a different type of starting point, within a very different world view. Thus, in the mystery of the Divine dispensation, it sometimes occurs that the free gift of God's grace is given to iconographers whose personal lives may not be in perfect order, and they may sometimes write icons of unexpected depth and spiritual beauty. That, however, does not invalidate the Church's insistence on the best circumstances for the writing of icons.

Icons and Their Place in Eastern Christian Worship

Icons are fundamentally a liturgical art, just as Eastern Christianity is a fundamentally liturgical way of life. The Liturgy is what the Church "does," its essential mission to bring the human race and indeed the entire cosmos back into harmony with God. The Liturgy, *leitourgia,* is therefore "the work of the People of God." In another sense, the Liturgy is not so much what we human beings do, but rather what we allow to happen to us, as we become willing participants in the never-ending praise of God that is the heavenly life which has long preceded the creation of the material world. Icons function as windows unto that celestial liturgy. That is why the majority of icons do not depict the saints engaged in some particular outward activity. Their static, hieratic pose catches them at prayer, in worship. Long before the earthly members of the Church enter the temple, its celestial choirs of angels and saints are already in the midst of their eternal liturgy. It is the privilege of earthly believers to set aside the cares of life and to "mystically represent the Cherubim and sing the thrice-holy hymn to the life-creating Trinity." The icons represent those who surround the throne of God, and we represent them as well, for we too are the icons, the image of God (Genesis 1:26).

The Blessing of Icons

Icons can be blessed in two ways. The *Euchologion* or *Book of Needs* contains the order for the blessing of icons of the Holy Triad, of the Lord Jesus Christ, of the Theotokos, of the holy incorporeal powers and the saints, as well as those of the liturgical feasts or biblical events. All of them follow a similar pattern. After the usual beginning or opening prayers, psalmody is followed by prayers which invoke themes from the Old and New Testaments justifying, even commanding the making of images, from the seraphs on the Ark of the covenant, to the Incarnation of Christ and the extrabiblical account of "the icon not made by human hands," the imprinting of the face of Christ on the Mandylion. Through the invocation of the Holy Spirit and the sprinkling of blessed water, the icons are brought to full efficacy. Brief hymns or *Troparia* appropriate to the icon are then sung in worship.

There is an alternate form of blessing of icons. Sometimes they are placed on the Holy Table in the Sanctuary during the (Eucharistic) Divine Liturgy. After the words of institution and the *epiclesis,* or calling down of the

Holy Spirit, commemorations are quietly made of the living and the dead. At this time the priest takes the icon and traces the sign of the cross with it over the consecrated gifts, while commemorating the owners, donors or recipients of the icons. On occasion one might see an icon "baptised." After a baptism, if an icon is presented as a gift to the newly-baptised, but still needs to be blessed, it may sometimes be immersed in the baptismal font, or sprinkled with water from it.

Each method of blessing icons has its strengths and weaknesses. The official order of blessing icons has the advantage of offering prayers and hymnography that are a teaching moment. The Eucharistic blessing ties the icon more closely to the essential mystery of our salvation in Christ's self-offering, and the baptismal blessing gives it a special bond with the one baptised. In ant event, an icon which has not been blessed has not been fully brought into the life of the Church, even though the iconographer may have received a blessing at the beginning of the effort, and the materials may have been likewise blessed at the time. When an icon is finished, it must be blessed in its mature state, to fully mediate between the visible and invisible worlds.

Icons and Their Placement in the Church Building

Icons should never be thought of as decoration. While they clearly have an aesthetic role to play, expressing the beauty that saves, their placement in the temple is regulated not primarily by concerns of interior design, but by a rational exposition of the faith. After the triumph of Orthodoxy over iconoclasm, a gradual but steady implementation of a canon of icon placement began to be developed. For example, while Roman Catholic Churches until recently often had an image of the patron or patrons of the parish behind the main altar, that place in Eastern Churches became reserved for an icon of the Theotokos, either seated, with the infant Jesus, as the *Platytera ton ouranon*, or "wider than the heavens," (referring to her womb encompassing the one whom the cosmos cannot circumscribe), or in a praying or *orans* position, either with or without the sign of Emmanuel on her chest. Below this icon, one will usually find the great Fathers of the Church and the Mystical Supper. The altar or sanctuary is separated from the nave by the iconostasis, which bears a very standard arrangement of icons, although individual iconostases may have from one up to six tiers. What often astounds those who are not acquainted with the Byzantine tradition is that the altar side of the iconostasis is usually quite plain, and without icons. The icons all look out at the congregation, beckoning them to continue faithfully on their journey toward the fulfillment of God's Kingdom which is represented by the whole of the altar area.

The nave is most often surmounted by the main dome in which the usual icon is that of Christ the *Pantocrator*, or "ruler of all." The dome and its iconography serves as an expression of the Revelation of God through the *Logos* or Word (Jesus Christ). This revealed Word is set down in words by the Evangelists, whose icons are positioned in the four pendentives surrounding the dome. Between the two there may be several other levels of icons, all related to the revelation: angels, prophets, apostles, bishops. The upper walls of the nave most often carry icons of the earthly ministry of Jesus, while the lower walls, immediately surrounding the faithful hold icons of the saints, reminding the congregation that they are not alone in their worship and in their struggle to lead a Christian life.

The narthex or vestibule is a place of preparation for entry into the nave and according to the common tradition, its iconography usually relates to either the life of the patronal saint, or it bears icons that assist in preparation, such as the Last Judgment, a sobering image which helps one to focus on the ultimate reality of our lives. Thus, there is a clear linear thrust from the place of preparation for entry, to the assembly of the faithful in one Body under the headship of the *Pantocrator*, to the complete fulfillment of the Kingdom, glimpses of which we may see "through a glass, darkly," (1 Corinthians 13:12) as we peek, but cannot stare into the altar area, covered and revealed by the iconostasis.

While not *primarily* pedagogical, icons do assist greatly with catechesis, especially if the traditional scheme for the placement of icons in the church is used. Alas, in North America such dogmatically arranged icons are more the exception than the rule, as struggling pioneer communities of various Eastern Catholic and Orthodox jurisdictions did the best they could with what little they had, in terms of both material and theological resources. The wonderfully rational arrangement of icons that so lends itself to preaching and teaching the faith and simultaneously encapsulates in the church building what the Church is all about, is often replaced by a motley assortment of icons (sometimes mixed with non-iconographic images) which nevertheless expresses one crucial truth: the love of the faithful for their temple and their faith.

The Liturgical Use of Icons

Besides those icons which are permanently installed on the walls and ceilings of the temple, there are many others, which are venerated in numerous ways. They may be carried in procession (whether in panel form or on banners). They are used to impart blessings to the congregation, especially when they are solemnly brought out by the clergy for their particular feast days. They are surrounded with embroidery and flowers, kissed, incensed, and otherwise venerated with candles, anointing with fragrant oils, singing, prostrations, as the occasion merits, and as the Spirit moves the faithful. There is no question here of worshipping the icon. Eastern Christians do not treat icons as idols. They know that their veneration is directed toward and passes through to the prototype. The icon helps the unseen to be experienced within the visual realm. Hence they are sometimes referred to as "images of the invisible."

Icons and "the Liturgy after the Liturgy"

Christianity is a liturgical faith but not one that is cultic. The Liturgy, with all of its ritual, sights, sounds, smells and movement, with all of its didactic and doxological hymnography is not an end unto itself. The mission of Christ's Church is to transform the human race, one selfish will at a time, into an interwoven communion of "partakers of the Divine nature"(2 Peter 1:4). Along the way, the world around us is transformed as well, until that final day when God will be all in all (1 Corinthians 15:28). Thus, what is experienced during the liturgy must be brought into our daily lives, and our daily lives must be brought into the liturgy, until there is no longer a distinction, but only a consistent offering of self, and a humble receiving of God's love, which makes my neighbor and myself one with each other and with the God who gave us one life to live together, in the image and the likeness of the Three who are One.

If the liturgy must escape the confines of the parish church, and enter into the very fabric of our lives, then icons will be found there as well. The domestic church continues the Divine Liturgy throughout the schedule of our daily lives. Thus, in the Eastern Christian home, no room should be without its icon. Rooms without windows are oppressive places not fit for human habitation. Rooms without windows to eternity are equally pitiful.

There is a place in the Christian home, however, for a specially focused presence of icons. A place of gathering and family prayer, a place of personal devotion, the icon corner or icon wall is the centre of the domestic Church. Most pioneer families who came to this country from Ukraine or other Eastern Christian lands, brought with them their family icons, or at least the westernised sentimental religious images that had made tremendous inroads into the Eastern Churches during the centuries when icons were misunderstood and labeled primitive and backward. These were arranged either on the Eastern wall of the house, or in an Eastern corner, so that those praying before them might be facing the place of the rising sun and the Risen Son.

When arranged in a corner, the icons surround the person praying, filling one's field of vision and thereby saving the believer from visual distractions. The icons in the icon corner literally embrace the one at prayer. A hanging lamp, or a votive light on a shelf before the icons illuminates the icons with a living light. The flickering flames make the icons seem to come to life. What peace can be found in the embraces of one's icon corner!

The Lingering Effects of Icons on the Believer

As one gazes into the eyes of the icon (always disproportionately large and receptive) and notices how very small the lips in the icon so often are, the believer is called to silence, to a prayer that begins with words and visual contact, but ends in silent and imageless prayer of the heart. It seems so strange to my non-Eastern Christian friends when I tell them that I pray in my icon corner with my eyes closed. "What's the point?" they ask. The answer is that the icon is the very last thing that I see. That image, if I allow it to, can inscribe itself deeply into my conscious and subconscious mind. It is the point of departure for the imageless prayer "in Spirit and Truth" (John 4:24), which does God justice by not attempting to circumscribe the Limitless. In order to move from the world of a billion flickering images in a mind racing with the noise of half-thought thoughts, the place to gather oneself before God is the static, peaceful icon.

Some Special Questions about Icons

One often hears of wonder-working icons. Some icons exude a fragrant oil akin to myrrh. Some weep. Some miraculously restore and clean themselves (sometimes over an extended period of time, and sometimes quite rapidly). There are icons credited with healings. What is one to make of these phenomena, and how does one react? It is difficult to answer this question abstractly. The wonder needs to be experienced, and it is judged by its fruits. Unlike Western Christians, who sometimes rush to examine, dissect or X-ray the unusual image, or submit its excretions to laboratory testing, the Orthodox will usually make preliminary observations, looking for any obvious fraud, but leave it at that. If its spiritual fruits are good, the icon is venerated. But all icons are venerated. And not all wonders can be seen or touched. Is it not a miracle when one prays before an icon, any icon, and makes contact, even briefly, with God?

Considerable anxiety surrounds the question of non-traditional icons. By this one can mean icons which do not follow the Byzantine "style" or icons that follow that style, but depart from customary media or content. Perhaps the term non-traditional is the problem. The Holy Tradition of the Church is a living thing. It is not static. It can change. But in changing, it must always be true to itself, or else it is not the Holy Tradition which keeps us in living continuity with the fullness of Divine Revelation. Sometimes it is not entirely clear where the boundary lies between the Tradition, the handing forward of God's Truth, and traditions, the customs that we human beings cling to so tenaciously. What is handed on must be received. And reception, as we have seen above, is sometimes a question of hindsight. "By their fruits you shall know them. (Matthew 7:16)" Perhaps not immediately, but things will become known, as the Paraclete leads us into the Truth (John 16:13). If it does what an icon does, bringing the believer into closer contact with God, within the context of the living salvific reality of the worshipping Body of Christ, which is the Church, then it is probably an icon, even if it does not look quite right, or was not made quite correctly or by the well-prepared.

Conclusion

The folklorists, ethnographers, curators and art historians who have put together their reports in this volume have attempted to amass information about icons and iconographers in Canada. Theirs is a noble effort. They wish to leave the researchers of tomorrow a record of what could be known today about the external manifestations of a deeply interior reality: Eastern Christian Iconography. May it serve as a signpost along the way for those who will probe the depths of the icons described and listed herein. May they fall into those wide eyes of an icon and find God and themselves within.

They then go to the icon of Christ, and kiss it, saying:

We bow before Your most pure image,
    O kind Lord,
        and beg pardon for our sins...

       (from *The Hierarchical Liturgy of Saint John Chrysostom According to the Ukrainian Greek Catholic Usage,* Ottawa, circa 1988 and 1995, p. 2)

ABOUT THE AUTHORS

Radomir Bilash is a historian with Historic Sites and Service, Alberta Community Development, Edmonton.

Vladimir Blagonadejdin is a Russian iconographer practising in Vancouver, British Columbia.

Leslie Carlyle is a conservator with the Canadian Conservation Institute, Canadian Heritage, Ottawa.

Andriy Chirovsky is the Director and Peter and Doris Kule Professor of Eastern Christian Theology and Spirituality, Metropolitan Andrey Sheptytsky Institute of Eastern Christian Studies, Saint Paul University, Ottawa.

Lesya Granger is an artist based in Ottawa and the author of a master's thesis on "The Icon Tradition among Canadians of Ukrainian Descent", Carleton University,1996.

Pauline Greenhill is Associate Professor, Women's Studies, University of Winnipeg.

Stephen Inglis is Director General, Research, Canadian Museum of Civilization, Hull,Quebec.

Michael Owen Jones is Professor of History and Folklore and Director of the Center for the Study of Comparative Folklore and Mythology, University of California, Los Angeles.

Robert B.Klymasz is Curator, East European Programme, Canadian Centre for Folk Culture Studies, Canadian Museum of Civilization, Hull, Quebec.

Claire Labrecque is a doctoral candidate in medieval art history at Laval University, Quebec.

Anne-Marie Poulin is pursuing a doctorate at Laval University focusing on the ethnology of Francophone communities in North America.

Christina Senkiw of Etobicoke, Ontario, has authored, illustrated and published several books for children and a volume on the history of Ukrainian costume.

PaulaVachon of Hull, Quebec, is a graduate of the Universty of Bucharest, Romania, and has provided curatorial and various other services for the Canadian Museum of Civilization and other cultural agencies here and abroad.

Tatiana Vartanova lives in Ottawa where she specializes in fine arts restoration, icon painting and miniatures.

LIST OF ILLUSTRATIONS